# NATURALIZING WITH A CRIME

*A Guide to Overcoming Criminal Barriers to U.S. Citizenship*

Attorney Brian D. Lerner

**BDL** LAW OFFICES OF
**BRIAN D. LERNER**
A PROFESSIONAL CORPORATION

# ATTORNEY DRAFTED IMMIGRATION PETITIONS

## By

## Brian D. Lerner
## Attorney at Law

### Disclaimer and Terms of Use:

# TABLE OF CONTENTS

# INTRODUCTION

There are a multitude of different immigration petitions and applications. They are complex and full of requirements. Obviously it would be best to hire an immigration attorney to best prepare the petitions and applications. However, this can certainly cost thousands of dollars.

The next best option is to get a sample of the petition written by an experienced immigration attorney. The samples cost a fraction of what would be charged by an immigration attorney. However, while the reader has to alter, amend and change the parts of the sample petition to reflect their actual situation, it is a fantastic roadmap for them to use. If the reader has purchased the entire petition or application, they will have real live samples of cover letters, forms, declarations, affidavits and the necessary exhibits to use. The samples come from real cases and the names of those clients have been redacted to protect the privacy of that person or corporation.

These are petitions and applications that have been drafted by an experienced immigration attorney with over 25 years of experience. Get the benefits of that experience without the costs.

# About the Law Offices of Brian D. Lerner

The Law Offices of Brian D. Lerner, APC. The law practice consists of Immigration and Nationality Law and everything involved with and regarding immigration which includes citizenship, investment visas, family and employment visas, removal and deportation hearings, appeals, waivers, adjustment, consulate processing and all types of immigration and citizenship matters. Thousands of families have been reunited and/or permitted to stay in the U.S. and/or return to the U.S. because of the successful work of Immigration Attorney Brian D. Lerner.

This law office handles all types of immigration cases including family based and employment based. Immigration issues range from immigration court proceedings to trying to fix what paralegals may have done that was neither correct nor proper. Foreign nationals must have experienced lawyers admitted to practice law.

The Law Offices of Brian D. Lerner, APC, handles cases arising from business visas, work permits, Green Cards, non-immigrant visas, deportation, citizenship, appeals and all areas of immigration. The Law Offices of Brian D. Lerner, APC does EB-5 Investor Visas, H-1B Specialty Occupation, L-1 Intracompany Transferee, E-2 Treaty Investor, E-1 Treaty Trader, O-1 Extraordinary Ability among others. Regarding immigrant visas for the Green Card, the firm does PERM and advanced degree PERM, Family Petitions, and Extraordinary Alien Petitions. In addition to affirmative petitions, the Law Firm represents people in people in deportation and removal hearings, including political asylum, withholding of removal, and convention against torture cases.

Brian D. Lerner has been certified as an expert in Immigration & Nationality Law by the California State Bar, Board of Legal Specialization since 2000 and has been re-certified three times. He now passes on his decades of experience by allowing the Reader, Law Schools, Professors and other Immigration Attorneys to purchase sample petitions on every facet of Immigration Law.

## About Criminal Naturalization

Criminal Naturalization is a Foreign National applying for a United States Citizenship based on the fact that he/she has been a Lawful Permanent Resident for 5 years and was not born in the United States. One important question will be whether he/she has ever been arrested for, charged with, or convicted of a crime or other unlawful act. Although not every crime or civil violation creates an outright bar to receiving United States Citizenship, many do, while others will raise serious questions about whether he/she has the necessary good moral character to become a United States Citizen through naturalization.

# ATTORNEY COVER LETTER

# Law Offices of Brian D. Lerner

## A PROFESSIONAL CORPORATION

CERTIFIED SPECIALIST IN IMMIGRATION AND NATIONALITY LAW
ADMITTED TO THE U.S. SUPREME COURT

LONG BEACH, CALIFORNIA
(562) 495-0554

September 29, 2020

U.S. Citizenship and Immigration Services
Attn: N-400
1820 E. Skyharbor Circle S, Suite 100
Phoenix, AZ 85034

      Re:    **N-400, Application for Naturalization**
              **Applicant:** ███████████
              **Alien Number:** ███████

Dear Officer:

We hereby enclose the following in support of Applicant's N-400, Application for Naturalization:

| **Form:** | **Description:** |
|---|---|
| G-28 | Notice of Entry of Appearance as Attorney or Accredited Representative; and |
| N-400 | Application for Naturalization and $725.00 Filing Fee. |

## Table of Exhibits

| **Exhibit:** | **Description:** |
|---|---|
| 1. | Applicant's Permanent Resident Card; |
| 2. | Applicant's Mother's Naturalization Certificate; |
| 3. | Applicant's Notice to Appear; |
| 4. | Order of the Immigration Judge Dated March 1, 2019; |
| 5. | Applicant's Letter of Employment; |
| 6. | Applicant's 2019 Income Tax Return and W-2s. |
| 7. | Orange County Superior Court Docket Sheet – 96WF2961; |
| 8. | Orange County Superior Court Case Summary – 2415369; |
| 9. | Orange County Superior Court Case Summary – 2438069; |
| 10. | Orange County Superior Court Case Summary – 400031; |
| 11. | Orange County Superior Court Case Summary – 417974; |
| 12. | Orange County Superior Court Case Summary – 99HM07501; |
| 13. | Orange County Superior Court Case Summary – LJ55294; |
| 14. | Orange County Superior Court Case Summary – X007620; |
| 15. | Orange County Superior Court Docket Sheet – 03SF0869; |
| 16. | Orange County Superior Court Docket Sheet – 04HM01441; |
| 17. | Orange County Superior Court Docket Sheet – 04HF1326; |
| 18. | Orange County Superior Court Case Summary – 85932VK; |
| 19. | Orange County Superior Court Docket Sheet – 06HF2202; |
| 20. | Orange County Superior Court Docket Sheet – 07HF0020; |
| 21. | Orange County Superior Court Case Summary – IRM322200; and |

22.          Orange County Superior Court Case Summary – SH889199.

In the present case, Applicant is statutorily eligible for naturalization because he is at least 18-years-old, he has been a lawful permanent resident for at least five years, he has been physically present in the United States and resided in Orange County, California for the requisite period prior to the filing of his application and he has been a person of good moral character throughout the statutory period. *See* INA § 310 *et seq.*; 8 C.F.R. § 316.

Please note that Applicant's criminal history is limited to various California Vehicle Code violations. Exhibits 7-21. Importantly, said convictions does not make Application inadmissible to the Untied States under section 212 of the Act nor removable from the United States under section 237 of the Act. Applicant's other criminal cases were vacated and dismissed pursuant to either section 1203.43 or 1473.7, based on a ground of legal invalidity, and therefore, no longer exist for immigration purposes. *See Matter of Pickering*, 23 I&N Dec. 621 (BIA 2003) (a conviction vacated because it is legally defective will not constitute a conviction for immigration purposes); see also *Matter of Rodriguez-Ruiz*, 22 I&N Dec. 1378 (BIA 2000) (according full faith and credit to a New York court's vacatur of a conviction on the merits); *Matter of Adamiak*, 23 I&N Dec. 878 (BIA 2006) (conviction vacated for a failure to give legislatively required advisals of immigration consequences is eliminated for immigration purposes); *Nath v. Gonzales*, 467 F.3d 1185, 1187-89 (9th Cir. 2006) (conviction vacated because of a procedural or substantive defect is not considered a conviction for immigration purposes and cannot serve as the basis for removability).

In addition, because Applicant's convictions falls outside of the five-year statutory period for good moral character, they cannot be the sole basis for denying his application for naturalization. *See Lawson v. USCIS*, 795 F.Supp.2d 283, 296-97 (S.D.N.Y. 2011); *Gatcliffe v. Reno*, 23 F.Supp.2d 581, 585 (D.V.I. 1998); *Nyari v. Napolitano*, 562 F.3d 916 (8th Cir. 2009); *Santamaria-Ames v. INS*, 104 F.3d 1127 (9th Cir. 1996); *U.S. v. Hovsepian*, 422 F.3d 883 (9th Cir. 2005) (en banc). More importantly, Applicant acknowledges his past mistake and merely prays for the opportunity to move forward with her life. He has show genuine rehabilitation and has been a law abiding, contributing member of society ever since while at the same time, working diligently towards realizing his dream of becoming a U.S. citizen.

Based on the foregoing, we respectfully request that the instant application be approved. If you should have any questions, please feel free to contact our office at (562) 495-0554.

Sincerely,

Christopher A. Reed
Attorney at Law

# FORMS

Notice of Entry of Appearance
as Attorney or Accredited Representative

**Department of Homeland Security**

**DHS
Form G-28**
OMB No. 1615-0105
Expires 05/31/2021

## Part 1. Information About Attorney or Accredited Representative

1. USCIS Online Account Number (if any)

    ▶ [            ]

### Name of Attorney or Accredited Representative

2.a. Family Name (Last Name)  **Reed**

2.b. Given Name (First Name)  **Christopher**

2.c. Middle Name  **Allan**

### Address of Attorney or Accredited Representative

3.a. Street Number and Name  **3233 E. Broadway**

3.b. ☐ Apt. ☐ Ste. ☐ Flr. [          ]

3.c. City or Town  **Long Beach**

3.d. State **CA**   3.e. ZIP Code **90803**

3.f. Province [          ]

3.g. Postal Code [          ]

3.h. Country  **USA**

### Contact Information of Attorney or Accredited Representative

4. Daytime Telephone Number  **(562) 495-0554**

5. Mobile Telephone Number (if any) [          ]

6. Email Address (if any)  **creed@eimmigration.org**

7. Fax Number (if any)  **(562) 512-2038**

## Part 2. Eligibility Information for Attorney or Accredited Representative

Select all applicable items.

1.a. ☒ I am an attorney eligible to practice law in, and a member in good standing of, the bar of the highest courts of the following states, possessions, territories, commonwealths, or the District of Columbia. If you need extra space to complete this section, use the space provided in **Part 6. Additional Information.**

Licensing Authority

**California Supreme Court**

1.b. Bar Number (if applicable)

**235438**

1.c. I (select only one box) ☒ am not ☐ am subject to any order suspending, enjoining, restraining, disbarring, or otherwise restricting me in the practice of law. If you are subject to any orders, use the space provided in **Part 6. Additional Information** to provide an explanation.

1.d. Name of Law Firm or Organization (if applicable)

**Law Offices of Brian D. Lerner, APC**

2.a. ☐ I am an accredited representative of the following qualified nonprofit religious, charitable, social service, or similar organization established in the United States and recognized by the Department of Justice in accordance with 8 CFR part 1292.

2.b. Name of Recognized Organization

[          ]

2.c. Date of Accreditation (mm/dd/yyyy)

[          ]

3. ☐ I am associated with

[          ] ,

the attorney or accredited representative of record who previously filed Form G-28 in this case, and my appearance as an attorney or accredited representative for a limited purpose is at his or her request.

4.a. ☐ I am a law student or law graduate working under the direct supervision of the attorney or accredited representative of record on this form in accordance with the requirements in 8 CFR 292.1(a)(2).

4.b. Name of Law Student or Law Graduate

[          ]

4547

## Part 3. Notice of Appearance as Attorney or Accredited Representative

If you need extra space to complete this section, use the space provided in **Part 6. Additional Information.**

This appearance relates to immigration matters before (select **only one** box):

**1.a.** ☒ U.S. Citizenship and Immigration Services (USCIS)

**1.b.** List the form numbers or specific matter in which appearance is entered.

> N-400

**2.a.** ☐ U.S. Immigration and Customs Enforcement (ICE)

**2.b.** List the specific matter in which appearance is entered.

**3.a.** ☐ U.S. Customs and Border Protection (CBP)

**3.b.** List the specific matter in which appearance is entered.

**4.** Receipt Number (if any)

▶

**5.** I enter my appearance as an attorney or accredited representative at the request of the (select **only one** box):

☒ Applicant ☐ Petitioner ☐ Requestor
☐ Beneficiary/Derivative ☐ Respondent (ICE, CBP)

## Information About Client (Applicant, Petitioner, Requestor, Beneficiary or Derivative, Respondent, or Authorized Signatory for an Entity)

**6.a.** Family Name (Last Name) ▊

**6.b.** Given Name (First Name) ▊

**6.c.** Middle Name

**7.a.** Name of Entity (if applicable)

**7.b.** Title of Authorized Signatory for Entity (if applicable)

**8.** Client's USCIS Online Account Number (if any)

▶

**9.** Client's Alien Registration Number (A-Number) (if any)

▶ A- ▊

## Client's Contact Information

**10.** Daytime Telephone Number

▊

**11.** Mobile Telephone Number (if any)

▊

**12.** Email Address (if any)

▊

## Mailing Address of Client

**NOTE:** Provide the client's mailing address. **Do not** provide the business mailing address of the attorney or accredited representative **unless** it serves as the safe mailing address on the application or petition being filed with this Form G-28.

**13.a.** Street Number and Name ▊

**13.b.** ☐ Apt. ☐ Ste. ☐ Flr.

**13.c.** City or Town | Mission Viejo

**13.d.** State | CA | **13.e.** ZIP Code | 92691

**13.f.** Province

**13.g.** Postal Code

**13.h.** Country

> USA

## Part 4. Client's Consent to Representation and Signature

### Consent to Representation and Release of Information

I have requested the representation of and consented to being represented by the attorney or accredited representative named in **Part 1.** of this form. According to the Privacy Act of 1974 and U.S. Department of Homeland Security (DHS) policy, I also consent to the disclosure to the named attorney or accredited representative of any records pertaining to me that appear in any system of records of USCIS, ICE, or CBP.

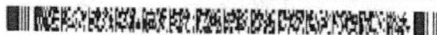

## Part 4. Client's Consent to Representation and Signature (continued)

### Options Regarding Receipt of USCIS Notices and Documents

USCIS will send notices to both a represented party (the client) and his, her, or its attorney or accredited representative either through mail or electronic delivery. USCIS will send all secure identity documents and Travel Documents to the client's U.S. mailing address.

If you want to have notices and/or secure identity documents sent to your attorney or accredited representative of record rather than to you, please select **all applicable** items below. You may change these elections through written notice to USCIS.

1.a. ☒ I request that USCIS send original notices on an application or petition to the business address of my attorney or accredited representative as listed in this form.

1.b. ☐ I request that USCIS send any secure identity document (Permanent Resident Card, Employment Authorization Document, or Travel Document) that I receive to the U.S. business address of my attorney or accredited representative (or to a designated military or diplomatic address in a foreign country (if permitted)).

**NOTE:** If your notice contains Form I-94, Arrival-Departure Record, USCIS will send the notice to the U.S. business address of your attorney or accredited representative. If you would rather have your Form I-94 sent directly to you, select **Item Number 1.c.**

1.c. ☐ I request that USCIS send my notice containing Form I-94 to me at my U.S. mailing address.

### Signature of Client or Authorized Signatory for an Entity

2.a. Signature of Client or Authorized Signatory for an Entity

➡

2.b. Date of Signature (mm/dd/yyyy) | 09/22/2020

## Part 5. Signature of Attorney or Accredited Representative

I have read and understand the regulations and conditions contained in 8 CFR 103.2 and 292 governing appearances and representation before DHS. I declare under penalty of perjury under the laws of the United States that the information I have provided on this form is true and correct.

1. a. Signature of Attorney or Accredited Representative

1.b. Date of Signature (mm/dd/yyyy) | 09/22/2020

2.a. Signature of Law Student or Law Graduate

2.b. Date of Signature (mm/dd/yyyy)

## Part 6. Additional Information

If you need extra space to provide any additional information within this form, use the space below. If you need more space than what is provided, you may make copies of this page to complete and file with this form or attach a separate sheet of paper. Type or print your name at the top of each sheet; indicate the **Page Number**, **Part Number**, and **Item Number** to which your answer refers; and sign and date each sheet.

**1.a** Family Name
(Last Name) ██████████

**1.b.** Given Name
(First Name) █████

**1.c.** Middle Name

**2.a.** Page Number   **2.b.** Part Number   **2.c.** Item Number

**2.d.**

**3.a.** Page Number   **3.b.** Part Number   **3.c.** Item Number

**3.d.**

**4.a.** Page Number   **4.b.** Part Number   **4.c.** Item Number

**4.d.**

**5.a.** Page Number   **5.b.** Part Number   **5.c.** Item Number

**5.d.**

**6.a.** Page Number   **6.b.** Part Number   **6.c.** Item Number

**6.d.**

 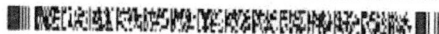

## Application for Naturalization

**Department of Homeland Security**

U.S. Citizenship and Immigration Services

**USCIS**
**Form N-400**
OMB No. 1615-0052
Expires 09/30/2022

| For USCIS Use Only | Date Stamp | Receipt | Action Block |
|---|---|---|---|
| | | | |
| Remarks | | | |

▶ **START HERE - Type or print in black ink.** Type or print "N/A" if an item is not applicable or the answer is none, unless otherwise indicated. Failure to answer all of the questions may delay U.S. Citizenship and Immigration Services (USCIS) processing your Form N-400. **NOTE: You must complete Parts 1. - 15.**

If your biological or legal adoptive mother or father is a U.S. citizen by birth, or was naturalized before you reached your 18th birthday, you may already be a U.S. citizen. Before you consider filing this application, please visit the USCIS Website at www.uscis.gov for more information on this topic and to review the instructions for Form N-600, Application for Certificate of Citizenship, and Form N-600K, Application for Citizenship and Issuance of Certificate Under Section 322.

**NOTE:** Are either of your parents a United States citizen? If you answer "Yes," then complete **Part 6. Information About Your Parents** as part of this application. If you answer "No," then skip **Part 6.** and go to **Part 7. Biographic Information.**

### Part 1. Information About Your Eligibility (Select only one box or your Form N-400 may be delayed)

Enter Your 9 Digit A-Number:
▶ A-

1. You are at least 18 years of age **and**:

   A. ☒ Have been a lawful permanent resident of the United States for at least 5 years.

   B. ☐ Have been a lawful permanent resident of the United States for at least 3 years. In addition, you have been married to and living with the same U.S. citizen spouse for the last 3 years, **and** your spouse has been a U.S. citizen for the last 3 years at the time you filed your Form N-400.

   C. ☐ Are a lawful permanent resident of the United States **and** you are the spouse of a U.S. citizen **and** your U.S. citizen spouse is regularly engaged in specified employment abroad. (See the Immigration and Nationality Act (INA) section 319(b).) If your residential address is outside the United States and you are filing under Section 319(b), select the USCIS Field Office from the list below where you would like to have your naturalization interview:

   D. ☐ Are applying on the basis of qualifying military service.

   E. ☐ Other (Explain):

### Part 2. Information About You (Person applying for naturalization)

1. Your Current Legal Name (**do not** provide a nickname)

| Family Name (Last Name) | Given Name (First Name) | Middle Name (if applicable) |
|---|---|---|
| ▮▮▮▮▮ | ▮▮▮▮ | N/A |

2. Your Name Exactly As It Appears on Your Permanent Resident Card (if applicable)

| Family Name (Last Name) | Given Name (First Name) | Middle Name (if applicable) |
|---|---|---|
| ▮▮▮▮▮ | ▮▮▮▮ | N/A |

3. Other Names You Have Used Since Birth (include nicknames, aliases, and maiden name, if applicable)

| Family Name (Last Name) | Given Name (First Name) | Middle Name (if applicable) |
|---|---|---|
| N/A | N/A | N/A |
| N/A | N/A | N/A |

4. Name Change (Optional)

   **Read the Form N-400 Instructions before you decide whether or not you would like to legally change your name.**

   Would you like to legally change your name?　　　　　　　　　　　　　　　　☐ Yes ☒ No

   If you answered "Yes," type or print the new name you would like to use in the spaces provided below.

| Family Name (Last Name) | Given Name (First Name) | Middle Name (if applicable) |
|---|---|---|
|  |  |  |

5. U.S. Social Security Number (if applicable)　　6. USCIS Online Account Number (if any)

   ► ██████████　　　　　　　　　　► N A

7. Gender　　　8. Date of Birth　　　9. Date You Became a Lawful
   ☒ Male ☐ Female　　(mm/dd/yyyy)　　　Permanent Resident (mm/dd/yyyy)
   　　　　　　　　　　03/21/1976　　　　　08/29/1991

10. Country of Birth　　　　　　11. Country of Citizenship or Nationality

| Iran | Iran |
|---|---|

12. Do you have a physical or developmental disability or mental impairment that prevents you from demonstrating your knowledge and understanding of the English language and/or civics requirements for naturalization?　　　　☐ Yes ☒ No

    If you answered "Yes," submit a completed Form N-648, Medical Certification for Disability Exceptions, when you file your Form N-400.

13. Exemptions from the English Language Test

    A. Are you **50** years of age or older **and** have you lived in the United States as a lawful permanent resident for periods totaling at least **20** years at the time you file your Form N-400?　　☐ Yes ☒ No

    B. Are you **55** years of age or older **and** have you lived in the United States as a lawful permanent resident for periods totaling at least **15** years at the time you file your Form N-400?　　☐ Yes ☒ No

    C. Are you **65** years of age or older **and** have you lived in the United States as a lawful permanent resident for periods totaling at least **20** years at the time you file your Form N-400? (If you meet this requirement, you will also be given a simplified version of the civics test.)　　☐ Yes ☒ No

## Part 3. Accommodations for Individuals With Disabilities and/or Impairments

**NOTE:** Read the information in the Form N-400 Instructions before completing this part.

1. Are you requesting an accommodation because of your disabilities and/or impairments?　　☐ Yes ☒ No

   If you answered "Yes," select any applicable box.

   A. ☐ I am deaf or hard of hearing and request the following accommodation. (If you are requesting a sign-language interpreter, indicate for which language (for example, American Sign Language).)

   B. ☐ I am blind or have low vision and request the following accommodation:

C. ☐ I have another type of disability and/or impairment (for example, use a wheelchair). (Describe the nature of your disability and/or impairment and the accommodation you are requesting.)

---

## Part 4. Information to Contact You

1. Daytime Telephone Number

2. Work Telephone Number (if any)

3. Evening Telephone Number

4. Mobile Telephone Number (if any)

5. Email Address (if any)

---

## Part 5. Information About Your Residence

1. Where have you lived during the last five years? Provide your most recent residence and then list every location where you have lived during the last five years. If you need extra space, use additional sheets of paper.

   A. Current Physical Address

   | Street Number and Name | | | Apt. | Ste. | Flr. | Number |
   |---|---|---|---|---|---|---|
   | | | | ☐ | ☐ | ☐ | |

   | City or Town | County | State | ZIP Code + 4 |
   |---|---|---|---|
   | Mission Viejo | Orange County | CA | 92691 - |

   | Province or Region (foreign address only) | Postal Code (foreign address only) | Country (foreign address only) |
   |---|---|---|
   | | | USA |

   | Dates of Residence | From (mm/dd/yyyy) | To (mm/dd/yyyy) |
   |---|---|---|
   | | 04/28/2004 | Present |

   B. Current Mailing Address (if different from the address above)

   In Care Of Name (if any)

   | Street Number and Name | | | Apt. | Ste. | Flr. | Number |
   |---|---|---|---|---|---|---|
   | | | | ☐ | ☐ | ☐ | |

   | City or Town | County | State | ZIP Code + 4 |
   |---|---|---|---|
   | | | | - |

   | Province or Region (foreign address only) | Postal Code (foreign address only) | Country (foreign address only) |
   |---|---|---|
   | | | |

---

C.  Physical Address 2

Street Number and Name                                                          Apt. Ste. Flr. Number

| N/A | ☐ ☐ ☐ | N/A |

City or Town                            County                         State       ZIP Code + 4

| N/A | N/A | N/A | N/A | - |

Province or Region          Postal Code              Country
(foreign address only)      (foreign address only)   (foreign address only)

|  |  | N/A |

Dates of      From (mm/dd/yyyy)      To (mm/dd/yyyy)
Residence     N/A                    N/A

D.  Physical Address 3

Street Number and Name                                                          Apt. Ste. Flr. Number

| N/A | ☐ ☐ ☐ | N/A |

City or Town                            County                         State       ZIP Code + 4

| N/A | N/A | N/A | N/A | - |

Province or Region          Postal Code              Country
(foreign address only)      (foreign address only)   (foreign address only)

|  |  | N/A |

Dates of      From (mm/dd/yyyy)      To (mm/dd/yyyy)
Residence     N/A                    N/A

E.  Physical Address 4

Street Number and Name                                                          Apt. Ste. Flr. Number

| N/A | ☐ ☐ ☐ | N/A |

City or Town                            County                         State       ZIP Code + 4

| N/A | N/A | N/A | N/A | - |

Province or Region          Postal Code              Country
(foreign address only)      (foreign address only)   (foreign address only)

|  |  | N/A |

Dates of      From (mm/dd/yyyy)      To (mm/dd/yyyy)
Residence     N/A                    N/A

## Part 6. Information About Your Parents

If neither one of your parents is a United States citizen, then skip this part and go to Part 7.

1.  Were your parents married before your 18th birthday?                    ☐ Yes  ☒ No

### Information About Your Mother

2.  Is your mother a U.S. citizen?                                          ☒ Yes  ☐ No

    If you answered "Yes," complete the following information. If you answered "No," go to **Item Number 3.**

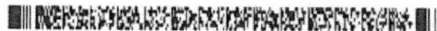

A. Current Legal Name of U.S. Citizen Mother

| Family Name (Last Name) | Given Name (First Name) | Middle Name (if applicable) |
|---|---|---|
| ▮ | Soheila | |

B. Mother's Country of Birth

Iran

C. Mother's Date of Birth (mm/dd/yyyy)

▮

D. Date Mother Became a U.S. Citizen (if known) (mm/dd/yyyy)

03/29/2000

E. Mother's A-Number (if any)

► A- ▮

*Information About Your Father*

3. Is your father a U.S. citizen?     ☐ Yes  ☒ No

If you answered "Yes," complete the information below. If you answered "No," go to **Part 7.**

A. Current Legal Name of U.S. Citizen Father

| Family Name (Last Name) | Given Name (First Name) | Middle Name (if applicable) |
|---|---|---|
| | | |

B. Father's Country of Birth

C. Father's Date of Birth (mm/dd/yyyy)

D. Date Father Became a U.S. Citizen (if known) (mm/dd/yyyy)

E. Father's A-Number (if any)

► A-

---

**Part 7. Biographic Information**

NOTE: USCIS requires you to complete the categories below to conduct background checks. (See the Form N-400 Instructions for more information.)

1. Ethnicity (Select **only one** box)

   ☐ Hispanic or Latino     ☒ Not Hispanic or Latino

2. Race (Select **all applicable** boxes)

   ☒ White  ☐ Asian  ☐ Black or African American  ☐ American Indian or Alaska Native  ☐ Native Hawaiian or Other Pacific Islander

3. Height  Feet 5  Inches 10     4. Weight  Pounds 1 8 5

5. Eye color (Select **only one** box)

   ☐ Black  ☐ Blue  ☒ Brown  ☐ Gray  ☐ Green  ☐ Hazel  ☐ Maroon  ☐ Pink  ☐ Unknown/Other

6. Hair color (Select **only one** box)

   ☐ Bald (No hair)  ☐ Black  ☐ Blond  ☒ Brown  ☐ Gray  ☐ Red  ☐ Sandy  ☐ White  ☐ Unknown/Other

## Part 8. Information About Your Employment and Schools You Attended

A- 0 4 3 0 6 0 7 1 8

List where you have worked or attended school full time or part time during the last five years. Provide information for the complete time period. Include all military, police, and/or intelligence service. Begin by providing information about your most recent or current employment, studies, or unemployment (if applicable). Provide the locations and dates where you worked, were self-employed, were unemployed, or have studied for the last five years. If you worked for yourself, type or print "self-employed." If you were unemployed, type or print "unemployed." If you need extra space, use additional sheets of paper.

1. Employer or School Name

| Street Number and Name | Apt. | Ste. | Flr. | Number |
|---|---|---|---|---|
| | ☐ | ☒ | ☐ | E |

| City or Town | State | ZIP Code + 4 |
|---|---|---|
| Tustin | CA | 92780 - |

| Province or Region (foreign address only) | Postal Code (foreign address only) | Country (foreign address only) |
|---|---|---|
| | | |

| Date From (mm/dd/yyyy) | Date To (mm/dd/yyyy) | Your Occupation |
|---|---|---|
| 03/2012 | PRESENT | Accounting/Logistics Manager |

2. Employer or School Name

N/A

| Street Number and Name | Apt. | Ste. | Flr. | Number |
|---|---|---|---|---|
| N/A | ☐ | ☐ | ☐ | N/A |

| City or Town | State | ZIP Code + 4 |
|---|---|---|
| N/A | N/A | N/A - |

| Province or Region (foreign address only) | Postal Code (foreign address only) | Country (foreign address only) |
|---|---|---|
| N/A | N/A | N/A |

| Date From (mm/dd/yyyy) | Date To (mm/dd/yyyy) | Your Occupation |
|---|---|---|
| N/A | N/A | N/A |

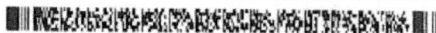

3. Employer or School Name

N/A

| Street Number and Name | Apt. | Ste. | Flr. | Number |
|---|---|---|---|---|
| N/A | ☐ | ☐ | ☐ | N/A |

| City or Town | State | ZIP Code + 4 |
|---|---|---|
| N/A | N/A | N/A - |

| Province or Region (foreign address only) | Postal Code (foreign address only) | Country (foreign address only) |
|---|---|---|
| N/A | N/A | N/A |

| Date From (mm/dd/yyyy) | Date To (mm/dd/yyyy) | Your Occupation |
|---|---|---|
| N/A | N/A | N/A |

**Part 9. Time Outside the United States**　　　　　　　A- ███████████

1. How many **total days (24 hours or longer)** did you spend outside the United States during the last 5 years?　　| 0 | days

2. How many trips of **24 hours or longer** have you taken outside the United States during the last 5 years?　　| 0 | trips

3. List below all the trips of **24 hours or longer** that you have taken outside the United States during the last 5 years. Start with your most recent trip and work backwards. If you need extra space, use additional sheets of paper.

| Date You Left the United States (mm/dd/yyyy) | Date You Returned to the United States (mm/dd/yyyy) | Did Trip Last 6 Months or More? | Countries to Which You Traveled | Total Days Outside the United States |
|---|---|---|---|---|
| | | ☐ Yes ☐ No | | |
| | | ☐ Yes ☐ No | | |
| | | ☐ Yes ☐ No | | |
| | | ☐ Yes ☐ No | | |
| | | ☐ Yes ☐ No | | |
| | | ☐ Yes ☐ No | | |

**Part 10. Information About Your Marital History**

1. What is your current marital status?

    ☒ Single, Never Married　☐ Married　☐ Divorced　☐ Widowed　☐ Separated　☐ Marriage Annulled

    If you are single and have **never** married, go to **Part 11**.

2. If you are married, is your spouse a current member of the U.S. armed forces?　　☐ Yes ☐ No

3. How many times have you been married (including annulled marriages, marriages to other people, and marriages to the same person)?　　| 0 |

4. If you are married now, provide the following information about your current spouse.

    A. Current Spouse's Legal Name

    | Family Name (Last Name) | Given Name (First Name) | Middle Name (if applicable) |
    |---|---|---|
    | N/A | N/A | N/A |

    B. Current Spouse's Previous Legal Name

    | Family Name (Last Name) | Given Name (First Name) | Middle Name (if applicable) |
    |---|---|---|
    | N/A | N/A | N/A |

    C. Other Names Used by Current Spouse (include nicknames, aliases, and maiden name, if applicable)

    | Family Name (Last Name) | Given Name (First Name) | Middle Name (if applicable) |
    |---|---|---|
    | N/A | N/A | N/A |

    D. Current Spouse's Date of Birth (mm/dd/yyyy)　　E. Date You Entered into Marriage with Current Spouse (mm/dd/yyyy)

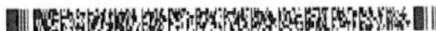

    | N/A | N/A |
    |---|---|

**F.** Current Spouse's Present Home Address

Street Number and Name                                                                  Apt. Ste. Flr. Number

N/A                                                                                ☐ ☐ ☐  N/A

City or Town                          County                          State          ZIP Code + 4

N/A                                   N/A                            N/A            N/A -

Province or Region            Postal Code                    Country
(foreign address only)        (foreign address only)        (foreign address only)

N/A                           N/A                            N/A

**G.** Current Spouse's Current Employer or Company

N/A

**5.** Is your current spouse a U.S. citizen?                                    ☐ Yes ☐ No

If you answered "Yes," answer **Item Number 6.** If you answered "No," go to **Item Number 7.**

**6.** If your current spouse is a U.S. citizen, complete the following information.

**A.** When did your current spouse become a U.S. citizen?

☐ At Birth - Go to **Item Number 8.**      ☐ Other - Complete the following information.

**B.** Date Your Current Spouse Became
a U.S. Citizen (mm/dd/yyyy)

N/A

**7.** If your current spouse is not a U.S. citizen, complete the following information.

**A.** Current Spouse's Country of Citizenship or Nationality    **B.** Current Spouse's A-Number (if any)

N/A                                                         ► A- N/A

**C.** Current Spouse's Immigration Status

☐ Lawful Permanent Resident    ☐ Other (Explain):

**8.** How many times has your current spouse been married (including annulled marriages, marriages to
other people, and marriages to the same person)? If your current spouse has been married before,
provide the following information about your current spouse's prior spouse.                N/A

If your current spouse has had more than one previous marriage, provide that information on additional sheets of paper.

**A.** Legal Name of My Current Spouse's Prior Spouse

Family Name (Last Name)               Given Name (First Name)           Middle Name (if applicable)

N/A                                   N/A                              N/A

**B.** Immigration Status of My Current Spouse's Prior Spouse (if known)

☐ U.S. Citizen    ☐ Lawful Permanent Resident    ☐ Other (Explain):

**C.** Date of Birth of My Current Spouse's    **D.** Country of Birth of My Current Spouse's
Prior Spouse (mm/dd/yyyy)                         Prior Spouse

N/A                                              N/A

**E.** Country of Citizenship or Nationality of My Current
Spouse's Prior Spouse

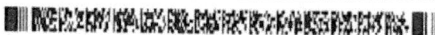

N/A

| Part 10. Information About Your Marital History (continued) | A- ████████ |
|---|---|

**F.** My Current Spouse's Date of Marriage with Prior Spouse (mm/dd/yyyy)

N/A

**G.** Date My Current Spouse's Marriage Ended with Prior Spouse (mm/dd/yyyy)

N/A

**H.** How My Current Spouse's Marriage Ended with Prior Spouse

☐ Annulled  ☐ Divorced  ☐ Spouse Deceased  ☐ Other (Explain): _____

**9.** If you were married before, provide the following information about your prior spouse. If you have more than one previous marriage, provide that information on additional sheets of paper.

**A.** My Prior Spouse's Legal Name

| Family Name (Last Name) | Given Name (First Name) | Middle Name (if applicable) |
|---|---|---|
| N/A | N/A | N/A |

**B.** My Prior Spouse's Immigration Status When My Marriage Ended (if known)

☐ U.S. Citizen  ☐ Lawful Permanent Resident  ☐ Other (Explain): _____

**C.** My Prior Spouse's Date of Birth (mm/dd/yyyy)

N/A

**D.** My Prior Spouse's Country of Birth

N/A

**E.** My Prior Spouse's Country of Citizenship or Nationality

N/A

**F.** Date of Marriage with My Prior Spouse (mm/dd/yyyy)

N/A

**G.** Date Marriage Ended with My Prior Spouse (mm/dd/yyyy)

N/A

**H.** How Marriage Ended with My Prior Spouse

☐ Annulled  ☐ Divorced  ☐ Spouse Deceased  ☐ Other (Explain): _____

| Part 11. Information About Your Children |
|---|

**1.** Indicate your total number of children. (You must indicate **ALL** children, including: children who are alive, missing, or deceased; children born in the United States or in other countries; children under 18 years of age or older; children who are currently married or unmarried; children living with you or elsewhere; current stepchildren; legally adopted children; **and** children born when you were not married.)

`0`

**2.** Provide the following information about all your children (sons and daughters) listed in **Item Number 1.**, regardless of age. To list any additional children, use additional sheets of paper.

**A.** Child 1

Current Legal Name

| Family Name (Last Name) | Given Name (First Name) | Middle Name (if applicable) |
|---|---|---|
| N/A | N/A | N/A |

| A-Number (if any) | Date of Birth (mm/dd/yyyy) | Country of Birth |
|---|---|---|
| ► A- N/A | N/A | N/A |

 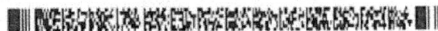

Current Address

Street Number and Name                                              Apt.  Ste.  Flr.  Number
N/A                                                                 ☐    ☐    ☐    N/A

City or Town                County                    State        ZIP Code + 4
N/A                         N/A                        N/A          N/A   -

Province or Region          Postal Code               Country
(foreign address only)      (foreign address only)    (foreign address only)
N/A                         N/A                        N/A

What is your child's relationship to you? (for example, biological child,    N/A
stepchild, legally adopted child)

**B.  Child 2**

Current Legal Name

Family Name (Last Name)        Given Name (First Name)        Middle Name (if applicable)
N/A                            N/A                            N/A

A-Number (if any)              Date of Birth (mm/dd/yyyy)  Country of Birth
► A-  N/A                       N/A                         N/A

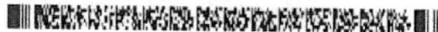

Current Address

Street Number and Name                                              Apt.  Ste.  Flr.  Number
N/A                                                                 ☐    ☐    ☐    N/A

City or Town                County                    State        ZIP Code + 4
N/A                         N/A                        N/A          N/A   -

Province or Region          Postal Code               Country
(foreign address only)      (foreign address only)    (foreign address only)
N/A                         N/A                        N/A

What is your child's relationship to you? (for example, biological child,    N/A
stepchild, legally adopted child)

**C.  Child 3**

Current Legal Name

Family Name (Last Name)        Given Name (First Name)        Middle Name (if applicable)
N/A                            N/A                            N/A

A-Number (if any)              Date of Birth (mm/dd/yyyy)  Country of Birth
► A-  N/A                       N/A                         N/A

## Part 11. Information About Your Children (continued)    A- ▮▮▮▮▮▮▮

Current Address

Street Number and Name | Apt. Ste. Flr. Number
N/A | ☐ ☐ ☐ N/A

City or Town | County | State | ZIP Code + 4
N/A | N/A | N/A | N/A -

Province or Region (foreign address only) | Postal Code (foreign address only) | Country (foreign address only)
N/A | N/A | N/A

What is your child's relationship to you? (for example, biological child, stepchild, legally adopted child) | N/A

### D. Child 4

Current Legal Name

Family Name (Last Name) | Given Name (First Name) | Middle Name (if applicable)
N/A | N/A | N/A

A-Number (if any) | Date of Birth (mm/dd/yyyy) | Country of Birth
▶ A- N/A | N/A | N/A

Current Address

Street Number and Name | Apt. Ste. Flr. Number
N/A | ☐ ☐ ☐ N/A

City or Town | County | State | ZIP Code + 4
N/A | N/A | N/A | N/A -

Province or Region (foreign address only) | Postal Code (foreign address only) | Country (foreign address only)
N/A | N/A | N/A

What is your child's relationship to you? (for example, biological child, stepchild, legally adopted child) | N/A

## Part 12. Additional Information About You (Person Applying for Naturalization)

Answer Item Numbers 1. - 21. If you answer "Yes" to any of these questions, include a typed or printed explanation on additional sheets of paper.

1. Have you **EVER** claimed to be a U.S. citizen (in writing or any other way)? ☐ Yes ☒ No

2. Have you **EVER** registered to vote in any Federal, state, or local election in the United States? ☐ Yes ☒ No

3. Have you **EVER** voted in any Federal, state, or local election in the United States? ☐ Yes ☒ No

4. A. Do you now have, or did you **EVER** have, a hereditary title or an order of nobility in any foreign country? ☐ Yes ☒ No

   B. If you answered "Yes," are you willing to give up any inherited titles or orders of nobility that you have in a foreign country at your naturalization ceremony? ☐ Yes ☐ No

5. Have you **EVER** been declared legally incompetent or been confined to a mental institution? ☐ Yes ☒ No

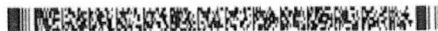

6. Do you owe any overdue Federal, state, or local taxes? ☐ Yes ☒ No

7. A. Have you **EVER** not filed a Federal, state, or local tax return since you became a lawful permanent resident? ☐ Yes ☒ No

   B. If you answered "Yes," did you consider yourself to be a "non-U.S. resident"? ☐ Yes ☐ No

8. Have you called yourself a "non-U.S. resident" on a Federal, state, or local tax return since you became a lawful permanent resident? ☐ Yes ☒ No

9. A. Have you **EVER** been a member of, involved in, or in any way associated with, any organization, association, fund, foundation, party, club, society, or similar group in the United States or in any other location in the world? ☐ Yes ☒ No

   B. If you answered "Yes," provide the information below. If you need extra space, attach the names of the other groups on additional sheets of paper and provide any evidence to support your answers.

| Name of the Group | Purpose of the Group | Dates of Membership | |
|---|---|---|---|
| | | From (mm/dd/yyyy) | To (mm/dd/yyyy) |
| | | | |
| | | | |
| | | | |
| | | | |

10. Have you **EVER** been a member of, or in any way associated (either directly or indirectly) with:

    A. The Communist Party? ☐ Yes ☒ No

    B. Any other totalitarian party? ☐ Yes ☒ No

    C. A terrorist organization? ☐ Yes ☒ No

11. Have you **EVER** advocated (either directly or indirectly) the overthrow of any government by force or violence? ☐ Yes ☒ No

12. Have you **EVER** persecuted (either directly or indirectly) any person because of race, religion, national origin, membership in a particular social group, or political opinion? ☐ Yes ☒ No

13. Between March 23, 1933 and May 8, 1945, did you work for or associate in any way (either directly or indirectly) with:

    A. The Nazi government of Germany? ☐ Yes ☒ No

    B. Any government in any area occupied by, allied with, or established with the help of the Nazi government of Germany? ☐ Yes ☒ No

    C. Any German, Nazi, or S.S. military unit, paramilitary unit, self-defense unit, vigilante unit, citizen unit, police unit, government agency or office, extermination camp, concentration camp, prisoner of war camp, prison, labor camp, or transit camp? ☐ Yes ☒ No

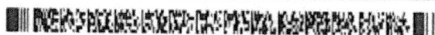

14. Were you **EVER** involved in any way with any of the following:

    A.  Genocide?    ☐ Yes ☒ No

    B.  Torture?    ☐ Yes ☒ No

    C.  Killing, or trying to kill, someone?    ☐ Yes ☒ No

    D.  Badly hurting, or trying to hurt, a person on purpose?    ☐ Yes ☒ No

    E.  Forcing, or trying to force, someone to have any kind of sexual contact or relations?    ☐ Yes ☒ No

    F.  Not letting someone practice his or her religion?    ☐ Yes ☒ No

15. Were you **EVER** a member of, or did you **EVER** serve in, help, or otherwise participate in, any of the following groups:

    A.  Military unit?    ☐ Yes ☒ No

    B.  Paramilitary unit (a group of people who act like a military group but are not part of the official military)?    ☐ Yes ☒ No

    C.  Police unit?    ☐ Yes ☒ No

    D.  Self-defense unit?    ☐ Yes ☒ No

    E.  Vigilante unit (a group of people who act like the police, but are not part of the official police)?    ☐ Yes ☒ No

    F.  Rebel group?    ☐ Yes ☒ No

    G.  Guerrilla group (a group of people who use weapons against or otherwise physically attack the military, police, government, or other people)?    ☐ Yes ☒ No

    H.  Militia (an army of people, not part of the official military)?    ☐ Yes ☒ No

    I.  Insurgent organization (a group that uses weapons and fights against a government)?    ☐ Yes ☒ No

16. Were you **EVER** a worker, volunteer, or soldier, or did you otherwise **EVER** serve in any of the following:

    A.  Prison or jail?    ☐ Yes ☒ No

    B.  Prison camp?    ☐ Yes ☒ No

    C.  Detention facility (a place where people are forced to stay)?    ☐ Yes ☒ No

    D.  Labor camp (a place where people are forced to work)?    ☐ Yes ☒ No

    E.  Any other place where people were forced to stay?    ☐ Yes ☒ No

17. Were you **EVER** a part of any group, or did you **EVER** help any group, unit, or organization that used a weapon against any person, or threatened to do so?    ☐ Yes ☒ No

    A.  If you answered "Yes," when you were part of this group, or when you helped this group, did you ever use a weapon against another person?    ☐ Yes ☐ No

    B.  If you answered "Yes," when you were part of this group, or when you helped this group, did you ever tell another person that you would use a weapon against that person?    ☐ Yes ☐ No

18. Did you **EVER** sell, give, or provide weapons to any person, or help another person sell, give, or provide weapons to any person?    ☐ Yes ☒ No

    A.  If you answered "Yes," did you know that this person was going to use the weapons against another person?    ☐ Yes ☐ No

    B.  If you answered "Yes," did you know that this person was going to sell or give the weapons to someone who was going to use them against another person?    ☐ Yes ☐ No

19. Did you **EVER** receive any type of military, paramilitary (a group of people who act like a military group but are not part of the official military), or weapons training? ☐ Yes ☒ No

20. Did you **EVER** recruit (ask), enlist (sign up), conscript (require), or use any person under 15 years of age to serve in or help an armed force or group? ☐ Yes ☒ No

21. Did you **EVER** use any person under 15 years of age to do anything that helped or supported people in combat? ☐ Yes ☒ No

**If any of Item Numbers 22. - 28. apply to you, you must answer "Yes" even if your records have been sealed, expunged, or otherwise cleared.** You must disclose this information even if someone, including a judge, law enforcement officer, or attorney, told you that it no longer constitutes a record or told you that you do not have to disclose the information.

22. Have you **EVER** committed, assisted in committing, or attempted to commit, a crime or offense for which you were **NOT** arrested? ☐ Yes ☒ No

23. Have you **EVER** been arrested, cited, or detained by any law enforcement officer (including any immigration official or any official of the U.S. armed forces) for any reason? ☒ Yes ☐ No

24. Have you **EVER** been charged with committing, attempting to commit, or assisting in committing a crime or offense? ☒ Yes ☐ No

25. Have you **EVER** been convicted of a crime or offense? ☒ Yes ☐ No

26. Have you **EVER** been placed in an alternative sentencing or a rehabilitative program (for example, diversion, deferred prosecution, withheld adjudication, deferred adjudication)? ☐ Yes ☐ No

27. A. Have you **EVER** received a suspended sentence, been placed on probation, or been paroled? ☒ Yes ☐ No

    B. If you answered "Yes," have you completed the probation or parole? ☒ Yes ☐ No

28. A. Have you **EVER** been in jail or prison? ☒ Yes ☐ No

    B. If you answered "Yes," how long were you in jail or prison? Years `0` Months `0` Days `1233`

29. If you answered "No" to ALL questions in Item Numbers 23. - 28., then skip this item and go to **Item Number 30.**

    If you answered "Yes" to any question in Item Numbers 23. - 28., then complete this table. If you need extra space, use additional sheets of paper and provide any evidence to support your answers.

| Why were you arrested, cited, detained, or charged? | Date arrested, cited, detained, or charged. (mm/dd/yyyy) | Where were you arrested, cited, detained, or charged? (City or Town, State, Country) | Outcome or disposition of the arrest, citation, detention, or charge (no charges filed, charges dismissed, jail, probation, etc.) |
|---|---|---|---|
| Speeding | 06/22/1998 | Orange County, CA USA | Fine |
| No Registration/Seat Belt | 09/29/1999 | Orange County, CA USA | Fine |
| No License | 05/01/1999 | Orange County, CA USA | Fine |
| Driving On Suspended | 06/01/1999 | Orange County, CA USA | Fine |
| See Attached. | See Attached. | See Attached. | See Attached |

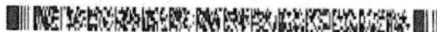

Answer **Item Numbers 30. - 46.** If you answer "Yes" to any of these questions, except **Item Numbers 37.** and **38.**, include a typed or printed explanation on additional sheets of paper and provide any evidence to support your answers.

30. Have you **EVER**:

    A. Been a habitual drunkard? ☐ Yes ☒ No

    B. Been a prostitute, or procured anyone for prostitution? ☐ Yes ☒ No

    C. Sold or smuggled controlled substances, illegal drugs, or narcotics? ☐ Yes ☒ No

    D. Been married to more than one person at the same time? ☐ Yes ☒ No

    E. Married someone in order to obtain an immigration benefit? ☐ Yes ☒ No

    F. Helped anyone to enter, or try to enter, the United States illegally? ☐ Yes ☒ No

    G. Gambled illegally or received income from illegal gambling? ☐ Yes ☒ No

    H. Failed to support your dependents or to pay alimony? ☐ Yes ☒ No

    I. Made any misrepresentation to obtain any public benefit in the United States? ☐ Yes ☒ No

31. Have you **EVER** given any U.S. Government officials **any** information or documentation that was false, fraudulent, or misleading? ☐ Yes ☒ No

32. Have you **EVER** lied to any U.S. Government officials to gain entry or admission into the United States or to gain immigration benefits while in the United States? ☐ Yes ☒ No

33. Have you **EVER** been removed, excluded, or deported from the United States? ☒ Yes ☐ No

34. Have you **EVER** been ordered removed, excluded, or deported from the United States? ☒ Yes ☐ No

35. Have you **EVER** been placed in removal, exclusion, rescission, or deportation proceedings? ☒ Yes ☐ No

36. Are removal, exclusion, rescission, or deportation proceedings (including administratively closed proceedings) **currently** pending against you? ☐ Yes ☒ No

37. Have you **EVER** served in the U.S. armed forces? ☐ Yes ☒ No

38. A. Are you **currently** a member of the U.S. armed forces? ☐ Yes ☒ No

    B. If you answered "Yes," are you scheduled to deploy overseas, including to a vessel, within the next three months? (Refer to the **Address Change** section in the Instructions on how to notify USCIS if you learn of your deployment plans after you file your Form N-400.) ☐ Yes ☐ No

    C. If you answered "Yes," are you **currently** stationed overseas? ☐ Yes ☐ No

39. Have you **EVER** been court-martialed, administratively separated, or disciplined, or have you received an other than honorable discharge, while in the U.S. armed forces? ☐ Yes ☒ No

40. Have you **EVER** been discharged from training or service in the U.S. armed forces because you were an alien? ☐ Yes ☒ No

41. Have you **EVER** left the United States to avoid being drafted in the U.S. armed forces? ☐ Yes ☒ No

42. Have you **EVER** applied for any kind of exemption from military service in the U.S. armed forces? ☐ Yes ☒ No

43. Have you **EVER** deserted from the U.S. armed forces? ☐ Yes ☒ No

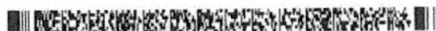

**Part 12. Additional Information About You** (Person Applying for Naturalization) (continued)

A- ▇▇▇▇▇▇▇▇▇

44. **A.** Are you a male who lived in the United States at any time between your 18th and 26th birthdays? (This does not include living in the United States as a lawful nonimmigrant.) ☒ Yes ☐ No

   **B.** If you answered "Yes," when did you register for the Selective Service? Provide the information below.

   | Date Registered (mm/dd/yyyy) | Selective Service Number |
   |---|---|
   | ᴎ/ᴀ | ᴎ/ᴀ |

   **C.** If you answered "Yes," but you **did not register** with the Selective Service System and you are:

   1. Still under 26 years of age, you must register before you apply for naturalization, and complete the Selective Service information above; **OR**

   2. Now 26 to 31 years of age (29 years of age if you are filing under INA section 319(a)), but you did not register with the Selective Service, you must attach a statement explaining why you did not register, and provide a status information letter from the Selective Service.

Answer **Item Numbers 45. - 50.** If you answer "No" to any of these questions, include a typed or printed explanation on additional sheets of paper and provide any evidence to support your answers.

45. Do you support the Constitution and form of Government of the United States? ☒ Yes ☐ No

46. Do you understand the full Oath of Allegiance to the United States? ☒ Yes ☐ No

47. Are you willing to take the full Oath of Allegiance to the United States? ☒ Yes ☐ No

48. If the law requires it, are you willing to bear arms on behalf of the United States? ☒ Yes ☐ No

49. If the law requires it, are you willing to perform noncombatant services in the U.S. armed forces? ☒ Yes ☐ No

50. If the law requires it, are you willing to perform work of national importance under civilian direction? ☒ Yes ☐ No

---

**Part 13. Applicant's Statement, Certification, and Signature**

**NOTE:** Read the **Penalties** section of the Form N-400 Instructions before completing this part.

*Applicant's Statement*

**NOTE:** Select the box for either **Item A.** or **B.** in **Item Number 1.** If applicable, select the box for **Item Number 2.**

1. Applicant's Statement Regarding the Interpreter

   **A.** ☒ I can read and understand English, and I have read and understand every question and instruction on this application and my answer to every question.

   **B.** ☐ The interpreter named in **Part 14.** read to me every question and instruction on this application and my answer to every question in _____, a language in which I am fluent, and I understood everything.

2. Applicant's Statement Regarding the Preparer

   ☒ At my request, the preparer named in **Part 15.,** | Christopher A. Reed | , prepared this application for me based only upon information I provided or authorized.

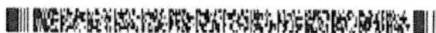

## Applicant's Certification

Copies of any documents I have submitted are exact photocopies of unaltered, original documents, and I understand that USCIS may require that I submit original documents to USCIS at a later date. Furthermore, I authorize the release of any information from any of my records that USCIS may need to determine my eligibility for the immigration benefit that I seek.

I further authorize release of information contained in this application, in supporting documents, and in my USCIS records to other entities and persons where necessary for the administration and enforcement of U.S. immigration laws.

I understand that USCIS will require me to appear for an appointment to take my biometrics (fingerprints, photograph, and/or signature) and, at that time, I will be required to sign an oath reaffirming that:

1) I reviewed and provided or authorized all of the information in my application;

2) I understood all of the information contained in, and submitted with, my application; and

3) All of this information was complete, true, and correct at the time of filing.

I certify, under penalty of perjury, that I provided or authorized all of the information in my application, I understand all of the information contained in, and submitted with, my application, and that all of this information is complete, true, and correct.

### Applicant's Signature

| | | |
|---|---|---|
| 3. | Applicant's Signature | Date of Signature (mm/dd/yyyy) |
| ➡ | *K. A. Shaany* | 09/22/2020 |

**NOTE TO ALL APPLICANTS:** If you do not completely fill out this application or fail to submit required documents listed in the Instructions, USCIS may deny your application.

---

**Part 14. Interpreter's Contact Information, Certification, and Signature**

Provide the following information about the interpreter.

### Interpreter's Full Name

1. Interpreter's Family Name (Last Name)      Interpreter's Given Name (First Name)

2. Interpreter's Business or Organization Name (if any)

### Interpreter's Mailing Address

3. Street Number and Name     Apt.   Ste.   Flr.   Number

    City or Town     State    ZIP Code + 4

    Province     Postal Code    Country

**Part 14. Interpreter's Contact Information, Certification, and Signature** (continued)

### *Interpreter's Contact Information*

4. Interpreter's Daytime Telephone Number

5. Interpreter's Mobile Telephone Number (if any)

6. Interpreter's Email Address (if any)

### *Interpreter's Certification*

I certify, under penalty of perjury, that:

I am fluent in English and [                              ], which is the same language specified in **Part 13., Item B.** in **Item Number 1.**, and I have read to this applicant in the identified language every question and instruction on this application and his or her answer to every question. The applicant informed me that he or she understands every instruction, question and answer on the application, including the **Applicant's Certification** and has verified the accuracy of every answer.

### *Interpreter's Signature*

7. Interpreter's Signature

Date of Signature (mm/dd/yyyy)

➡

**Part 15. Contact Information, Declaration, and Signature of the Person Preparing This Application, if Other Than the Applicant**

Provide the following information about the preparer.

### *Preparer's Full Name*

1. Preparer's Family Name (Last Name)

   Reed

   Preparer's Given Name (First Name)

   Christopher

2. Preparer's Business or Organization Name (if any)

   Law Offices of Brian D. Lerner, APC

### *Preparer's Mailing Address*

3. Street Number and Name

   3233 E. Broadway

   Apt. Ste. Flr. □ □ □  Number

   City or Town

   Long Beach

   State  CA

   ZIP Code + 4  90803 -

   Province

   Postal Code

   Country  USA

**Part 15. Contact Information, Declaration, and Signature of the Person Preparing This Application, if Other Than the Applicant** (continued)

A- ▓▓▓▓▓▓▓▓▓▓▓

*Preparer's Contact Information*

4. Preparer's Daytime Telephone Number

(562) 495-0554

5. Preparer's Mobile Telephone Number (if any)

N/A

6. Preparer's Email Address (if any)

creed@eimmigration.org

*Preparer's Statement*

7. A. ☐ I am not an attorney or accredited representative but have prepared this application on behalf of the applicant and with the applicant's consent.

B. ☒ I am an attorney or accredited representative and my representation of the applicant in this case
☒ extends ☐ does not extend beyond the preparation of this application.

**NOTE:** If you are an attorney or accredited representative whose representation extends beyond preparation of this application, you may be obliged to submit a completed Form G-28, Notice of Entry of Appearance as Attorney or Accredited Representative, with this application.

*Preparer's Certification*

By my signature, I certify, under penalty of perjury, that I prepared this application at the request of the applicant. The applicant then reviewed this completed application and informed me that he or she understands all of the information contained in, and submitted with, his or her application, including the **Applicant's Certification**, and that all of this information is complete, true, and correct. I completed this application based only on information that the applicant provided to me or authorized me to obtain or use.

*Preparer's Signature*

8. Preparer's Signature

➡

Date of Signature (mm/dd/yyyy)

09/22/2020

**NOTE: Do not complete Parts 16., 17., or 18. until the USCIS Officer instructs you to do so at the interview.**

**Part 16. Signature at Interview**

I swear (affirm) and certify under penalty of perjury under the laws of the United States of America that I know that the contents of this Form N-400, Application for Naturalization, subscribed by me, including corrections number 1 through _____ , are complete, true, and correct. The evidence submitted by me on numbered pages 1 through _____ are complete, true, and correct.

Subscribed to and sworn to (affirmed) before me

|  |  |
|---|---|
| USCIS Officer's Printed Name or Stamp | Date of Signature (mm/dd/yyyy) |

| Applicant's Signature | USCIS Officer's Signature |
|---|---|
|  |  |

| Part 17. Renunciation of Foreign Titles | A- ▇▇▇▇▇▇▇▇ |
|---|---|

If you answered "Yes" to **Part 12., Items A.** and **B.** in **Item Number 4.**, then you must affirm the following before a USCIS officer:

I further renounce the title of _____ which I have heretofore held; or
                              (list titles)

I further renounce the order of nobility of _____ to which I have heretofore belonged.
                                         (list order of nobility)

Applicant's Printed Name

Applicant's Signature

USCIS Officer's Printed Name

USCIS Officer's Signature

Date of Signature (mm/dd/yyyy)

| Part 18. Oath of Allegiance |
|---|

If your application is approved, you will be scheduled for a public oath ceremony at which time you will be required to take the following Oath of Allegiance immediately prior to becoming a naturalized citizen. By signing below you acknowledge your willingness and ability to take this oath:

I hereby declare on oath, that I absolutely and entirely renounce and abjure all allegiance and fidelity to any foreign prince, potentate, state, or sovereignty, of whom or which I have heretofore been a subject or citizen;

that I will support and defend the Constitution and laws of the United States of America against all enemies, foreign, and domestic;

that I will bear true faith and allegiance to the same;

that I will bear arms on behalf of the United States when required by the law;

that I will perform noncombatant service in the armed forces of the United States when required by the law;

that I will perform work of national importance under civilian direction when required by the law; and

that I take this obligation freely, without any mental reservation or purpose of evasion; so help me God.

**Applicant's Printed Name**

| Family Name (Last Name) | Given Name (First Name) | Middle Name (if applicable) |
|---|---|---|
| | | |

**Applicant's Signature**

| Applicant's Signature | Date of Signature (mm/dd/yyyy) |
|---|---|
| | |

## Addendum

Part 12 Number 23.:
Applicant has been convicted of various vehicle code violations, some infractions and others misdemeanors.
Applicant also had 6 other criminal cases that were vacated and dismissed pursuant to PC § 1204.43 and PC
§ 1473.7.

Part 12 Number 24.:
See Above.

Part 12 Number 25.:
See Above.

Part 12 Number 26.:
See Above.

Part 12 Number 27A.:
See Above.

Part 12 Number 27B.:
See Above.

Part 12 Number 28A.:
See Above.

Part 12 Number 33.:
Applicant was ordered removed on October 17, 2011. On March 1, 2019, his removal proceedings were
reopened and terminated by the Immigration Judge in Los Angeles, CA.

Part 12 Number 34.:
See above.

Part 12 Number 35.:
See above.

# EXHIBIT 'I'

## Applicant's Permanent Resident Card

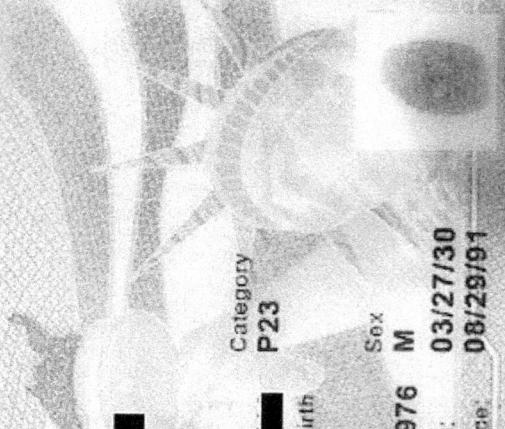

UNITED STATES OF AMERICA
**PERMANENT RESIDENT**

Surname

Given Name

USCIS#

Category
P23

Country of Birth

Date of Birth
21 MAR 1976

Sex
M

Card Expires: 03/27/30

Resident Since: 08/29/91

6400586

122

62276780

FORM I-551
Rev (00-0000)

# EXHIBIT '2'

## Naturalization Certificate of Applicant's Mother

UNITED STATES OF AMERICA

No. 25532337

CERTIFICATE OF NATURALIZATION

INS Registration No.

Personal description of holder
as of date of naturalization:

Date of birth: JANUARY 1, 1949

Sex: FEMALE

Height: 5 feet 3 inches

Marital status: DIVORCED

Country of former nationality:
IRAN

I certify that the description given is true, and that the photograph affixed
hereto is a likeness of me.

_____
(Complete and true signature of holder)

Be it known that, pursuant to an application filed with the Attorney General

at: LOS ANGELES, CA

The Attorney General having found that:

then residing in the United States, intends to reside in the United States when so
required by the Naturalization Laws of the United States, and had in all other
respects complied with the applicable provisions of such naturalization laws and was
entitled to be admitted to citizenship, such person having taken the oath of allegiance
in a ceremony conducted by the

U.S. DISTRICT COURT
FOR THE CENTRAL DIST. OF CALIFORNIA

at: LOS ANGELES, CA
on:
MARCH 29, 2000

that such person is admitted as a citizen of the United States of America.

_____
Commissioner of Immigration and Naturalization

FORM N-550 REV. C-91

# EXHIBIT '3'

Applicant's Notice to Appear

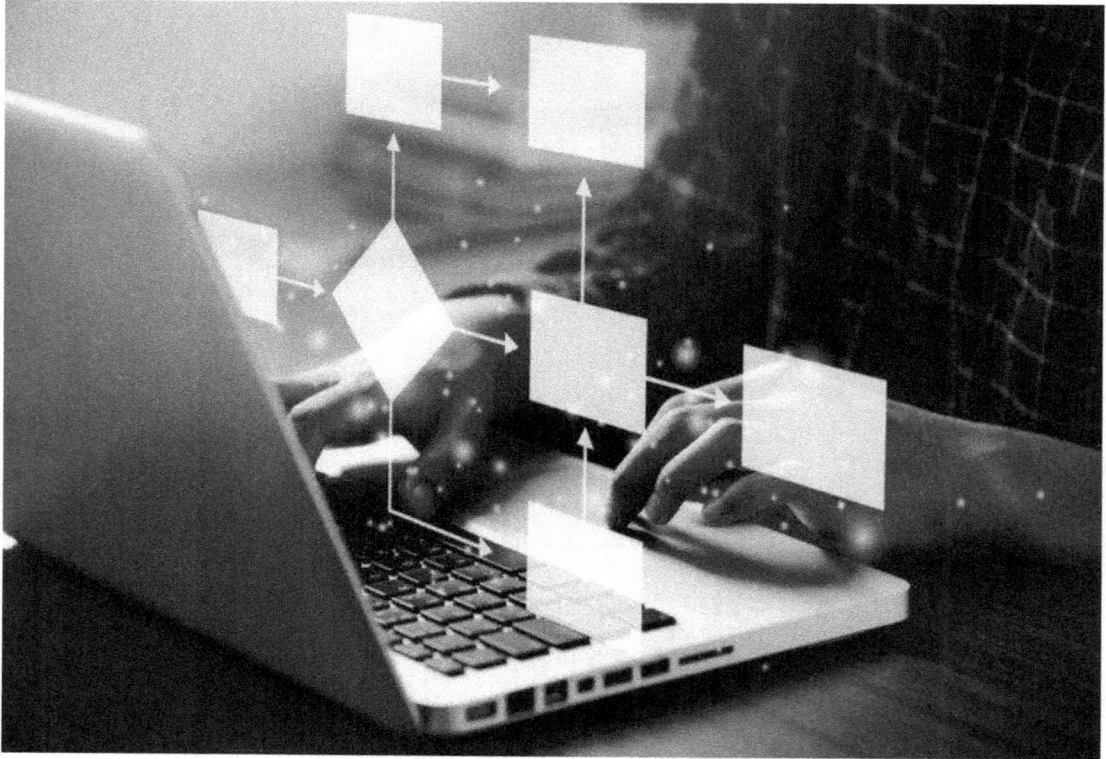

U.S. Department of Homeland Security

Notice to Appear

## In removal proceedings under section 240 of the Immigration and Nationality Act:

Subject ID : 340760698       FIN #: 1122706063       File No: ▓▓▓▓▓▓▓▓

                          DOB: 03/21/1976       Event No: SBD1108000559

In the Matter of: ███████████████████████████████████

Respondent: _____ currently residing at:

4500 NORTH 60TH STREET WEST , LANCASTER CALIFORNIA 93536            (661) 940-3555

                      (Number, street, city and ZIP code)           (Area code and phone number)

☐ 1. You are an arriving alien.

☐ 2. You are an alien present in the United States who has not been admitted or paroled.

☒ 3. You have been admitted to the United States, but are removable for the reasons stated below.

The Department of Homeland Security alleges that you:
       See Continuation Page Made a Part Hereof

On the basis of the foregoing, it is charged that you are subject to removal from the United States pursuant to the following provision(s) of law:
       See Continuation Page Made a Part Hereof

☐ This notice is being issued after an asylum officer has found that the respondent has demonstrated a credible fear of persecution or torture.

☒ Section 235(b)(1) order was vacated pursuant to: ☒ 8CFR 208.30(f)(2) ☐ 8CFR 235.3(b)(5)(iv)

YOU ARE ORDERED to appear before an immigration judge of the United States Department of Justice at:
TO BE DETERMINED

_____
           (Complete Address of Immigration Court including Room Number, if any)

on   a date to be set   at   a time to be set   to show why you should not be removed from the United States based on the

        (Date)                  (Time)

charge(s) set forth above.                 SDDU

Date:   8-26-11                   (Signature and Title of Issuing Officer)

                                 (City and State)

See reverse for important information

Form I-862 (Rev. 08/01/07)

Subject ID : 340760698     Event No: SBD1108000559
FINS #: 1122706063
File No:

Name: Kiarash ASHAARY (AKA : SINI, KIARASH ASHAARY; ASHAARY, KIARASH HKN; ASHAARY, KIARASH; ASHARRY, KIARASHSINI; ASHAARY, SINI)

## NOTICE OF RIGHTS

You have been arrested because immigration officers believe that you are illegally in the United States. You have the right to a hearing before the Immigration Court to determine whether you may remain in the United States. If you request a hearing, you may be detained in custody or you may be eligible to be released on bond, until your hearing date. In the alternative, you may request to return to your country as soon as possible, without a hearing.

You have the right to contact an attorney or other legal representative to represent you at your hearings, or to answer any questions regarding your legal rights in the United States. Upon your request, the officer who gave you this notice will provide you with a list of legal organizations that may represent you for free or for a small fee. You have the right to communicate with the consular or diplomatic officer from your country. You may use a telephone to call a lawyer, other legal representative, or consular officer at any time prior to your departure from the United States.

## REQUEST FOR DISPOSITION

_____ ☐ I request a hearing before the Immigration Court to determine whether or not I may remain in the
Initials    United States.

_____ ☒ I believe I face harm if I return to my country. My case will be referred to the Immigration Court
Initials    for a hearing.

_____ ☒ I admit that I am in the United States illegally, and I believe that I do not face harm if I return to my
Initials    country. I give up my right to a hearing before the Immigration Court. I wish to return to my country
as soon as arrangements can be made to effect my departure. I understand that I may be held in
detention until my departure.

_____        8-26-11
Signature of Subject                            Date

## CERTIFICATION OF SERVICE

☒ Notice read by subject.

☐ Notice read to subject by _____, in the _____ language.

JAVIER LEMUS
_____        _____
Name of Officer (Print)                         Name of Interpreter (Print)

_____        August 26, 2011   12:00 AM
Signature of Officer                             Date and Time of Service

Form I-826 (Rev. 08/01/07)

45

U.S. Department of Homeland Security.        Continuation  ge for Form __I200__

| Alien's Name | File Number | Date |
|---|---|---|
| ████ | ████  Event No: SBD1108000559 | August 26, 2011 |

OTHER ALIASES KNOWN BY:
-------------------------

████████████

| Signature | Title |
|---|---|
| ████ | IMMIGRATION ENFORCEMENT AGENT |

2__ of __2__ Pages

Form I-831 Continuation Page (Rev. 08/01/07)

| Alien's Name | File Number | Date |
|---|---|---|
| ███████████ | ██████████ | August 26, 2011 |
| | Event No: SBD1108000559 | |

```
THE SERVICE ALLEGES THAT YOU:
===================================
1. You are not a citizen or national of the United States;
2. You are a native of IRAN and a citizen of IRAN;
3. You were admitted to the United States as a Legal Permanent Resident in LOS ANGELES,
CALIFORNIA on or about August 29, 1991;
4. You were, on December 11, 2007, convicted in the Superior Court of California county of
Orange, Harbor Justice Center for the offense of unauthorized use of personal
identification, a felony, in violation of California Penal Code section number 530.5(a).
5. For this offence you were sentences to a period of confinement of two (2) years prison.
6. You were, on or about December 2, 2004 you were convicted in the Superior Court of the
state of California county of Orange for Possession of a Controlled Substance,
Methamphetamine a felony in violation of Section 11377(a) of the California Health and
Safety Code.
7.  For this offence you were sentences to a period of confinement of 180 days jail.
```

```
ON THE BASIS OF THE FOREGOING, IT IS CHARGED THAT YOU ARE SUBJECT TO REMOVAL FROM THE UNITED
STATES PURSUANT TO THE FOLLOWING PROVISION(S) OF LAW:
==================================================================================================
```

Section 237(a)(2)(A)(iii) of the Immigration and Nationality Act (Act), as amended, in that,
at any time after admission, you have been convicted of an aggravated felony as defined in
section 101(a)(43)(G) of the Act, a law relating to a theft offense (including receipt of
stolen property) or burglary offense for which the term of imprisonment at least 1 year was
imposed.

Section 237(a)(2)(B)(i) of the Immigration and Nationality Act, as amended, in that, at any
time after admission, you have been convicted of a violation of (or a conspiracy or attempt
to violate) any law or regulation of a State, the United States, or a foreign country
relating to a controlled substance (as defined in Section 102 of the Controlled Substances
Act, 21 U.S.C. 802), other than a single offense involving possession for one's own use of
30 grams or less of marijuana.

| Signature | Title |
|---|---|
| _(signature)_ | SDD |

3 of 3 Pages

Form I-831 Continuation Page (Rev. 08/01/07)

EXHIBIT '4'

Order of the Immigration Judge dated March 1, 2019

Law Offices of Brian D. Lerner, APC
Reed, Christopher Allan
3233 E. Broadway
Long Beach, CA  90803

File A 043-060-718        DATE: Mar 1, 2019

___ Unable to forward - No address provided.

_X_ Attached is a copy of the decision of the Immigration Judge. This decision
is final unless an appeal is filed with the Board of Immigration Appeals
within 30 calendar days of the date of the mailing of this written decision.
See the enclosed forms and instructions for properly preparing your appeal.
Your notice of appeal, attached documents, and fee or fee waiver request
must be mailed to:      Board of Immigration Appeals
                        Office of the Clerk
                        5107 Leesburg Pike, Suite 2000
                        Falls Church, VA 22041

___ Attached is a copy of the decision of the immigration judge as the result
of your Failure to Appear at your scheduled deportation or removal hearing.
This decision is final unless a Motion to Reopen is filed in accordance
with Section 242b(c)(3) of the Immigration and Nationality Act, 8 U.S.C. §
1252b(c)(3) in deportation proceedings or section 240(b)(5)(C), 8 U.S.C. §
1229a(b)(5)(C) in removal proceedings.  If you file a motion to reopen, your
motion must be filed with this court:
                        IMMIGRATION COURT
                 300 N. LOS ANGELES ST, RM 4330
                    LOS ANGELES, CA 90012

___ Attached is a copy of the decision of the immigration judge relating to a
Reasonable Fear Review. This is a final order. Pursuant to 8 C.F.R. §
1208.31(g)(1), no administrative appeal is available. However, you may file
a petition for review within 30 days with the appropriate Circuit Court of
Appeals to appeal this decision pursuant to 8 U.S.C. § 1252; INA §242.

___ Attached is a copy of the decision of the immigration judge relating to a
Credible Fear Review. This is a final order. No appeal is available.

___ Other: _____
       _____


                              _____
                              COURT CLERK
                              IMMIGRATION COURT                    FF

    cc: OFFICE OF CHIEF COUNSEL
        300 N. LOS ANGELES ST, RM 8108
        LOS ANGELES, CA 90012

United States Department of Justice
Executive Office for Immigration Review
Immigration Court
Los Angeles, California

In the Matter of: ███████████████

## ORDER OF THE IMMIGRATION JUDGE

Upon consideration of Respondent's Motion to Reopen and Terminate Removal Proceedings
Based on Convictions Vacated Pursuant to Section 1473.7 of the California Penal Code, it is
HEREBY ORDERED that the motion be [X] GRANTED [ ] DENIED because:

[ ] DHS does not oppose the motion.
[ ] Respondent does not oppose the motion.
[X] A response to the motion has not been filed with the Court.
[X] Good case has been established for the motion.
[ ] The Court agrees with the reasons stated in the opposition to the motion.
[ ] The motion is untimely per _____.
[X] Other: Motion to Reopen granted sua sponte pursuant to
Matter of J-J-. Evidence demonstrates that respondent
is no longer subject to removal as convictions vacated
due to legal infirmity and dismissed. Motion to Terminate
Granted.

Deadlines:

[ ] The application (s) for relief must be filed by _____.
[ ] Respondent must comply with DHS biometrics instructions by _____.

_____3-1-2019_____                           _____
Date                                          Kevin W. Riley
                                              Immigration Judge

_____

Certificate of Service
This document was served by: ⌣ Mail ⌣ Personal Service
To: [ ] Alien [ ] Alien c/o Custodial Officer [✓] Alien's Atty/Rep [ ] DHS
    Date: March 1, 2019                    By: Court Staff: _____

Applicant's Letter of Employment

**3S** Network, Inc.

1541 Parkway Loop, Ste. E
Tustin, CA 92780
Tel: (949) 916 4561
Fax: (949) 916-4563

May 19, 2020

Re: ▮▮▮▮▮▮▮▮▮

To Whom It May Concern:

The purpose of this letter is to confirm that Mr. Ashaary has been providing services as both an Accounting Manager and Logistics Manager since March, 2012. Mr. Ashaary receives $80,000 per year for the services he provides.

Regards,

Katy Lindsay
HR Manager

EXHIBIT '6'

Applicant's 2019 Income Tax Return and W-2s

# Form 1040 — Department of the Treasury—Internal Revenue Service (99)

## U.S. Individual Income Tax Return — 2019

OMB No. 1545-0074 IRS Use Only—Do not write or staple in this space.

**Filing Status**
Check only one box.

[X] Single  [ ] Married filing jointly  [ ] Married filing separately (MFS)  [ ] Head of household (HOH)  [ ] Qualifying widow(er) (QW)

If you checked the MFS box, enter the name of spouse. If you checked the HOH or QW box, enter the child's name if the qualifying person is a child but not your dependent. ▶

| Your first name and middle initial | Last name | | Your social security number |
|---|---|---|---|
| ▓▓▓▓▓ | ▓▓▓▓▓ | | ▓▓▓▓▓ |
| If joint return, spouse's first name and middle initial | Last name | | Spouse's social security number |

Home address (number and street). If you have a P.O. box, see instructions. ▓▓▓▓▓ — Apt. no.

City, town or post office, state, and ZIP code. If you have a foreign address, also complete spaces below (see instructions). ▓▓▓▓▓

Foreign country name — Foreign province/state/county — Foreign postal code

**Presidential Election Campaign**
Check here if you, or your spouse if filing jointly, want $3 to go to this fund. Checking a box below will not change your tax or refund.  [ ] You  [ ] Spouse

If more than four dependents, see instructions and ✓ here ▶ [ ]

**Standard Deduction**
Someone can claim:  [ ] You as a dependent   [ ] Your spouse as a dependent
[ ] Spouse itemizes on a separate return or you were a dual-status alien

**Age/Blindness**  You:  [ ] Were born before January 2, 1955  [ ] Are blind   Spouse:  [ ] Was born before January 2, 1955  [ ] Is blind

**Dependents** (see instructions):

| (1) First name    Last name | (2) Social security number | (3) Relationship to you | (4) ✓ if qualifies for (see instructions): | |
|---|---|---|---|---|
| | | | Child tax credit | Credit for other dependents |
| ▓▓▓▓▓ | | Parent | [ ] | [X] |
| | | | [ ] | [ ] |
| | | | [ ] | [ ] |
| | | | [ ] | [ ] |

**Standard Deduction for—**
- Single or Married filing separately, $12,200
- Married filing jointly or Qualifying widow(er), $24,400
- Head of household, $18,350
- If you checked any box under Standard Deduction, see instructions.

| | | |  |
|---|---|---|---|
| 1 | Wages, salaries, tips, etc. Attach Form(s) W-2 | 1 | 0. |
| 2a | Tax-exempt interest . . . . | | |
| 2b | b Taxable interest. Attach Sch. B if required | 2b | 36. |
| 3a | Qualified dividends . . . . | | |
| 3b | b Ordinary dividends. Attach Sch. B if required | 3b | |
| 4a | IRA distributions . . . . | | |
| 4b | b Taxable amount . . . . . | 4b | |
| 4c | c Pensions and annuities . . . | | |
| 4d | d Taxable amount . . . . . | 4d | |
| 5a | Social security benefits . . . | | |
| 5b | b Taxable amount . . . . . | 5b | |
| 6 | Capital gain or (loss). Attach Schedule D if required. If not required, check here ▶ [ ] | 6 | |
| 7a | Other income from Schedule 1, line 9 | 7a | 41,704. |
| 7b | b Add lines 1, 2b, 3b, 4b, 4d, 5b, 6, and 7a. This is your total income ▶ | 7b | 41,740. |
| 8a | Adjustments to income from Schedule 1, line 22 | 8a | 2,947. |
| 8b | b Subtract line 8a from line 7b. This is your adjusted gross income ▶ | 8b | 38,793. |
| 9 | Standard deduction or itemized deductions (from Schedule A) . . . . .  9  33,812. | | |
| 10 | Qualified business income deduction. Attach Form 8995 or Form 8995-A . . . 10  996. | | |
| 11a | Add lines 9 and 10 . . . . . . . . . . . . . . . . . . . . . . | 11a | 34,808. |
| 11b | b Taxable income. Subtract line 11a from line 8b. If zero or less, enter -0- . . . . . . . | 11b | 3,985. |

For Disclosure, Privacy Act, and Paperwork Reduction Act Notice, see separate instructions.

Form **1040** (2019)

| | | | | | | | |
|---|---|---|---|---|---|---|---|
| | 12a | Tax (see inst.) Check if any from Form(s): 1 ☐ 8814  2 ☐ 4972  3 ☐ ___ | | 12a | 398. | | |
| | b | Add Schedule 2, line 3, and line 12a and enter the total | | | | 12b | 1,198. |
| | 13a | Child tax credit or credit for other dependents | | 13a | 500. | | |
| | b | Add Schedule 3, line 7, and line 13a and enter the total | | | | 13b | 500. |
| | 14 | Subtract line 13b from line 12b. If zero or less, enter -0- | | | | 14 | 698. |
| | 15 | Other taxes, including self-employment tax, from Schedule 2, line 10 | | | | 15 | 5,893. |
| | 16 | Add lines 14 and 15. This is your total tax | | | | 16 | 6,591. |
| | 17 | Federal income tax withheld from Forms W-2 and 1099 | | | | 17 | |
| • If you have a qualifying child, attach Sch. EIC. | 18 | Other payments and refundable credits: | | | | | |
| | a | Earned income credit (EIC) . . . . . . . . . . No . . | | 18a | | | |
| • If you have nontaxable combat pay, see instructions. | b | Additional child tax credit. Attach Schedule 8812 | | 18b | | | |
| | c | American opportunity credit from Form 8863, line 8 | | 18c | | | |
| | d | Schedule 3, line 14 | | 18d | 2,000. | | |
| | e | Add lines 18a through 18d. These are your total other payments and refundable credits | | | | 18e | 2,000. |
| | 19 | Add lines 17 and 18e. These are your total payments | | | | 19 | 2,000. |
| **Refund** | 20 | If line 19 is more than line 16, subtract line 16 from line 19. This is the amount you **overpaid** | | | | 20 | |
| | 21a | Amount of line 20 you want refunded to you. If Form 8888 is attached, check here ☐ | | | | 21a | |
| Direct deposit? See instructions. | ▶ b | Routing number  X X X X X X X X  ▶ c Type: ☐ Checking  ☐ Savings | | | | | |
| | ▶ d | Account number  X X X X X X X X X X X X X X X X | | | | | |
| | 22 | Amount of line 20 you want applied to your 2020 estimated tax  ▶ | | 22 | | | |
| **Amount You Owe** | 23 | **Amount you owe.** Subtract line 19 from line 16. For details on how to pay, see instructions | | | | 23 | 4,688. |
| | 24 | Estimated tax penalty (see instructions) . . . . . . . . . . ▶ | | 24 | 97. | | |

**Third Party Designee**
(Other than paid preparer)

Do you want to allow another person (other than your paid preparer) to discuss this return with the IRS? See instructions. ☐ **Yes. Complete below.** ☒ **No**

| Designee's name ▶ | Phone no. ▶ | Personal identification number (PIN) ▶ [  ][  ][  ][  ][  ] |
|---|---|---|

**Sign Here**

Joint return? See instructions. Keep a copy for your records.

Under penalties of perjury, I declare that I have examined this return and accompanying schedules and statements, and to the best of my knowledge and belief, they are true, correct, and complete. Declaration of preparer (other than taxpayer) is based on all information of which preparer has any knowledge.

| Your signature  *K. Ashaary* | Date  7/8/20 | Your occupation  S/E | If the IRS sent you an Identity Protection PIN, enter it here (see inst.) [  ][  ][  ][  ][  ][  ] |
|---|---|---|---|
| Spouse's signature. If a joint return, both must sign. | Date | Spouse's occupation | If the IRS sent your spouse an Identity Protection PIN, enter it here (see inst.) [  ][  ][  ][  ][  ][  ] |
| Phone no. | | Email address | |

**Paid Preparer Use Only**

| Preparer's name  REZA AZADI | Preparer's signature  REZA AZADI  *Reza Azadi* | Date | PTIN  P01513002 | Check if: ☐ 3rd Party Designee |
|---|---|---|---|---|
| Firm's name ▶ Professional Financial Services | | | Phone no. (714)290-7180 | ☐ Self-employed |
| Firm's address ▶ 151 Kalmus Dr C 210 Costa Mesa CA 92626 | | | | Firm's EIN ▶ 33-0891189 |

Go to *www.irs.gov/Form1040* for instructions and the latest information.         BAA         REV 05/19/20 PRO         Form **1040** (2019)

# Additional Income and Adjustments to Income

► Attach to Form 1040 or 1040-SR.
► Go to *www.irs.gov/Form1040* for instructions and the latest information.

OMB No. 1545-0074

**2019**

Attachment
Sequence No. 01

Name(s) shown on Form 1040 or 1040-SR

Your social security number

At any time during 2019, did you receive, sell, send, exchange, or otherwise acquire any financial interest in any virtual currency? . . . . . . . . . . . . . . . . . . . . . . . . . . . . . . . . ☐ Yes ☒ No

## Part I   Additional Income

| | | | |
|---|---|---|---|
| 1 | Taxable refunds, credits, or offsets of state and local income taxes . . . . . . . . . . | 1 | |
| 2a | Alimony received . . . . . . . . . . . . . . . . . . . . . . . . | 2a | |
| b | Date of original divorce or separation agreement (see instructions) ► | | |
| 3 | Business income or (loss). Attach Schedule C . . . . . . . . . . . . . . . | 3 | 41,704. |
| 4 | Other gains or (losses). Attach Form 4797 . . . . . . . . . . . . . . . . | 4 | |
| 5 | Rental real estate, royalties, partnerships, S corporations, trusts, etc. Attach Schedule E . . . . | 5 | |
| 6 | Farm income or (loss). Attach Schedule F . . . . . . . . . . . . . . . . | 6 | |
| 7 | Unemployment compensation . . . . . . . . . . . . . . . . . . . . | 7 | |
| 8 | Other income. List type and amount ► | | |
| | | 8 | |
| 9 | Combine lines 1 through 8. Enter here and on Form 1040 or 1040-SR, line 7a . . . . . . . . | 9 | 41,704. |

## Part II   Adjustments to Income

| | | | |
|---|---|---|---|
| 10 | Educator expenses . . . . . . . . . . . . . . . . . . . . . . . . | 10 | |
| 11 | Certain business expenses of reservists, performing artists, and fee-basis government officials. Attach Form 2106 . . . . . . . . . . . . . . . . . . . . . . . . . . . | 11 | |
| 12 | Health savings account deduction. Attach Form 8889 . . . . . . . . . . . . . | 12 | |
| 13 | Moving expenses for members of the Armed Forces. Attach Form 3903 . . . . . . . . | 13 | |
| 14 | Deductible part of self-employment tax. Attach Schedule SE . . . . . . . . . . . | 14 | 2,947. |
| 15 | Self-employed SEP, SIMPLE, and qualified plans . . . . . . . . . . . . . . | 15 | |
| 16 | Self-employed health insurance deduction . . . . . . . . . . . . . . . . | 16 | |
| 17 | Penalty on early withdrawal of savings . . . . . . . . . . . . . . . . . | 17 | |
| 18a | Alimony paid . . . . . . . . . . . . . . . . . . . . . . . . . . | 18a | |
| b | Recipient's SSN . . . . . . . . . . . . . . . . . . . . . . ► | | |
| c | Date of original divorce or separation agreement (see instructions) ► | | |
| 19 | IRA deduction . . . . . . . . . . . . . . . . . . . . . . . . . | 19 | |
| 20 | Student loan interest deduction . . . . . . . . . . . . . . . . . . . | 20 | |
| 21 | Tuition and fees. Attach Form 8917 . . . . . . . . . . . . . . . . . . | 21 | |
| 22 | Add lines 10 through 21. These are your **adjustments to income**. Enter here and on Form 1040 or 1040-SR, line 8a . . . . . . . . . . . . . . . . . . . . . . . | 22 | 2,947. |

# SCHEDULE 2
(Form 1040 or 1040-SR)

Department of the Treasury
Internal Revenue Service

# Additional Taxes

▶ Attach to Form 1040 or 1040-SR.
▶ Go to www.irs.gov/Form1040 for instructions and the latest information.

OMB No. 1545-0074

2019

Attachment
Sequence No. 02

Name(s) shown on Form 1040 or 1040-SR

Your social security number

| Part I | Tax | | |
|---|---|---|---|
| 1 | Alternative minimum tax. Attach Form 6251 | 1 | |
| 2 | Excess advance premium tax credit repayment. Attach Form 8962 | 2 | 800. |
| 3 | Add lines 1 and 2. Enter here and include on Form 1040 or 1040-SR, line 12b | 3 | 800. |

| Part II | Other Taxes | | |
|---|---|---|---|
| 4 | Self-employment tax. Attach Schedule SE | 4 | 5,893. |
| 5 | Unreported social security and Medicare tax from Form: a ☐ 4137   b ☐ 8919 | 5 | |
| 6 | Additional tax on IRAs, other qualified retirement plans, and other tax-favored accounts. Attach Form 5329 if required | 6 | |
| 7a | Household employment taxes. Attach Schedule H | 7a | |
| b | Repayment of first-time homebuyer credit from Form 5405. Attach Form 5405 if required | 7b | |
| 8 | Taxes from:  a ☐ Form 8959   b ☐ Form 8960 | | |
| | c ☐ Instructions; enter code(s) | 8 | |
| 9 | Section 965 net tax liability installment from Form 965-A . . . . . . . . 9 | | |
| 10 | Add lines 4 through 8. These are your **total other taxes.** Enter here and on Form 1040 or 1040-SR, line 15 | 10 | 5,893. |

For Paperwork Reduction Act Notice, see your tax return instructions.          REV 05/19/20 PRO          Schedule 2 (Form 1040 or 1040-SR) 2019

# Additional Credits and Payments

▶ Attach to Form 1040 or 1040-SR.
▶ Go to *www.irs.gov/Form1040* for instructions and the latest information.

OMB No. 1545-0074

2019

Attachment
Sequence No. 03

Name(s) shown on Form 1040 or 1040-SR

▮▮▮▮▮▮▮

Your social security number

▮▮▮▮▮▮▮

## Part I  Nonrefundable Credits

| | | | |
|---|---|---|---|
| 1 | Foreign tax credit. Attach Form 1116 if required | 1 | |
| 2 | Credit for child and dependent care expenses. Attach Form 2441 | 2 | |
| 3 | Education credits from Form 8863, line 19 | 3 | |
| 4 | Retirement savings contributions credit. Attach Form 8880 | 4 | |
| 5 | Residential energy credits. Attach Form 5695 | 5 | |
| 6 | Other credits from Form:  a ☐ 3800   b ☐ 8801   c ☐ | 6 | |
| 7 | Add lines 1 through 6. Enter here and include on Form 1040 or 1040-SR, line 13b | 7 | |

## Part II  Other Payments and Refundable Credits

| | | | |
|---|---|---|---|
| 8 | 2019 estimated tax payments and amount applied from 2018 return | 8 | 2,000. |
| 9 | Net premium tax credit. Attach Form 8962 | 9 | |
| 10 | Amount paid with request for extension to file (see instructions) | 10 | |
| 11 | Excess social security and tier 1 RRTA tax withheld | 11 | |
| 12 | Credit for federal tax on fuels. Attach Form 4136 | 12 | |
| 13 | Credits from Form:  a ☐ 2439   b ☐ Reserved   c ☐ 8885   d ☐ | 13 | |
| 14 | Add lines 8 through 13. Enter here and on Form 1040 or 1040-SR, line 18d | 14 | 2,000. |

For Paperwork Reduction Act Notice, see your tax return instructions.　　　REV 05/19/20 PRO　　　Schedule 3 (Form 1040 or 1040-SR) 2019

| SCHEDULE A<br>(Form 1040 or 1040-SR)<br>(Rev. January 2020)<br>Department of the Treasury<br>Internal Revenue Service (99) | Itemized Deductions<br>▶ Go to *www.irs.gov/ScheduleA* for instructions and the latest information.<br>▶ Attach to Form 1040 or 1040-SR.<br>Caution: If you are claiming a net qualified disaster loss on Form 4684, see the instructions for line 16. | OMB No. 1545-0074<br>2019<br>Attachment<br>Sequence No. 07 |
|---|---|---|

Name(s) shown on Form 1040 or 1040-SR ▮▮▮▮                                       Your social security number ▮▮▮▮

| Medical and Dental Expenses | | | Caution: Do not include expenses reimbursed or paid by others. | | | | |
|---|---|---|---|---|---|---|---|
| | | 1 | Medical and dental expenses (see instructions) . . . . . . . | 1 | | 12,134. | |
| | | 2 | Enter amount from Form 1040 or 1040-SR, line 8b | **2** | 38,793. | | |
| | | 3 | Multiply line 2 by 7.5% (0.075) . . . . . . . . . . . . | 3 | | 2,909. | |
| | | 4 | Subtract line 3 from line 1. If line 3 is more than line 1, enter -0-. . . . . . | | | 4 | 9,225. |
| **Taxes You Paid** | | 5 | State and local taxes. | | | | |
| | | a | State and local income taxes or general sales taxes. You may include either income taxes or general sales taxes on line 5a, but not both. If you elect to include general sales taxes instead of income taxes, check this box . . . . . . . . . . . . . . . ▶ ☒ | 5a | 681. | | |
| | | b | State and local real estate taxes (see instructions) . . . . . . . | 5b | 6,114. | | |
| | | c | State and local personal property taxes . . . . . . . . . | 5c | 385. | | |
| | | d | Add lines 5a through 5c . . . . . . . . . . . . . | 5d | 7,180. | | |
| | | e | Enter the smaller of line 5d or $10,000 ($5,000 if married filing separately) . . . . . . . . . . . . . . . . | 5e | 7,180. | | |
| | | 6 | Other taxes. List type and amount ▶ _____ | 6 | | | |
| | | 7 | Add lines 5e and 6 . . . . . . . . . . . . . . . . . . . | | | 7 | 7,180. |
| **Interest You Paid**<br>Caution: Your mortgage interest deduction may be limited (see instructions). | | 8 | Home mortgage interest and points. If you didn't use all of your home mortgage loan(s) to buy, build, or improve your home, see instructions and check this box . . . . . . . . . . . ▶ ☐ | | | | |
| | | a | Home mortgage interest and points reported to you on Form 1098. See instructions if limited . . . . . . . . . . | 8a | 13,308. | | |
| | | b | Home mortgage interest not reported to you on Form 1098. See instructions if limited. If paid to the person from whom you bought the home, see instructions and show that person's name, identifying no., and address . . . . . . . . . . . . . . .<br>▶ _____ _____ | 8b | | | |
| | | c | Points not reported to you on Form 1098. See instructions for special rules . . . . . . . . . . . . . . . . . | 8c | | | |
| | | d | Mortgage insurance premiums (see instructions) . . . . . . . | 8d | 1,039. | | |
| | | e | Add lines 8a through 8d . . . . . . . . . . | 8e | 14,347. | | |
| | | 9 | Investment interest. Attach Form 4952 if required. See instructions . | 9 | | | |
| | | 10 | Add lines 8e and 9 . . . . . . . . . . . . . . . . . . . | | | 10 | 14,347. |
| **Gifts to Charity**<br>Caution: If you made a gift and got a benefit for it, see instructions. | | 11 | Gifts by cash or check. If you made any gift of $250 or more, see instructions . . . . . . . . . . . . . . . | 11 | 3,060. | | |
| | | 12 | Other than by cash or check. If you made any gift of $250 or more, see instructions. You **must** attach Form 8283 if over $500. . . . | 12 | | | |
| | | 13 | Carryover from prior year . . . . . . . . . . . | 13 | | | |
| | | 14 | Add lines 11 through 13 . . . . . . . . . . . . . . . . | | | 14 | 3,060. |
| **Casualty and Theft Losses** | | 15 | Casualty and theft loss(es) from a federally declared disaster (other than net qualified disaster losses). Attach Form 4684 and enter the amount from line 18 of that form. See instructions . . . . . . . . . . . . . . . . . . . . . . . . | | | 15 | |
| **Other Itemized Deductions** | | 16 | Other—from list in instructions. List type and amount ▶ _____ _____ | | | 16 | |
| **Total Itemized Deductions** | | 17 | Add the amounts in the far right column for lines 4 through 16. Also, enter this amount on Form 1040 or 1040-SR, line 9 . . . . . . . . . . . . . . . . . . . . | | | 17 | 33,812. |
| | | 18 | If you elect to itemize deductions even though they are less than your standard deduction, check this box . . . . . . . . . . . . . . . . . . . . . ▶ ☐ | | | | |

For Paperwork Reduction Act Notice, see the Instructions for Forms 1040 and 1040-SR.  BAA  REV 05/19/20 PRO   Schedule A (Form 1040 or 1040-SR) 2019

| SCHEDULE C<br>(Form 1040 or 1040-SR)<br><br>Department of the Treasury<br>Internal Revenue Service (99) | **Profit or Loss From Business**<br>(Sole Proprietorship)<br>▶ Go to www.irs.gov/ScheduleC for instructions and the latest information.<br>▶ Attach to Form 1040, 1040-SR, 1040-NR, or 1041; partnerships generally must file Form 1065. | OMB No. 1545-0074<br><br>2019<br>Attachment<br>Sequence No. 09 |

| Name of proprietor | Social security number (SSN) |
|---|---|
| ▉▉▉▉▉▉ | ▉▉▉▉▉ |

| A | Principal business or profession, including product or service (see instructions)<br>NETWORKING | B | Enter code from instructions<br>▶ 5 1 9 1 0 0 |
|---|---|---|---|
| C | Business name. If no separate business name, leave blank.<br>3 S. NETWORK, INC. | D | Employer ID number (EIN) (see instr.)<br>▉▉▉▉▉ |

E  Business address (including suite or room no.) ▶ 26702 ARACENA DR.
City, town or post office, state, and ZIP code   MISSION VIEJO, CA 92691

F  Accounting method:   (1) ☒ Cash   (2) ☐ Accrual   (3) ☐ Other (specify) ▶ _____

| | | | |
|---|---|---|---|
| G | Did you "materially participate" in the operation of this business during 2019? If "No," see instructions for limit on losses | ☒ Yes | ☐ No |
| H | If you started or acquired this business during 2019, check here ▶ ☐ | | |
| I | Did you make any payments in 2019 that would require you to file Form(s) 1099? (see instructions) | ☐ Yes | ☒ No |
| J | If "Yes," did you or will you file required Forms 1099? | ☐ Yes | ☒ No |

## Part I  Income

| | | | |
|---|---|---|---|
| 1 | Gross receipts or sales. See instructions for line 1 and check the box if this income was reported to you on Form W-2 and the "Statutory employee" box on that form was checked  ▶ ☐ | 1 | 76,767. |
| 2 | Returns and allowances | 2 | |
| 3 | Subtract line 2 from line 1 | 3 | 76,767. |
| 4 | Cost of goods sold (from line 42) | 4 | |
| 5 | Gross profit. Subtract line 4 from line 3 | 5 | 76,767. |
| 6 | Other income, including federal and state gasoline or fuel tax credit or refund (see instructions) | 6 | |
| 7 | Gross income. Add lines 5 and 6  ▶ | 7 | 76,767. |

## Part II  Expenses. Enter expenses for business use of your home only on line 30.

| | | | | | | | |
|---|---|---|---|---|---|---|---|
| 8 | Advertising | 8 | 1,346. | 18 | Office expense (see instructions) | 18 | 1,709. |
| 9 | Car and truck expenses (see instructions) | 9 | 8,055. | 19 | Pension and profit-sharing plans | 19 | |
| 10 | Commissions and fees | 10 | | 20 | Rent or lease (see instructions): | | |
| 11 | Contract labor (see instructions) | 11 | | a | Vehicles, machinery, and equipment | 20a | |
| 12 | Depletion | 12 | | b | Other business property | 20b | |
| 13 | Depreciation and section 179 expense deduction (not included in Part III) (see Instructions). | 13 | 1,587. | 21 | Repairs and maintenance | 21 | 5,572. |
| | | | | 22 | Supplies (not included in Part III) | 22 | 3,880. |
| | | | | 23 | Taxes and licenses | 23 | 785. |
| 14 | Employee benefit programs (other than on line 19). | 14 | | 24 | Travel and meals: | | |
| | | | | a | Travel | 24a | 1,056. |
| 15 | Insurance (other than health) | 15 | 3,324. | b | Deductible meals (see instructions) | 24b | 1,867. |
| 16 | Interest (see instructions): | | | 25 | Utilities | 25 | 1,230. |
| a | Mortgage (paid to banks, etc.) | 16a | | 26 | Wages (less employment credits) | 26 | |
| b | Other | 16b | | 27a | Other expenses (from line 48) | 27a | 4,202. |
| 17 | Legal and professional services | 17 | 450. | b | Reserved for future use | 27b | |

| | | | |
|---|---|---|---|
| 28 | Total expenses before expenses for business use of home. Add lines 8 through 27a  ▶ | 28 | 35,063. |
| 29 | Tentative profit or (loss). Subtract line 28 from line 7 | 29 | 41,704. |
| 30 | Expenses for business use of your home. Do not report these expenses elsewhere. Attach Form 8829 unless using the simplified method (see instructions).<br>Simplified method filers only: enter the total square footage of: (a) your home: _____<br>and (b) the part of your home used for business: _____. Use the Simplified Method Worksheet in the instructions to figure the amount to enter on line 30 | 30 | |
| 31 | Net profit or (loss). Subtract line 30 from line 29.<br>• If a profit, enter on both Schedule 1 (Form 1040 or 1040-SR), line 3 (or Form 1040-NR, line 13) and on Schedule SE, line 2. (If you checked the box on line 1, see instructions). Estates and trusts, enter on Form 1041, line 3.<br>• If a loss, you must go to line 32. | 31 | 41,704. |
| 32 | If you have a loss, check the box that describes your investment in this activity (see instructions).<br>• If you checked 32a, enter the loss on both Schedule 1 (Form 1040 or 1040-SR), line 3 (or Form 1040-NR, line 13) and on Schedule SE, line 2. (If you checked the box on line 1, see the line 31 instructions). Estates and trusts, enter on Form 1041, line 3.<br>• If you checked 32b, you must attach Form 6198. Your loss may be limited. | 32a ☐ All investment is at risk.<br>32b ☐ Some investment is not at risk. | |

For Paperwork Reduction Act Notice, see the separate instructions.  BAA   REV 05/19/20 PRO   Schedule C (Form 1040 or 1040-SR) 2019

**Part III** Cost of Goods Sold (see instructions)

33 Method(s) used to value closing inventory: a ☐ Cost  b ☐ Lower of cost or market  c ☐ Other (attach explanation)

34 Was there any change in determining quantities, costs, or valuations between opening and closing inventory? If "Yes," attach explanation . . . . . . . . . . . . . . . . . . . . . . . . . . . ☐ Yes ☐ No

| | | |
|---|---|---|
| 35 | Inventory at beginning of year. If different from last year's closing inventory, attach explanation . . . | 35 | |
| 36 | Purchases less cost of items withdrawn for personal use . . . . . . . . . . . . | 36 | |
| 37 | Cost of labor. Do not include any amounts paid to yourself . . . . . . . . . . . | 37 | |
| 38 | Materials and supplies . . . . . . . . . . . . . . . . . . . . | 38 | |
| 39 | Other costs . . . . . . . . . . . . . . . . . . . . . . . | 39 | |
| 40 | Add lines 35 through 39 . . . . . . . . . . . . . . . . . . . | 40 | |
| 41 | Inventory at end of year . . . . . . . . . . . . . . . . . . . | 41 | |
| 42 | Cost of goods sold. Subtract line 41 from line 40. Enter the result here and on line 4 . . . . . . | 42 | |

**Part IV** Information on Your Vehicle. Complete this part **only** if you are claiming car or truck expenses on line 9 and are not required to file Form 4562 for this business. See the instructions for line 13 to find out if you must file Form 4562.

43 When did you place your vehicle in service for business purposes? (month, day, year) ▶ 01/01/2019

44 Of the total number of miles you drove your vehicle during 2019, enter the number of miles you used your vehicle for:

a Business ___9,500___ b Commuting (see instructions) ___3,000___ c Other ___3,500___

45 Was your vehicle available for personal use during off-duty hours? . . . . . . . . . . . ☒ Yes ☐ No

46 Do you (or your spouse) have another vehicle available for personal use? . . . . . . . . . . ☐ Yes ☒ No

47a Do you have evidence to support your deduction? . . . . . . . . . . . . . . . ☐ Yes ☒ No

b If "Yes," is the evidence written? . . . . . . . . . . . . . . . . . . . . ☐ Yes ☐ No

**Part V** Other Expenses. List below business expenses not included on lines 8–26 or line 30.

| | |
|---|---|
| TELPHONE & CELL | 2,452. |
| SUIT & ASS. | 1,750. |
| | |
| | |
| | |
| | |
| | |
| | |
| | |
| | |

| | | |
|---|---|---|
| 48 | Total other expenses. Enter here and on line 27a . . . . . . . . . . . . . . | 48 | 4,202. |

# SCHEDULE SE
**(Form 1040 or 1040-SR)**

Department of the Treasury
Internal Revenue Service (99)

# Self-Employment Tax

▶ Go to *www.irs.gov/ScheduleSE* for instructions and the latest information.
▶ Attach to Form 1040, 1040-SR, or 1040-NR.

OMB No. 1545-0074

**2019**

Attachment
Sequence No. **17**

| Name of person with self-employment income (as shown on Form 1040, 1040-SR, or 1040-NR) | Social security number of person with self-employment income ▶ |
|---|---|
| KIARASH ASHAARY | 607-44-7640 |

***Before you begin:*** To determine if you must file Schedule SE, see the instructions.

## May I Use Short Schedule SE or Must I Use Long Schedule SE?

**Note:** Use this flowchart **only** if you must file Schedule SE. If unsure, see *Who Must File Schedule SE* in the instructions.

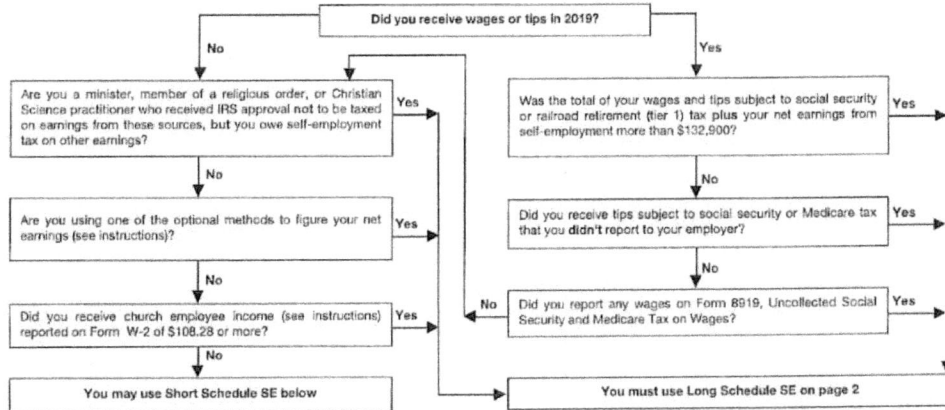

```
                        ┌─────────────────────────────────────────┐
                        │   Did you receive wages or tips in 2019? │
                        └─────────────────────────────────────────┘
           No                                              Yes

┌─────────────────────────────────────┐        ┌──────────────────────────────────────────┐
│ Are you a minister, member of a      │ Yes    │ Was the total of your wages and tips        │ Yes
│ religious order, or Christian        │───▶    │ subject to social security or railroad      │───▶
│ Science practitioner who received    │        │ retirement (tier 1) tax plus your net       │
│ IRS approval not to be taxed on      │        │ earnings from self-employment more than     │
│ earnings from these sources, but you │        │ $132,900?                                   │
│ owe self-employment tax on other     │        └──────────────────────────────────────────┘
│ earnings?                            │                            No
└─────────────────────────────────────┘        ┌──────────────────────────────────────────┐
            No                                  │ Did you receive tips subject to social      │ Yes
┌─────────────────────────────────────┐        │ security or Medicare tax that you didn't    │───▶
│ Are you using one of the optional    │ Yes    │ report to your employer?                    │
│ methods to figure your net earnings  │───▶    └──────────────────────────────────────────┘
│ (see instructions)?                  │                            No
└─────────────────────────────────────┘        ┌──────────────────────────────────────────┐
            No                          No      │ Did you report any wages on Form 8919,      │ Yes
┌─────────────────────────────────────┐ ◀──────│ Uncollected Social Security and Medicare    │───▶
│ Did you receive church employee      │ Yes    │ Tax on Wages?                               │
│ income (see instructions) reported   │───▶    └──────────────────────────────────────────┘
│ on Form W-2 of $108.28 or more?      │
└─────────────────────────────────────┘
            No

┌─────────────────────────────────────┐        ┌──────────────────────────────────────────┐
│  You may use Short Schedule SE below │───▶    │  You must use Long Schedule SE on page 2   │
└─────────────────────────────────────┘        └──────────────────────────────────────────┘
```

## Section A—Short Schedule SE. Caution: Read above to see if you can use Short Schedule SE.

| | | | |
|---|---|---|---:|
| **1a** | Net farm profit or (loss) from Schedule F, line 34, and farm partnerships, Schedule K-1 (Form 1065), box 14, code A | **1a** | |
| **b** | If you received social security retirement or disability benefits, enter the amount of Conservation Reserve Program payments included on Schedule F, line 4b, or listed on Schedule K-1 (Form 1065), box 20, code AH | **1b** | ( ) |
| **2** | Net profit or (loss) from Schedule C, line 31; and Schedule K-1 (Form 1065), box 14, code A (other than farming). Ministers and members of religious orders, see instructions for types of income to report on this line. See instructions for other income to report | **2** | 41,704. |
| **3** | Combine lines 1a, 1b, and 2 | **3** | 41,704. |
| **4** | Multiply line 3 by 92.35% (0.9235). If less than $400, you don't owe self-employment tax; **don't file** this schedule unless you have an amount on line 1b ▶ | **4** | 38,514. |
| | **Note:** If line 4 is less than $400 due to Conservation Reserve Program payments on line 1b, see instructions. | | |
| **5** | Self-employment tax. If the amount on line 4 is: | | |
| | • $132,900 or less, multiply line 4 by 15.3% (0.153). Enter the result here and on **Schedule 2 (Form 1040 or 1040-SR), line 4,** or Form 1040-NR, line 55. | | |
| | • More than $132,900, multiply line 4 by 2.9% (0.029). Then, add $16,479.60 to the result. Enter the total here and on **Schedule 2 (Form 1040 or 1040-SR), line 4,** or Form 1040-NR, line 55 . | **5** | 5,893. |
| **6** | Deduction for one-half of self-employment tax. Multiply line 5 by 50% (0.50). Enter the result here and on **Schedule 1 (Form 1040 or 1040-SR), line 14,** or Form 1040-NR, line 27 | **6** | 2,947. |

For Paperwork Reduction Act Notice, see your tax return instructions.    BAA    REV 05/19/20 PRO    Schedule SE (Form 1040 or 1040-SR) 2019

Form **8995**

Department of the Treasury
Internal Revenue Service

**Qualified Business Income Deduction
Simplified Computation**

▶ Attach to your tax return.
▶ Go to *www.irs.gov/Form8995* for instructions and the latest information.

OMB No. 1545-0123

**2019**

Attachment
Sequence No. **55**

Name(s) shown on return

Your taxpayer identification number

| 1 | (a) Trade, business, or aggregation name | (b) Taxpayer identification number | (c) Qualified business income or (loss) |
|---|---|---|---|
| i | NETWORKING | | 38,757. |
| ii | | | |
| iii | | | |
| iv | | | |
| v | | | |

| | | | |
|---|---|---|---|
| 2 | Total qualified business income or (loss). Combine lines 1i through 1v, column (c) . . . . . . . . . . . . . . . . . . . . | **2** | 38,757. |
| 3 | Qualified business net (loss) carryforward from the prior year . . . . . . . | **3** ( | 0. ) |
| 4 | Total qualified business income. Combine lines 2 and 3. If zero or less, enter -0- | **4** | 38,757. |
| 5 | Qualified business income component. Multiply line 4 by 20% (0.20) . . . . . . . . . | **5** | 7,751. |
| 6 | Qualified REIT dividends and publicly traded partnership (PTP) income or (loss) (see instructions) . . . . . . . . . . . . . . . . . . . . . | **6** | |
| 7 | Qualified REIT dividends and qualified PTP (loss) carryforward from the prior year . . . . . . . . . . . . . . . . . . . . . . . . | **7** ( | 0. ) |
| 8 | Total qualified REIT dividends and PTP income. Combine lines 6 and 7. If zero or less, enter -0- . . . . . . . . . . . . . . . . . . . | **8** | 0. |
| 9 | REIT and PTP component. Multiply line 8 by 20% (0.20) . . . . . . . . . . . | **9** | 0. |
| 10 | Qualified business income deduction before the income limitation. Add lines 5 and 9 . . . . . . | **10** | 7,751. |
| 11 | Taxable income before qualified business income deduction . . . . . . | **11** | 4,981. |
| 12 | Net capital gain (see instructions) . . . . . . . . . . . . . . . | **12** | 0. |
| 13 | Subtract line 12 from line 11. If zero or less, enter -0- . . . . . | **13** | 4,981. |
| 14 | Income limitation. Multiply line 13 by 20% (0.20) . . . . . . . . . . . | **14** | 996. |
| 15 | Qualified business income deduction. Enter the lesser of line 10 or line 14. Also enter this amount on the applicable line of your return . . . . . . . . . . . . . . . . . . . ▶ | **15** | 996. |
| 16 | Total qualified business (loss) carryforward. Combine lines 2 and 3. If greater than zero, enter -0- . . | **16** ( | 0. ) |
| 17 | Total qualified REIT dividends and PTP (loss) carryforward. Combine lines 6 and 7. If greater than zero, enter -0- . . . . . . . . . . . . . . . . . . . . . . . . . . . . . . . . . . | **17** ( | 0. ) |

For Privacy Act and Paperwork Reduction Act Notice, see instructions.     REV 05/19/20 PRO     Form **8995** (2019)

| Form **8867** | **Paid Preparer's Due Diligence Checklist** | OMB No. 1545-0074 |
|---|---|---|
| Department of the Treasury Internal Revenue Service | Earned Income Credit (EIC), American Opportunity Tax Credit (AOTC), Child Tax Credit (CTC) (including the Additional Child Tax Credit (ACTC) and Credit for Other Dependents (ODC)), and Head of Household (HOH) Filing Status ▶ To be completed by preparer and filed with Form 1040, 1040-SR, 1040-NR, 1040-PR, or 1040-SS. ▶ Go to *www.irs.gov/Form8867* for instructions and the latest information. | **2019** Attachment Sequence No. **70** |

| Taxpayer name(s) shown on return | Taxpayer identification number |
|---|---|
| ▆▆▆▆▆▆ | ▆▆▆▆▆▆ |

Enter preparer's name and PTIN

P01513002

**Part I  Due Diligence Requirements**

Please check the appropriate box for the credit(s) and/or HOH filing status claimed on the return and complete the related Parts I–V for the benefit(s) claimed (check all that apply).  ☐ EIC  ☒ CTC/ACTC/ODC  ☐ AOTC  ☐ HOH

| | | Yes | No | N/A |
|---|---|---|---|---|
| 1 | Did you complete the return based on information for tax year 2019 provided by the taxpayer or reasonably obtained by you? | ☒ | ☐ | |
| 2 | If credits are claimed on the return, did you complete the applicable EIC and/or CTC/ACTC/ODC worksheets found in the Form 1040, 1040-SR, 1040-NR, 1040-PR, or 1040-SS instructions, and/or the AOTC worksheet found in the Form 8863 instructions, or your own worksheet(s) that provides the same information, and all related forms and schedules for each credit claimed? | ☐ | ☐ | ☒ |
| 3 | Did you satisfy the knowledge requirement? To meet the knowledge requirement, you must do both of the following. | | | |
| | • Interview the taxpayer, ask questions, and contemporaneously document the taxpayer's responses to determine that the taxpayer is eligible to claim the credit(s) and/or HOH filing status. | | | |
| | • Review information to determine that the taxpayer is eligible to claim the credit(s) and/or HOH filing status and to compute the amount(s) of any credit(s) | ☒ | ☐ | |
| 4 | Did any information provided by the taxpayer or a third party for use in preparing the return, or information reasonably known to you, appear to be incorrect, incomplete, or inconsistent? (If "Yes," answer questions 4a and 4b. If "No," go to question 5.) | ☐ | ☒ | |
| a | Did you make reasonable inquiries to determine the correct, complete, and consistent information? | ☐ | ☐ | |
| b | Did you contemporaneously document your inquiries? (Documentation should include the questions you asked, whom you asked, when you asked, the information that was provided, and the impact the information had on your preparation of the return.) | ☐ | ☐ | |
| 5 | Did you satisfy the record retention requirement? To meet the record retention requirement, you must keep a copy of your documentation referenced in 4b, a copy of this Form 8867, a copy of any applicable worksheet(s), a record of how, when, and from whom the information used to prepare Form 8867 and any applicable worksheet(s) was obtained, and a copy of any document(s) provided by the taxpayer that you relied on to determine eligibility for the credit(s) and/or HOH filing status or to compute the amount(s) of the credit(s) | ☒ | ☐ | |
| | List those documents, if any, that you relied on. | | | |
| 6 | Did you ask the taxpayer whether he/she could provide documentation to substantiate eligibility for the credit(s) and/or HOH filing status and the amount(s) of any credit(s) claimed on the return if his/her return is selected for audit? | ☒ | ☐ | |
| 7 | Did you ask the taxpayer if any of these credits were disallowed or reduced in a previous year? (If credits were disallowed or reduced, go to question 7a; if not, go to question 8.) | ☐ | ☐ | ☒ |
| a | Did you complete the required recertification Form 8862? | ☐ | ☐ | ☐ |
| 8 | If the taxpayer is reporting self-employment income, did you ask questions to prepare a complete and correct Schedule C (Form 1040 or 1040-SR)? | ☐ | ☐ | ☒ |

For Paperwork Reduction Act Notice, see separate instructions.    REV 05/19/20 PRO    Form **8867** (2019)

| **Part II** | Due Diligence Questions for Returns Claiming EIC (If the return does not claim EIC, go to Part III.) | | | |
|---|---|---|---|---|
| | | Yes | No | N/A |
| 9a | Have you determined that the taxpayer is, in fact, eligible to claim the EIC for the number of qualifying children claimed, or is eligible to claim the EIC without a qualifying child? (Skip 9b and 9c if the taxpayer is claiming the EIC and does not have a qualifying child.) . . . . . . . . . . . . . . . | ☐ | ☐ | |
| b | Did you ask the taxpayer if the child lived with the taxpayer for over half of the year, even if the taxpayer has supported the child the entire year? . . . . . . . . . . . . . . . . . . . | ☐ | ☐ | |
| c | Did you explain to the taxpayer the rules about claiming the EIC when a child is the qualifying child of more than one person (tiebreaker rules)? . . . . . . . . . . . . . . . . . | ☐ | ☐ | ☐ |

| **Part III** | Due Diligence Questions for Returns Claiming CTC/ACTC/ODC (If the return does not claim CTC, ACTC, or ODC, go to Part IV.) | | | |
|---|---|---|---|---|
| | | Yes | No | N/A |
| 10 | Have you determined that each qualifying person for the CTC/ACTC/ODC is the taxpayer's dependent who is a citizen, national, or resident of the United States? . . . . . . . . . . . . . | ☒ | ☐ | |
| 11 | Did you explain to the taxpayer that he/she may not claim the CTC/ACTC if the taxpayer has not lived with the child for over half of the year, even if the taxpayer has supported the child, unless the child's custodial parent has released a claim to exemption for the child? . . . . . . . . . . | ☐ | ☐ | ☐ |
| 12 | Did you explain to the taxpayer the rules about claiming the CTC/ACTC/ODC for a child of divorced or separated parents (or parents who live apart), including any requirement to attach a Form 8332 or similar statement to the return? . . . . . . . . . . . . . . . . . . . . . | ☐ | ☐ | ☒ |

| **Part IV** | Due Diligence Questions for Returns Claiming AOTC (If the return does not claim AOTC, go to Part V.) | | |
|---|---|---|---|
| | | Yes | No |
| 13 | Did the taxpayer provide substantiation for the credit, such as a Form 1098-T and/or receipts for the qualified tuition and related expenses for the claimed AOTC? . . . . . . . . . . . . | ☐ | ☐ |

| **Part V** | Due Diligence Questions for Claiming HOH (If the return does not claim HOH filing status, go to Part VI.) | | |
|---|---|---|---|
| | | Yes | No |
| 14 | Have you determined that the taxpayer was unmarried or considered unmarried on the last day of the tax year and provided more than half of the cost of keeping up a home for the year for a qualifying person? . . . . . | ☐ | ☐ |

| **Part VI** | Eligibility Certification |
|---|---|

▶ **You will have complied with all due diligence requirements for claiming the applicable credit(s) and/or HOH filing status on the return of the taxpayer identified above if you:**

A. Interview the taxpayer, ask adequate questions, contemporaneously document the taxpayer's responses on the return or in your notes, review adequate information to determine if the taxpayer is eligible to claim the credit(s) and/or HOH filing status and to compute the amount(s) of the credit(s);

B. Complete this Form 8867 truthfully and accurately and complete the actions described in this checklist for any applicable credit(s) claimed and HOH filing status, if claimed;

C. Submit Form 8867 in the manner required; **and**

D. Keep all five of the following records for 3 years from the latest of the dates specified in the Form 8867 instructions under *Document Retention*.

1. A copy of this Form 8867.

2. The applicable worksheet(s) or your own worksheet(s) for any credit(s) claimed.

3. Copies of any documents provided by the taxpayer on which you relied to determine the taxpayer's eligibility for the credit(s) and/or HOH filing status and to compute the amount(s) of the credit(s).

4. A record of how, when, and from whom the information used to prepare this form and the applicable worksheet(s) was obtained.

5. A record of any additional information you relied upon, including questions you asked and the taxpayer's responses, to determine the taxpayer's eligibility for the credit(s) and/or HOH filing status and to compute the amount(s) of the credit(s).

▶ **If you have not complied with all due diligence requirements, you may have to pay a $530 penalty for each failure to comply related to a claim of an applicable credit or HOH filing status.**

| | | Yes | No |
|---|---|---|---|
| 15 | Do you certify that all of the answers on this Form 8867 are, to the best of your knowledge, true, correct, and complete? . . . . . . . . . . . . . . . . . . . . . . . . . . . . . | ☒ | ☐ |

| Form **8962** | **Premium Tax Credit (PTC)** | OMB No. 1545-0074 |
|---|---|---|
| Department of the Treasury Internal Revenue Service | ▶ Attach to Form 1040, 1040-SR, or 1040-NR.  ▶ Go to *www.irs.gov/Form8962* for instructions and the latest information. | **2019** Attachment Sequence No. **73** |

Name shown on your return █████████

Your social security number █████████

You cannot take the PTC if your filing status is married filing separately unless you qualify for an exception (see instructions). If you qualify, check the box . . ▶ ☐

**Part I  Annual and Monthly Contribution Amount**

| | | | |
|---|---|---|---|
| **1** | Tax family size. Enter your tax family size (see instructions) . . . . . . . . . . . | **1** | 2 |
| **2a** | Modified AGI. Enter your modified AGI (see instructions) . . . . . . . . . **2a** | 38,793. | |
| **b** | Enter the total of your dependents' modified AGI (see instructions) . . . . . **2b** | | |
| **3** | Household income. Add the amounts on lines 2a and 2b (see instructions) . . . . . . . . . . | **3** | 38,793. |
| **4** | Federal poverty line. Enter the federal poverty line amount from Table 1-1, 1-2, or 1-3 (see instructions). Check the appropriate box for the federal poverty table used. **a** ☐ Alaska  **b** ☐ Hawaii  **c** ☒ Other 48 states and DC | **4** | 16,460. |
| **5** | Household income as a percentage of federal poverty line (see instructions) . . . . . . . . . | **5** | 235 % |
| **6** | Did you enter 401% on line 5? (See instructions if you entered less than 100%.)   ☒ **No.** Continue to line 7.   ☐ **Yes.** You are not eligible to take the PTC. If advance payment of the PTC was made, see the instructions for how to report your excess advance PTC repayment amount. | | |
| **7** | Applicable Figure. Using your line 5 percentage, locate your "applicable figure" on the table in the instructions . . | **7** | 0.0781 |
| **8a** | Annual contribution amount. Multiply line 3 by line 7. Round to nearest whole dollar amount **8a** 3,030. | **b** Monthly contribution amount. Divide line 8a by 12. Round to nearest whole dollar amount **8b** | 253. |

**Part II  Premium Tax Credit Claim and Reconciliation of Advance Payment of Premium Tax Credit**

**9** Are you allocating policy amounts with another taxpayer or do you want to use the alternative calculation for year of marriage (see instructions)?
☐ **Yes.** Skip to Part IV, Allocation of Policy Amounts, or Part V, Alternative Calculation for Year of Marriage.  ☒ **No.** Continue to line 10.

**10** See the instructions to determine if you can use line 11 or must complete lines 12 through 23.
☒ **Yes.** Continue to line 11. Compute your annual PTC. Then skip lines 12–23 and continue to line 24.   ☐ **No.** Continue to lines 12–23. Compute your monthly PTC and continue to line 24.

| Annual Calculation | (a) Annual enrollment premiums (Form(s)) 1095-A, line 33A) | (b) Annual applicable SLCSP premium (Form(s) 1095-A, line 33B) | (c) Annual contribution amount (line 8a) | (d) Annual maximum premium assistance (subtract (c) from (b), if zero or less, enter -0-) | (e) Annual premium tax credit allowed (smaller of (a) or (d)) | (f) Annual advance payment of PTC (Form(s) 1095-A, line 33C) |
|---|---|---|---|---|---|---|
| **11** Annual Totals | 6,084. | 5,256. | 3,030. | 2,226. | 2,226. | 3,600. |

| Monthly Calculation | (a) Monthly enrollment premiums (Form(s)) 1095-A, lines 21–32, column A) | (b) Monthly applicable SLCSP premium (Form(s) 1095-A, lines 21–32, column B) | (c) Monthly contribution amount (amount from line 8b or alternative marriage monthly calculation) | (d) Monthly maximum premium assistance (subtract (c) from (b), if zero or less, enter -0-) | (e) Monthly premium tax credit allowed (smaller of (a) or (d)) | (f) Monthly advance payment of PTC (Form(s) 1095-A, lines 21–32, column C) |
|---|---|---|---|---|---|---|
| **12** January | | | | | | |
| **13** February | | | | | | |
| **14** March | | | | | | |
| **15** April | | | | | | |
| **16** May | | | | | | |
| **17** June | | | | | | |
| **18** July | | | | | | |
| **19** August | | | | | | |
| **20** September | | | | | | |
| **21** October | | | | | | |
| **22** November | | | | | | |
| **23** December | | | | | | |

| | | | |
|---|---|---|---|
| **24** | Total premium tax credit. Enter the amount from line 11(e) or add lines 12(e) through 23(e) and enter the total here | **24** | 2,226. |
| **25** | Advance payment of PTC. Enter the amount from line 11(f) or add lines 12(f) through 23(f) and enter the total here | **25** | 3,600. |
| **26** | Net premium tax credit. If line 24 is greater than line 25, subtract line 25 from line 24. Enter the difference here and on Schedule 3 (Form 1040 or 1040-SR), line 9, or Form 1040-NR, line 65. If line 24 equals line 25, enter -0-. Stop here. If line 25 is greater than line 24, leave this line blank and continue to line 27 . . . . . . . . . | **26** | |

**Part III  Repayment of Excess Advance Payment of the Premium Tax Credit**

| | | | |
|---|---|---|---|
| **27** | Excess advance payment of PTC. If line 25 is greater than line 24, subtract line 24 from line 25. Enter the difference here | **27** | 1,374. |
| **28** | Repayment limitation (see instructions) . . . . . . . . . . . . . . . . . . . | **28** | 800. |
| **29** | Excess advance premium tax credit repayment. Enter the smaller of line 27 or line 28 here and on Schedule 2 (Form 1040 or 1040-SR), line 2, or Form 1040-NR, line 44 . . . . . . . . . . . . . . . . | **29** | 800. |

For Paperwork Reduction Act Notice, see your tax return instructions.  56  BA     REV 05/19/20 PR                Form **8962** (2019)

## Part IV · Allocation of Policy Amounts

Complete the following information for up to four policy amount allocations. See instructions for allocation details.

**Allocation 1**

| 30 | (a) Policy Number (Form 1095-A, line 2) | (b) SSN of other taxpayer | (c) Allocation start month | (d) Allocation stop month |
|---|---|---|---|---|
| | **Allocation percentage applied to monthly amounts** | **(e) Premium Percentage** | **(f) SLCSP Percentage** | **(g) Advance Payment of the PTC Percentage** |
| | | | | |

**Allocation 2**

| 31 | (a) Policy Number (Form 1095-A, line 2) | (b) SSN of other taxpayer | (c) Allocation start month | (d) Allocation stop month |
|---|---|---|---|---|
| | **Allocation percentage applied to monthly amounts** | **(e) Premium Percentage** | **(f) SLCSP Percentage** | **(g) Advance Payment of the PTC Percentage** |
| | | | | |

**Allocation 3**

| 32 | (a) Policy Number (Form 1095-A, line 2) | (b) SSN of other taxpayer | (c) Allocation start month | (d) Allocation stop month |
|---|---|---|---|---|
| | **Allocation percentage applied to monthly amounts** | **(e) Premium Percentage** | **(f) SLCSP Percentage** | **(g) Advance Payment of the PTC Percentage** |
| | | | | |

**Allocation 4**

| 33 | (a) Policy Number (Form 1095-A, line 2) | (b) SSN of other taxpayer | (c) Allocation start month | (d) Allocation stop month |
|---|---|---|---|---|
| | **Allocation percentage applied to monthly amounts** | **(e) Premium Percentage** | **(f) SLCSP Percentage** | **(g) Advance Payment of the PTC Percentage** |
| | | | | |

34 Have you completed all policy amount allocations?

☐ **Yes.** Multiply the amounts on Form 1095-A by the allocation percentages entered by policy. Add all allocated policy amounts and non-allocated policy amounts from Forms 1095-A, if any, to compute a combined total for each month. Enter the combined total for each month on lines 12–23, columns (a), (b), and (f). Compute the amounts for lines 12–23, columns (c)–(e), and continue to line 24.

☐ **No.** See the instructions to report additional policy amount allocations.

## Part V · Alternative Calculation for Year of Marriage

Complete line(s) 35 and/or 36 to elect the alternative calculation for year of marriage. For eligibility to make the election, see the instructions for line 9. To complete line(s) 35 and/or 36 and compute the amounts for lines 12–23, see the instructions for this Part V.

| | | (a) Alternative family size | (b) Alternative monthly contribution amount | (c) Alternative start month | (d) Alternative stop month |
|---|---|---|---|---|---|
| 35 | Alternative entries for your SSN | | | | |
| 36 | Alternative entries for your spouse's SSN | | | | |

Form **4562**

Department of the Treasury
Internal Revenue Service (99)

## Depreciation and Amortization
### (Including Information on Listed Property)
► Attach to your tax return.
► Go to *www.irs.gov/Form4562* for instructions and the latest information.

OMB No. 1545-0172

**2019**

Attachment
Sequence No. **179**

| Name(s) shown on return | Business or activity to which this form relates | Identifying number |
|---|---|---|
| | Sch C NETWORKING | |

**Part I  Election To Expense Certain Property Under Section 179**
**Note:** If you have any listed property, complete Part V before you complete Part I.

| | | | |
|---|---|---|---|
| 1 | Maximum amount (see instructions) . . . . . . . . . . . . . . . . . . . | 1 | 1,020,000. |
| 2 | Total cost of section 179 property placed in service (see instructions) . . . . . . . . . . | 2 | 1,450. |
| 3 | Threshold cost of section 179 property before reduction in limitation (see instructions) . . . . . . | 3 | 2,550,000. |
| 4 | Reduction in limitation. Subtract line 3 from line 2. If zero or less, enter -0- . . . . . . . | 4 | 0. |
| 5 | Dollar limitation for tax year. Subtract line 4 from line 1. If zero or less, enter -0-. If married filing separately, see instructions . . . . . . . . . . . . . . . . . . . . . . | 5 | 1,020,000. |

| 6 | (a) Description of property | (b) Cost (business use only) | (c) Elected cost |
|---|---|---|---|
| | PRITER & ASS | 1,450. | 1,450. |
| | | | |

| | | | |
|---|---|---|---|
| 7 | Listed property. Enter the amount from line 29 . . . . . . . . . .  **7** | | |
| 8 | Total elected cost of section 179 property. Add amounts in column (c), lines 6 and 7 . . . . . | 8 | 1,450. |
| 9 | Tentative deduction. Enter the **smaller** of line 5 or line 8 . . . . . . . . . . . . . | 9 | 1,450. |
| 10 | Carryover of disallowed deduction from line 13 of your 2018 Form 4562 . . . . . . . . . | 10 | |
| 11 | Business income limitation. Enter the smaller of business income (not less than zero) or line 5. See instructions | 11 | 43,154. |
| 12 | Section 179 expense deduction. Add lines 9 and 10, but don't enter more than line 11 . . . . . | 12 | 1,450. |
| 13 | Carryover of disallowed deduction to 2020. Add lines 9 and 10, less line 12 ► | 13 | 0. | |

**Note:** Don't use Part II or Part III below for listed property. Instead, use Part V.

**Part II  Special Depreciation Allowance and Other Depreciation (Don't include listed property. See instructions.)**

| | | | |
|---|---|---|---|
| 14 | Special depreciation allowance for qualified property (other than listed property) placed in service during the tax year. See instructions . . . . . . . . . . . . . . . . . . . | 14 | 0. |
| 15 | Property subject to section 168(f)(1) election . . . . . . . . . . . . . . . . . | 15 | |
| 16 | Other depreciation (including ACRS) . . . . . . . . . . . . . . . . . . . . | 16 | |

**Part III  MACRS Depreciation (Don't include listed property. See instructions.)**

**Section A**

| | | | |
|---|---|---|---|
| 17 | MACRS deductions for assets placed in service in tax years beginning before 2019 . . . . . . | 17 | 137. |
| 18 | If you are electing to group any assets placed in service during the tax year into one or more general asset accounts, check here . . . . . . . . . . . . . . . . . . . . ► ☐ | | |

**Section B—Assets Placed in Service During 2019 Tax Year Using the General Depreciation System**

| (a) Classification of property | (b) Month and year placed in service | (c) Basis for depreciation (business/investment use only—see instructions) | (d) Recovery period | (e) Convention | (f) Method | (g) Depreciation deduction |
|---|---|---|---|---|---|---|
| 19a  3-year property | | | | | | |
| b  5-year property | | | | | | |
| c  7-year property | | | | | | |
| d  10-year property | | | | | | |
| e  15-year property | | | | | | |
| f  20-year property | | | | | | |
| g  25-year property | | | 25 yrs. | | S/L | |
| h  Residential rental property | | | 27.5 yrs. | MM | S/L | |
| | | | 27.5 yrs. | MM | S/L | |
| i  Nonresidential real property | | | 39 yrs. | MM | S/L | |
| | | | | MM | S/L | |

**Section C—Assets Placed in Service During 2019 Tax Year Using the Alternative Depreciation System**

| | | | | | | |
|---|---|---|---|---|---|---|
| 20a  Class life | | | | | S/L | |
| b  12-year | | | 12 yrs. | | S/L | |
| c  30-year | | | 30 yrs. | MM | S/L | |
| d  40-year | | | 40 yrs. | MM | S/L | |

**Part IV  Summary** (See instructions.)

| | | | |
|---|---|---|---|
| 21 | Listed property. Enter amount from line 28 . . . . . . . . . . . . . . . . . . | 21 | |
| 22 | **Total.** Add amounts from line 12, lines 14 through 17, lines 19 and 20 in column (g), and line 21. Enter here and on the appropriate lines of your return. Partnerships and S corporations—see instructions . | 22 | 1,587. |
| 23 | For assets shown above and placed in service during the current year, enter the portion of the basis attributable to section 263A costs . . . . . . . . . .  **23** | | |

For Paperwork Reduction Act Notice, see separate instructions.  **BAA**

REV 05/15/20 PRO

Form **4562** (2019)

58

APE                          ATTACH FEDERAL RETURN

19    PBA    519100

---

**Filing Status**

If your California filing status is different from your federal filing status, check the box here . . . . . . . . . . . . . . ☐

1  ☒ Single

4  ☐ Head of household (with qualifying person). See instructions.

2  ☐ Married/RDP filing jointly. See inst.

5  ☐ Qualifying widow(er). Enter year spouse/RDP died. [____]

See instructions. [_____]

3  ☐ Married/RDP filing separately. Enter spouse's/RDP's SSN or ITIN above and full name here [_____]

6  If someone can claim you (or your spouse/RDP) as a dependent, check the box here. See inst . . . . . . . ● 6 ☐

---

**Exemptions**

► For line 7, line 8, line 9, and line 10: Multiply the number you enter in the box by the pre-printed dollar amount for that line.    **Whole dollars only**

7  **Personal:** If you checked box 1, 3, or 4 above, enter 1 in the box. If you checked box 2 or 5, enter 2 in the box. If you checked the box on line 6, see instructions. ● 7 [1] X $122 = ● $ | 122

8  **Blind:** If you (or your spouse/RDP) are visually impaired, enter 1; if both are visually impaired, enter 2. . . . . . . . . . . . . . . . . . . . . . . . . . . . . . . . ● 8 [  ] X $122 = ● $

9  **Senior:** If you (or your spouse/RDP) are 65 or older, enter 1; if both are 65 or older, enter 2 . . . . . . . . . . . . . . . . . . . . . . . . . . . . . . . . . . . . ● 9 [  ] X $122 = ● $

10  **Dependents: Do not include yourself or your spouse/RDP.**

| | Dependent 1 | Dependent 2 | Dependent 3 |
|---|---|---|---|
| First Name | ● ▇▇▇▇ | ● | ● |
| Last Name | ● ▇▇▇▇ | ● | ● |
| SSN | ● ▇▇▇▇ | ● | ● |
| Dependent's relationship to you | ● ▇▇▇▇ | ● | ● |

Total dependent exemptions . . . . . . . . . . . . . . . . . . . . . . . . . . . . . . . . . . . ● 10 [1] X $378 = ● $ | 378

REV 05/01/20 PRO

175    3101194    Form 540 2019 **Side 1**
59

Your name: ASHAARY  Your SSN or ITIN: 607-44-7640

| | | | |
|---|---|---|---|
| 11 | **Exemption amount:** Add line 7 through line 10. Transfer this amount to line 32 . . . . . . . . . | ● 11 $ | 500 |

**Taxable Income**

| | | | |
|---|---|---|---|
| 12 | State wages from your federal Form(s) W-2, box 16 . . . . . . . . . . . . . . . . . . . . . . . . . . . . ● 12 | 0 | .00 |
| 13 | Enter federal adjusted gross income from federal Form 1040 or 1040-SR, line 8b . . . . . . . ● 13 | | 38793 .00 |
| 14 | California adjustments – subtractions. Enter the amount from Schedule CA (540), Part I, line 23, column B. . . . . . . . . . . . . . . . . . . . . . . . . . . . . . . . . . . . . ● 14 | | 137 .00 |
| 15 | Subtract line 14 from line 13. If less than zero, enter the result in parentheses. . See instructions . . . . . . . . . . . . . . . . . . . . . . . . . 15 | | 38656 .00 |
| 16 | California adjustments – additions. Enter the amount from Schedule CA (540), Part I, line 23, column C. . . . . . . . . . . . . . . . . . . . . . . . . . . . . . . . . . . . ● 16 | | .00 |
| 17 | California adjusted gross income. Combine line 15 and line 16 . . . . . . . . . . . . . . . . . . . . . ● 17 | | 38656 .00 |

18 Enter the larger of
{ Your California **itemized deductions** from Schedule CA (540), Part II, line 30; **OR**
Your California **standard deduction** shown below for your filing status:
• Single or Married/RDP filing separately. . . . . . . . . . . . . . . . . . . . . . . . . . . . . . $4,537
• Married/RDP filing jointly, Head of household, or Qualifying widow(er) . . . . $9,074 }
If Married/RDP filing separately or the box on line 6 is checked, STOP. See instructions ● 18   | 32092 .00

| | | | |
|---|---|---|---|
| 19 | Subtract line 18 from line 17. This is your **taxable income.** If less than zero, enter -0- . . . . . . . . . . . . . . . . . . . . . . . . . . . . . . . . . . . ● 19 | | 6564 .00 |

**Tax**

| | | | |
|---|---|---|---|
| 31 | Tax. Check the box if from: [X] Tax Table   [ ] Tax Rate Schedule ● [ ] FTB 3800 ● [ ] FTB 3803 . . . . . . . . . . . . . . . . ● 31 | | 66 .00 |
| 32 | Exemption credits. Enter the amount from line 11. If your federal AGI is more than $200,534, see instructions. . . . . . . . . . . . . . . . . . . . . . . . . . . . . . . . . . . . . . ● 32 | | 500 .00 |
| 33 | Subtract line 32 from line 31. If less than zero, enter -0- . . . . . . . . . . . . . . . . . . . . . . . . . ● 33 | | 0 .00 |
| 34 | Tax. See instructions. Check the box if from: ● [ ] Schedule G-1 ● [ ] FTB 5870A . . ● 34 | | .00 |
| 35 | Add line 33 and line 34. . . . . . . . . . . . . . . . . . . . . . . . . . . . . . . . . . . . . . . . . . ● 35 | | 0 .00 |

**Special Credits**

| | | | |
|---|---|---|---|
| 40 | Nonrefundable Child and Dependent Care Expenses Credit. See instructions. . . . . . . . . . . . ● 40 | | .00 |
| 43 | Enter credit name [ ] code ● [ ] and amount. . . ● 43 | | .00 |
| 44 | Enter credit name [ ] code ● [ ] and amount. . . ● 44 | | .00 |
| 45 | To claim more than two credits. See instructions. Attach Schedule P (540). . . . . . . . . . . . . ● 45 | | .00 |
| 46 | Nonrefundable renter's credit. See instructions . . . . . . . . . . . . . . . . . . . . . . . . . . . . . . ● 46 | | .00 |
| 47 | Add line 40 through line 46. These are your total credits . . . . . . . . . . . . . . . . . . . . . . . . . ● 47 | | .00 |
| 48 | Subtract line 47 from line 35. If less than zero, enter -0-. . . . . . . . . . . . . . . . . . . . . . . . . . ● 48 | | 0 .00 |

Your name: [REDACTED]     Your SSN or ITIN: [REDACTED]

**Other Taxes**

| | | | |
|---|---|---|---|
| 61 | Alternative minimum tax. Attach Schedule P (540) | ● 61 | .00 |
| 62 | Mental Health Services Tax. See instructions | ● 62 | .00 |
| 63 | Other taxes and credit recapture. See instructions | ● 63 | .00 |
| 64 | Add line 48, line 61, line 62, and line 63. This is your total tax. | ● 64 | 0 .00 |

**Payments**

| | | | |
|---|---|---|---|
| 71 | California income tax withheld. See instructions | ● 71 | .00 |
| 72 | 2019 CA estimated tax and other payments. See instructions | ● 72 | .00 |
| 73 | Withholding (Form 592-B and/or 593). See instructions | ● 73 | .00 |
| 74 | Excess SDI (or VPDI) withheld. See instructions | ● 74 | .00 |
| 75 | Earned Income Tax Credit (EITC) | ● 75 | .00 |
| 76 | Young Child Tax Credit (YCTC). See instructions | ● 76 | .00 |
| 77 | Add lines 71 through 76. These are your total payments. See instructions | ◉ 77 | .00 |

**Use Tax**

91 **Use Tax.** Do not leave blank. See instructions ...... ● 91  0 .00

If line 91 is zero, check if:  [X]  No use tax is owed.

[ ]  You paid your use tax obligation directly to CDTFA.

**Overpaid Tax/Tax Due**

| | | | |
|---|---|---|---|
| 92 | Payments balance. If line 77 is more than line 91, subtract line 91 from line 77 | ◉ 92 | .00 |
| 93 | **Use Tax balance.** If line 91 is more than line 77, subtract line 77 from line 91 | ◉ 93 | 0 .00 |
| 94 | Overpaid tax. If line 92 is more than line 64, subtract line 64 from line 92 | ◉ 94 | .00 |
| 95 | Amount of line 94 you want applied to your **2020** estimated tax | ● 95 | .00 |
| 96 | Overpaid tax available this year. Subtract line 95 from line 94 | ● 96 | .00 |
| 97 | Tax due. If line 92 is less than line 64, subtract line 92 from line 64 | ◉ 97 | 0 .00 |

Your name: ▮▮▮▮▮  Your SSN or ITIN: ▮▮▮▮▮

| | Code | Amount |
|---|---|---|
| California Seniors Special Fund. See instructions................................. | ● 400 | .00 |
| Alzheimer's Disease and Related Dementia Voluntary Tax Contribution Fund.............. | ● 401 | .00 |
| Rare and Endangered Species Preservation Voluntary Tax Contribution Program.......... | ● 403 | .00 |
| California Breast Cancer Research Voluntary Tax Contribution Fund.................... | ● 405 | .00 |
| California Firefighters' Memorial Fund............................................. | ● 406 | .00 |
| Emergency Food for Families Voluntary Tax Contribution Fund........................ | ● 407 | .00 |
| California Peace Officer Memorial Foundation Fund................................. | ● 408 | .00 |
| California Sea Otter Fund......................................................... | ● 410 | .00 |
| California Cancer Research Voluntary Tax Contribution Fund......................... | ● 413 | .00 |
| School Supplies for Homeless Children Fund........................................ | ● 422 | .00 |
| State Parks Protection Fund/Parks Pass Purchase.................................. | ● 423 | .00 |
| Protect Our Coast and Oceans Voluntary Tax Contribution Fund...................... | ● 424 | .00 |
| Keep Arts in Schools Voluntary Tax Contribution Fund............................. | ● 425 | .00 |
| Prevention of Animal Homelessness and Cruelty Voluntary Tax Contribution Fund......... | ● 431 | .00 |
| California Senior Citizen Advocacy Voluntary Tax Contribution Fund................... | ● 438 | .00 |
| Native California Wildlife Rehabilitation Voluntary Tax Contribution Fund............... | ● 439 | .00 |
| Rape Kit Backlog Voluntary Tax Contribution Fund................................. | ● 440 | .00 |
| Organ and Tissue Donor Registry Voluntary Tax Contribution Fund.................... | ● 441 | .00 |
| National Alliance on Mental Illness California Voluntary Tax Contribution Fund........... | ● 442 | .00 |
| Schools Not Prisons Voluntary Tax Contribution Fund.............................. | ● 443 | .00 |
| Suicide Prevention Voluntary Tax Contribution Fund............................... | ● 444 | .00 |
| **110** Add code 400 through code 444. This is your total contribution.................... | ● 110 | .00 |

Your name: [redacted]    Your SSN or ITIN: [redacted]

**Amount You Owe**

**111** AMOUNT YOU OWE. If you do not have an amount on line 96, add line 93, line 97, and line 110. See instructions. **Do not send cash.**
Mail to:   FRANCHISE TAX BOARD, PO BOX 942867, SACRAMENTO CA 94267-0001 ..... ● 111 [_____] . 00
Pay Online – Go to ftb.ca.gov/pay for more information.

**Interest and Penalties**

**112** Interest, late return penalties, and late payment penalties ........................ 112 [_____] . 00

**113** Underpayment of estimated tax.

Check the box:  ●  [  ] FTB 5805 attached ●  [  ] FTB 5805F attached ........... ● 113 [_____] . 00

**114** Total amount due. See instructions. Enclose, but **do not** staple, any payment ............ 114 [_____] . 00

**115** REFUND OR NO AMOUNT DUE. Subtract the sum of 110, line 112 and line 113 from line 96. See instructions.

Mail to: FRANCHISE TAX BOARD, PO BOX 942840, SACRAMENTO CA 94240-0001 ....... ● 115 [          0] . 00

**Refund and Direct Deposit**

Fill in the information to authorize direct deposit of your refund into one or two accounts. Do not attach a voided check or a deposit slip.
See instructions. **Have you verified the routing and account numbers?** Use whole dollars only.
All or the following amount of my refund (line 115) is authorized for direct deposit into the account shown below:

● Routing number [_____]   ● Type [ ] Checking / [ ] Savings   ● Account number [_____]   ● 116 Direct deposit amount [_____] . 00

The remaining amount of my refund (line 115) is authorized for direct deposit into the account shown below:

● Routing number [_____]   ● Type [ ] Checking / [ ] Savings   ● Account number [_____]   ● 117 Direct deposit amount [_____] . 00

IMPORTANT: See the instructions to find out if you should attach a copy of your complete federal tax return.

To learn about your privacy rights, how we may use your information, and the consequences for not providing the requested information, go to ftb.ca.gov/forms and search for 1131. To request this notice by mail, call 800.852.5711.

Under penalties of perjury, I declare that I have examined this tax return, including accompanying schedules and statements, and to the best of my knowledge and belief, it is true, correct, and complete.

Your signature [_____]   Date [_____]   Spouse's/RDP's signature (if a joint tax return, both must sign) [_____]

**Sign Here**

It is unlawful to forge a spouse's/RDP's signature.

Joint tax return? (See instructions)

● Your email address. Enter only one email address. [_____]   ● Preferred phone number  9493058088

Paid preparer's signature (declaration of preparer is based on all information of which preparer has any knowledge) [redacted]

Firm's name (or yours, if self-employed)
PROFESSIONAL FINANCIAL SERVICES    ● PTIN [redacted]

Firm's address
151 KALMUS DR C 210 COSTA MESA CA 92626    ● Firm's FEIN  330891189

Do you want to allow another person to discuss this tax return with us? See instructions ..... ●  [ ] Yes  [X] No

Print Third Party Designee's Name [_____]   Telephone Number [_____]

REV 05/01/20 PRO

175    3105194
63

Form 540 2019 Side 5

**Important: Attach this schedule to the back of your original or amended Form 540, 540 2EZ, or 540NR.**

**Caution:** If this schedule is filled out, **do not** send your federal Form(s) W-2 to the Franchise Tax Board. If your federal Form(s) W-2 are from multiple states, **attach** copies showing California tax withheld to this schedule. If this schedule is blank, attach your federal Form(s) W-2 to the lower front of your tax return. **DO NOT ATTACH PAYMENT TO THIS SCHEDULE.**

*Employee's social security number, name, and address must be the same as the information on federal Form(s) W-2.

## W-2 Information

a. Employee's social security number*

b. Employer identification number (EIN)

c. Employer's name

Employer's address

P.O. BOX 940

| City | State | ZIP code |
|---|---|---|
| ROSEVILLE | CA | 95678 |

e. Employee's first name*   Initial*   Last name*   Suffix*

f. Employee's address*

| City* | State* | ZIP code* |
|---|---|---|
| | CA | 92691 |

| | Wages, tips, other compensation | | Social security tax withheld | | Allocated tips (not included in box 1) |
|---|---|---|---|---|---|
| 1. | 0. | 4. | 922. | 8. | |
| | Federal income tax withheld | | Medicare tax withheld | | Dependent care benefits |
| 2. | 0. | 6. | 216. | 10. | |
| | Social security wages | | Social security tips | | Nonqualified plans |
| 3. | 14,874. | 7. | | 11. | |

### 12. Codes and amounts

| | Code | Amount | | Code | Amount |
|---|---|---|---|---|---|
| 12a. | | | 12c. | | |
| 12b. | | | 12d. | | |

13. Check the appropriate box for: Statutory employee, Retirement plan, or Third-party sick pay

☐ Statutory employee   ☐ Retirement plan   ☐ Third-party sick pay

14. SDI, VPDI, or CA SDI (from box 14 or 19)

| Type | Amount | | 16. | State wages, tips, etc. |
|---|---|---|---|---|
| CA-SDI | 149. | | | 0. |

15. State and employer's state ID number

| State | Employer's state ID number | | 17. | State income tax |
|---|---|---|---|---|
| CA | | | | 0. |

REV 05/01/20 PRO

TAXABLE YEAR

# 2019 California Adjustments — Residents

SCHEDULE
CA (540)

**Important:** Attach this schedule behind Form 540, Side 5 as a supporting California schedule.

Name(s) as shown on tax return

SSN or ITIN

## Part I   Income Adjustment Schedule
### Section A – Income from federal Form 1040 or 1040-SR

| | | | A Federal Amounts (taxable amounts from your federal tax return) | B Subtractions See instructions | C Additions See instructions |
|---|---|---|---|---|---|
| 1 | Wages, salaries, tips, etc. See instructions before making an entry in column B or C | 1 | 0. | | |
| 2 | Taxable interest. a | 2b | 36. | | |
| 3 | Ordinary dividends. See instructions. a | 3b | | | |
| 4 | IRA distributions. See instructions. a | 4b | | | |
| | c Pensions and annuities. See instructions. c | 4d | | | |
| 5 | Social security benefits. a | 5b | | | |
| 6 | Capital gain or (loss). See instructions | 6 | | | |

### Section B – Additional Income from federal Schedule 1 (Form 1040 or 1040-SR)

| | | | A | B | C |
|---|---|---|---|---|---|
| 1 | Taxable refunds, credits, or offsets of state and local income taxes | 1 | | | |
| 2a | Alimony received | 2a | | | |
| 3 | Business income or (loss) | 3 | 41,704. | 137. | |
| 4 | Other gains or (losses) | 4 | | | |
| 5 | Rental real estate, royalties, partnerships, S corporations, trusts, etc | 5 | | | |
| 6 | Farm income or (loss) | 6 | | | |
| 7 | Unemployment compensation | 7 | | | |
| 8 | Other income. | 8 | | a b c d e f g | a b c d e f g |

a California lottery winnings
b Disaster loss deduction from FTB 3805V
c Federal NOL (federal Schedule 1 (Form 1040 or 1040-SR), line 8)
d NOL deduction from FTB 3805V

e NOL from FTB 3805Z, 3806, 3807, or 3809
f Other (describe):

g Student loan discharged due to closure of a for-profit school

| | | | A | B | C |
|---|---|---|---|---|---|
| 9 | Total. Combine Section A, line 1 through line 6, and Section B, line 1 through line 8 in column A. Add Section A, line 1 through line 6, and Section B, line 1 through line 8g in column B and column C. Go to Section C. | 9 | 41,740. | 137. | |

### Section C – Adjustments to Income from federal Schedule 1 (Form 1040 or 1040-SR)

| | | | A | B | C |
|---|---|---|---|---|---|
| 10 | Educator expenses | 10 | | | |
| 11 | Certain business expenses of reservists, performing artists, and fee-basis government officials | 11 | | | |
| 12 | Health savings account deduction | 12 | | | |
| 13 | Moving expenses. Attach federal Form 3903. See instructions | 13 | | | |
| 14 | Deductible part of self-employment tax | 14 | 2,947. | | |
| 15 | Self-employed SEP, SIMPLE, and qualified plans | 15 | | | |
| 16 | Self-employed health insurance deduction | 16 | | | |
| 17 | Penalty on early withdrawal of savings | 17 | | | |
| 18a | Alimony paid. b Recipient's:  SSN | | | | |
| | Last name | 18a | | | |
| 19 | IRA deduction | 19 | | | |
| 20 | Student loan interest deduction | 20 | | | |
| 21 | Tuition and fees | 21 | | | |
| 22 | Add line 10 through line 18a and line 19 through line 21 in columns A, B, and C. See instructions | 22 | 2,947. | | |
| 23 | Total. Subtract line 22 from line 9 in columns A, B, and C. See instructions | 23 | 38,793. | 137. | |

**Part II  Adjustments to Federal Itemized Deductions**

Check the box if you did NOT itemize for federal but will itemize for California . . . . . . . . . ◉☐

| | | | **A** Federal Amounts (from federal Schedule A (Form 1040 or 1040-SR)) | **B** Subtractions See instructions | **C** Additions See instructions |
|---|---|---|---|---|---|
| **Medical and Dental Expenses** See instructions. | | | | | |
| 1 | Medical and dental expenses . . . . . . . . . . . . . . . . . . . . . . . ◉ 12,134. | 1 | | | |
| 2 | Enter amount from federal Form 1040 or 1040-SR, line 8b ◉ 38,793. | 2 | | | |
| 3 | Multiply line 2 by 7.5% (0.075) . . . . . . . . . . . . . . . . . . . . . ◉ 2,909. | 3 | | | |
| 4 | Subtract line 3 from line 1. If line 3 is more than line 1, enter 0 . . . . . . . . . . . . . . . . . . . . 4 | ◉ | 9,225. | | ◉ 0. |
| **Taxes You Paid** | | | | | |
| 5a | State and local income tax or general sales taxes. . . . . . . . . . . . . . . . . . . . . . . . . . . . 5a | ◉ | 681. | ◉ 681. | |
| 5b | State and local real estate taxes . . . . . . . . . . . . . . . . . . . . . . . . . . . . . . . . . . . 5b | ◉ | 6,114. | | |
| 5c | State and local personal property taxes . . . . . . . . . . . . . . . . . . . . . . . . . . . . . . . 5c | ◉ | 385. | | |
| 5d | Add lines 5a through 5c . . . . . . . . . . . . . . . . . . . . . . . . . . . . . . . . . . . . . . . . 5d | ◉ | 7,180. | | |
| 5e | Enter the smaller of line 5d or $10,000 ($5,000 if married filing separately) in column A . . Enter the amount from line 5a, column B in line 5e, column B . . . . . . . . . . . . . . . . . . . . Enter the difference from line 5d and line 5e, column A in line 5e, column C . . . . . . . . . . 5e | ◉ | 7,180. | ◉ 681. | ◉ 0. |
| 6 | Other taxes. List type ◉ _____ . . . . . . . . . . . . . 6 | ◉ | | ◉ | ◉ |
| 7 | Add lines 5e and 6 . . . . . . . . . . . . . . . . . . . . . . . . . . . . . . . . . . . . . . . . . . . 7 | ◉ | 7,180. | ◉ 681. | ◉ 0. |
| **Interest You Paid** | | | | | |
| 8a | Home mortgage interest and points reported to you on Form 1098. . . . . . . . . . . . . . . . . 8a | ◉ | 13,308. | | ◉ |
| 8b | Home mortgage interest not reported to you on Form 1098 . . . . . . . . . . . . . . . . . . . . . 8b | ◉ | | | ◉ |
| 8c | Points not reported to you on Form 1098. . . . . . . . . . . . . . . . . . . . . . . . . . . . . . . . 8c | ◉ | | | ◉ |
| 8d | Mortgage insurance premiums . . . . . . . . . . . . . . . . . . . . . . . . . . . . . . . . . . . . . 8d | ◉ | 1,039. | ◉ 1,039. | ◉ |
| 8e | Add lines 8a through 8d . . . . . . . . . . . . . . . . . . . . . . . . . . . . . . . . . . . . . . . . . 8e | ◉ | 14,347. | ◉ 1,039. | ◉ |
| 9 | Investment interest. . . . . . . . . . . . . . . . . . . . . . . . . . . . . . . . . . . . . . . . . . . . 9 | ◉ | | ◉ | ◉ |
| 10 | Add lines 8e and 9 . . . . . . . . . . . . . . . . . . . . . . . . . . . . . . . . . . . . . . . . . . . 10 | ◉ | 14,347. | ◉ 1,039. | ◉ |
| **Gifts to Charity** | | | | | |
| 11 | Gifts by cash or check . . . . . . . . . . . . . . . . . . . . . . . . . . . . . . . . . . . . . . . . . 11 | ◉ | 3,060. | ◉ | ◉ |
| 12 | Other than by cash or check. . . . . . . . . . . . . . . . . . . . . . . . . . . . . . . . . . . . . . . 12 | ◉ | | ◉ | ◉ |
| 13 | Carryover from prior year. . . . . . . . . . . . . . . . . . . . . . . . . . . . . . . . . . . . . . . . 13 | ◉ | | ◉ | ◉ |
| 14 | Add lines 11 through 13 . . . . . . . . . . . . . . . . . . . . . . . . . . . . . . . . . . . . . . . . . 14 | ◉ | 3,060. | ◉ | ◉ |
| **Casualty and Theft Losses** | | | | | |
| 15 | Casualty or theft loss(es) (other than net qualified disaster losses). Attach federal Form 4684. See instructions. . . . . . . . . . . . . . . . . . . . . . . . . . . . . . . . . . . . . 15 | ◉ | | ◉ | ◉ |
| **Other Itemized Deductions** | | | | | |
| 16 | Other—from list in federal instructions . . . . . . . . . . . . . . . . . . . . . . . . . . . . . . . . 16 | ◉ | | ◉ | ◉ |
| 17 | Add lines 4, 7, 10, 14, 15, and 16 in columns A, B, and C . . . . . . . . . . . . . . . . . . . . . . 17 | ◉ | 33,812. | ◉ 1,720. | ◉ 0. |
| 18 | Total. Combine line 17 column A less column B plus column C . . . . . . . . . . . . . . . . . . . . . . . . . . . ◉ 18 | | **32,092.** | | |

### Job Expenses and Certain Miscellaneous Deductions

19  Unreimbursed employee expenses - job travel, union dues, job education, etc.
    Attach federal Form 2106 if required. See instructions........................ ⊙ 19 [          ]

20  Tax preparation fees. ...................................................... ⊙ 20 [          ]

21  Other expenses - investment, safe deposit box, etc. List type ⊙ _____ ⊙ 21 [      0.  ]

22  Add lines 19 through 21.................................................... ⊙ 22 [      0.  ]

23  Enter amount from federal Form 1040 or 1040-SR, line 8b ⊙ ____ 38,793.

24  Multiply line 23 by 2% (0.02). If less than zero, enter 0. .................. ⊙ 24 [    776.  ]

25  Subtract line 24 from line 22. If line 24 is more than line 22, enter 0. .......... ⊙ 25 [          0. ]

26  Total Itemized Deductions. Add line 18 and line 25. ........................ ⊙ 26 [     32,092. ]

27  Other adjustments. See instructions. Specify. ⊙ _____ ....... ⊙ 27 [          ]

28  Combine line 26 and line 27. ............................................. ⊙ 28 [     32,092. ]

29  Is your federal AGI (Form 540, line 13) more than the amount shown below for your filing status?

    Single or married/RDP filing separately ........................... $200,534
    Head of household................................................. $300,805
    Married/RDP filing jointly or qualifying widow(er) .................. $401,072
    No. Transfer the amount on line 28 to line 29.

    Yes. Complete the Itemized Deductions Worksheet in the instructions for Schedule CA (540), line 29. ................... ⊙ 29 [     32,092. ]

30  Enter the larger of the amount on line 29 or your standard deduction listed below

    Single or married/RDP filing separately. See instructions............. $4,537
    Married/RDP filing jointly, head of household, or qualifying widow(er) .... $9,074

    Transfer the amount on line 30 to Form 540, line 18. ......................... ⊙ 30 [     32,092. ]

| TAXABLE YEAR | **Depreciation and** | | CALIFORNIA FORM |
|---|---|---|---|
| **2019** | **Amortization Adjustments** | | **3885A** |

Do not complete this form if your California depreciation amounts are the same as federal amounts.

| Name(s) as shown on tax return | SSN or ITIN |
|---|---|
| ▓▓▓▓ | |

**Part I  Identify the Activity as Passive or Nonpassive. (See instructions.)**

1  ☐ This form is being completed for a passive activity.
   ☒ This form is being completed for a nonpassive activity.

Business or activity to which form FTB 3885A relates

NETWORKING

**Part II  Election to Expense Certain Tangible Property (IRC Section 179).**

2  Enter the amount from line 12 of the Tangible Property Expense Worksheet in the instructions ............... ⊙ 2 _____ 1,450.

**Part III  Depreciation**

| 3 | (a) Description of property placed in service | (b) Date placed in service mm/dd/yyyy | (c) California basis for depreciation | (d) Method | (e) Life or rate | (f) California depreciation deduction |
|---|---|---|---|---|---|---|
| 3 | PRITER & ASS | 05/25/2019 | 0. | 200DB | 5.0 | 0. |
| | | | | | | |
| | | | | | | |
| | | | | | | |

4  Add the amounts on line 3, column (f) .................................................. 4 _____ 0.
5  California depreciation for assets placed in service prior to 2019........................ 5 _____ 274.
6  Total California depreciation from this activity. Add the amounts on line 2, line 4, and line 5 ........... 6 _____ 1,724.
7  Total federal depreciation from this activity. Enter depreciation from federal Form 4562, line 22 .......... 7 _____ 1,587.
8  a  If line 6 is **more** than line 7, enter the difference here and see instructions............................. 8a _____ 137.
   b  If line 6 is **less** than line 7, enter the difference here and see instructions............................. 8b _____

**Part IV  Amortization**

| 9 | (a) Description of cost | (b) Date amortization begins mm/dd/yyyy | (c) California basis for amortization | (d) Code section | (e) Period or percentage | (f) California amortization deduction |
|---|---|---|---|---|---|---|
| 9 | | | | | | |
| | | | | | | |
| | | | | | | |
| | | | | | | |

10  Total California amortization from this activity. Add the amounts on line 9, column (f) ...................... 10 _____
11  California amortization of costs that began before 2019.................................................. 11 _____
12  Total California amortization from this activity. Add the amounts on line 10 and line 11....................... 12 _____
13  Total federal amortization from this activity. Enter amortization from federal Form 4562, line 44.................. 13 _____
14  a  If line 12 is **more** than line 13, enter the difference here and see instructions......................... 14a _____
    b  If line 12 is **less** than line 13, enter the difference here and see instructions......................... 14b _____

| Name as Shown on Return | | | Social Security Number |
|---|---|---|---|
| ▮▮▮▮▮▮ | | | 607-44-7640 |

| Section B, Line 3 — Business Income or (Loss) Adjustments | (B) California Amount | (C) Federal Amount | (d) California Adjustment |
|---|---|---|---|
| 3 S. NETWORK, INC. | 41,567. | 41,704. | |
| | | | |
| | | | |
| | | | |
| | | | |
| | | | |
| | | | |
| | | | |
| | | | |
| Totals . . . . . . . . . . . . . . . . . . . . . . . | 41,567. | 41,704. | -137. |

| Section B, Line 5 — Rents, Royalties, Partnerships, Estates, Trusts, Etc. Adjustments | (B) California | (C) Federal | (d) California Adjustment |
|---|---|---|---|
| | | | |
| | | | |
| | | | |
| | | | |
| | | | |
| | | | |
| | | | |
| | | | |
| | | | |
| Totals . . . . . . . . . . . . . . . . . . . . . . | | | |

| Section B, Line 6 — Farm Income or (Loss) Adjustments | (B) California | (C) Federal | (d) California Adjustment |
|---|---|---|---|
| | | | |
| | | | |
| | | | |
| | | | |
| | | | |
| | | | |
| | | | |
| | | | |
| Totals . . . . . . . . . . . . . . . . . . . . . . | | | |

OMB NO. 1545-0008    Department of the Treasury - Internal Revenue Service

| 1 Wages, tips, other compensation | 2 Federal income tax withheld |
|---|---|
| 0.00 | 0.00 |
| 3 Social security wages | 4 Social security tax withheld |
| 14874.09 | 922.19 |
| 5 Medicare wages and tips | 6 Medicare tax withheld |
| 14874.09 | 215.67 |

c Employer's name, address, and ZIP code

3004

| 7 Social security tips | 8 Allocated tips | 9 |
|---|---|---|
| 0.00 | 0.00 | |
| 10 Dependent care benefits | 11 Nonqualified plans | 12a See instructions for box 12 |
| 0.00 | 0.00 | |
| 12b | 12c | 12d |

b Employer identification number (EIN)    942629822
a Employee's social security number    607-44-7640

| 13 Statutory employee | Retirement plan | Third-party sick pay | 14 Other |
|---|---|---|---|
| | | | CA-SDI    148.74 |

e Employee's name, address and ZIP code

Form **W-2**
Wage and Tax Statement
**2019**
Copy 1 - To be Filed With Employee's State, City or Local Income Tax Return

| 15 State CA | Employer's state ID number 04407680 | 16 State wages, tips, etc. |
|---|---|---|
| | | 0.00 |
| | | 0.00 |
| | 17 State income tax | 18 Local wages, tips, etc. |
| | 0.00 | 0.00 |
| | 0.00 | 0.00 |
| | 19 Local income tax | 20 Locality name |
| | 0.00 | |
| | 0.00 | |

---

OMB NO. 1545-0008    Department of the Treasury - Internal Revenue Service

| 1 Wages, tips, other compensation | 2 Federal income tax withheld |
|---|---|
| 0.00 | 0.00 |
| 3 Social security wages | 4 Social security tax withheld |
| 14874.09 | 922.19 |
| 5 Medicare wages and tips | 6 Medicare tax withheld |
| 14874.09 | 215.67 |

c Employer's name, address, and ZIP code

| 7 Social security tips | 8 Allocated tips | 9 |
|---|---|---|
| 0.00 | 0.00 | |
| 10 Dependent care benefits | 11 Nonqualified plans | 12a See instructions for box 12 |
| 0.00 | 0.00 | |
| 12b | 12c | 12d |

b Employer identification number (EIN)    942629822
a Employee's social security number    607-44-7640

| 13 Statutory employee | Retirement plan | Third-party sick pay | 14 Other |
|---|---|---|---|
| | | | CA-SDI    148.74 |

e Employee's name, address and ZIP code

Form **W-2**
Wage and Tax Statement
**2019**
Copy 2 - To be Filed With Employee's State, City or Local Income Tax Return

| 15 State CA | Employer's state ID number 04407680 | 16 State wages, tips, etc. |
|---|---|---|
| | | 0.00 |
| | | 0.00 |
| | 17 State income tax | 18 Local wages, tips, etc. |
| | 0.00 | 0.00 |
| | 0.00 | 0.00 |
| | 19 Local income tax | 20 Locality name |
| | 0.00 | |
| | 0.00 | |

---

OMB NO. 1545-008
This information is being furnished to the Internal Revenue Service. If you are required to file a tax return, a negligence penalty or other sanction may be imposed on you if this income is taxable and you fail to report it.

Department of the Treasury - Internal Revenue Service

| 1 Wages, tips, other compensation | 2 Federal income tax withheld |
|---|---|
| 0.00 | 0.00 |
| 3 Social security wages | 4 Social security tax withheld |
| 14874.09 | 922.19 |
| 5 Medicare wages and tips | 6 Medicare tax withheld |
| 14874.09 | 215.67 |

c Employer's name, address and ZIP code

| 7 Social security tips | 8 Allocated tips | 9 |
|---|---|---|
| 0.00 | 0.00 | |
| 10 Dependent care benefits | 11 Nonqualified plans | 12a See instructions for box 12 |
| 0.00 | 0.00 | |
| 12b | 12c | 12d |

b Employer identification number (EIN)    942629822
a Employee's social security number    607-44-7640

| 13 Statutory employee | Retirement plan | Third-party sick pay | 14 Other |
|---|---|---|---|
| | | | CA-SDI    148.74 |

e Employee's name, address and ZIP code

Form **W-2**
Wage and Tax Statement
**2019**
Copy C - For EMPLOYEE'S RECORDS (See Notice to Employee on the back of Copy B)

| 15 State CA | Employer's state ID number 04407680 | 16 State wages, tips, etc. |
|---|---|---|
| | | 0.00 |
| | | 0.00 |
| | 17 State income tax | 18 Local wages, tips, etc. |
| | 0.00 | 0.00 |
| | 0.00 | 0.00 |
| | 19 Local income tax | 20 Locality name |
| | 0.00 | |
| | 0.00 | 70 |

---

OMB NO. 1545-008
This information is being furnished to the Internal Revenue Service

Department of the Treasury - Internal Revenue Service

| 1 Wages, tips, other compensation | 2 Federal income tax withheld |
|---|---|
| 0.00 | 0.00 |
| 3 Social security wages | 4 Social security tax withheld |
| 14874.09 | 922.19 |
| 5 Medicare wages and tips | 6 Medicare tax withheld |
| 14874.09 | 215.67 |

c Employer's name, address and ZIP code

| 7 Social security tips | 8 Allocated tips | 9 |
|---|---|---|
| 0.00 | 0.00 | |
| 10 Dependent care benefits | 11 Nonqualified plans | 12a See instructions for box 12 |
| 0.00 | 0.00 | |
| 12b | 12c | 12d |

b Employer identification number (EIN)    942629822
a Employee's social security number    607-44-7640

| 13 Statutory employee | Retirement plan | Third-party sick pay | 14 Other |
|---|---|---|---|
| | | | CA-SDI    148.74 |

e Employee's name, address and ZIP code

Form **W-2**
Wage and Tax Statement
**2019**
Copy B - To Be Filed With Employee's FEDERAL Tax Return

| 15 State CA | Employer's state ID number 04407680 | 16 State wages, tips, etc. |
|---|---|---|
| | | 0.00 |
| | | 0.00 |
| | 17 State income tax | 18 Local wages, tips, etc. |
| | 0.00 | 0.00 |
| | 0.00 | 0.00 |
| | 19 Local income tax | 20 Locality name |
| | 0.00 | |
| | 0.00 | |

☐ CORRECTED (if checked)

| PAYER'S name, street address, city or town, state or province, country, ZIP or foreign postal code, and telephone no. | 1 Rents $ | OMB No. 1545-0115 **2019** Form **1099-MISC** | **Miscellaneous Income** |
|---|---|---|---|
| ▉▉▉▉▉▉▉▉▉▉▉ US 949-616-4561 | 2 Royalties $ | | |
| | 3 Other income $ | 4 Federal income tax withheld $ | **Copy B** **For Recipient** |

| PAYER'S TIN | RECIPIENT'S TIN | 5 Fishing boat proceeds $ | 6 Medical and health care payments $ | |
|---|---|---|---|---|
| 77-0609275 | XXX-XX-7640 | | | |

| RECIPIENT'S name, street address, city or town, state or province, country, and ZIP or foreign postal code | 7 Nonemployee compensation $ 76,766.86 | 8 Substitute payments in lieu of dividends or interest $ | This is important tax information and is being furnished to the IRS. If you are required to file a return, a negligence penalty or other sanction may be imposed on you if this income is taxable and the IRS determines that it has not been reported. |
|---|---|---|---|
| ▉▉▉▉▉▉▉▉▉▉ ▉▉▉▉▉▉ | 9 Payer made direct sales of $5,000 or more of consumer products to a buyer (recipient) for resale ▶ ☐ | 10 Crop insurance proceeds $ | |
| | 11 | 12 | |

| Account number (see instructions) | FATCA filing requirement ☐ | 13 Excess golden parachute payments $ | 14 Gross proceeds paid to an attorney $ | |
|---|---|---|---|---|

| 15a Section 409A deferrals $ | 15b Section 409A income $ | 16 State tax withheld $ $ | 17 State/Payer's state no. | 18 State income $ $ |
|---|---|---|---|---|

Form **1099-MISC**     GRSNMOABSP1_deliveres_906408118400-1078157     (keep for your records)     Department of the Treasury - Internal Revenue Service

## Instructions for Recipient

Recipient's taxpayer identification number (TIN). For your protection, this form may show only the last four digits of your social security number (SSN), individual taxpayer identification number (ITIN), adoption taxpayer identification number (ATIN), or employer identification number (EIN). However, the payer has reported your complete TIN to the IRS.

Account number. May show an account or other unique number the payer assigned to distinguish your account.

FATCA filing requirement. If the FATCA filing requirement box is checked, the payer is reporting on this Form 1099 to satisfy its chapter 4 account reporting requirement. You also may have a filing requirement. See the Instructions for Form 8938.

Amounts shown may be subject to self-employment (SE) tax. If your net income from self-employment is $400 or more, you must file a return and compute your SE tax on Schedule SE (Form 1040). See Pub. 334 for more information. Note: If you are still receiving payments on which no income, social security, and Medicare taxes are withheld, you should make estimated tax payments. See Form 1040-ES (or Form 1040-ES(NR)). Individuals must report these amounts as explained in the box 7 instructions on this page. Corporations, fiduciaries, or partnerships must report the amounts on the proper line of their tax returns.

Form 1099-MISC incorrect? If this form is incorrect or has been issued in error, contact the payer. If you cannot get this form corrected, attach an explanation to your tax return and report your income correctly.

Box 1. Report rents from real estate on Schedule E (Form 1040). However, report rents on Schedule C (Form 1040) if you provided significant services to the tenant, sold real estate as a business, or rented personal property as a business. See Pub. 527.

Box 2. Report royalties from oil, gas, or mineral properties, copyrights, and patents on Schedule E (Form 1040). However, report payments for a working interest as explained in the box 7 instructions. For royalties on timber, coal, and iron ore, see Pub. 544.

Box 3. Generally, report this amount on the "Other income" line of Schedule 1 (Form 1040) (or Form 1040NR) and identify the payment. The amount shown may be payments received as the beneficiary of a deceased employee, prizes, awards, taxable damages, Indian gaming profits, or other taxable income. See Pub. 525. If it is trade or business income, report this amount on Schedule C or F (Form 1040).

Box 4. Shows backup withholding or withholding on Indian gaming profits. Generally, a payer must backup withhold if you did not furnish your TIN. See Form W-9 and Pub. 505 for more information. Report this amount on your income tax return as tax withheld.

Box 5. An amount in this box means the fishing boat operator considers you self-employed. Report this amount on Schedule C (Form 1040). See Pub. 334.

Box 6. For individuals, report on Schedule C (Form 1040).

Box 7. Shows nonemployee compensation. If you are in the trade or business of catching fish, box 7 may show cash you received for the sale of fish. If the amount in this box is SE income, report it on Schedule C or F (Form 1040), and complete Schedule SE (Form 1040). You received this form instead of Form W-2 because the payer did not consider you an employee and did not withhold income tax or social security and Medicare tax. If you believe you are an employee and cannot get the payer to correct this form, report this amount on the line for "Wages, salaries, tips, etc." of Form 1040 (or Form 1040NR). You also must complete Form 8919 and attach it to your return. If you are not an employee but the amount in this box is not SE income (for example, it is income from a sporadic activity or a hobby), report this amount on the "Other income" line of Schedule 1 (Form 1040) (or Form 1040NR).

Box 8. Shows substitute payments in lieu of dividends or tax-exempt interest received by your broker on your behalf as a result of a loan of your securities. Report on the "Other income" line of Schedule 1 (Form 1040) (or Form 1040NR).

Box 9. If checked, $5,000 or more of sales of consumer products was paid to you on a buy-sell, deposit-commission, or other basis. A dollar amount does not have to be shown. Generally, report any income from your sale of these products on Schedule C (Form 1040).

Box 10. Report this amount on Schedule F (Form 1040).

Box 13. Shows your total compensation of excess golden parachute payments subject to a 20% excise tax. See the Form 1040 (or Form 1040NR) instructions for where to report.

Box 14. Shows gross proceeds paid to an attorney in connection with legal services. Report only the taxable part as income on your return.

Box 15a. May show current year deferrals as a nonemployee under a nonqualified deferred compensation (NQDC) plan that is subject to the requirements of section 409A, plus any earnings on current and prior year deferrals.

Box 15b. Shows income as a nonemployee under an NQDC plan that does not meet the requirements of section 409A. This amount also is included in box 7 as nonemployee compensation. Any amount included in box 15b that is currently taxable is also included in this box. This income is also subject to a substantial additional tax to be reported on Form 1040 (or Form 1040NR). See the Form 1040 (or Form 1040NR) instructions.

Boxes 16-18. Show state or local income tax withheld from the payments.

Future developments. For the latest information about developments related to Form 1099-MISC and its instructions, such as legislation enacted after they were published, go to www.irs.gov/Form1099MISC.

**1099-MISC / COPY B**

EXHIBIT '7'

Orange County Superior Court Docket Sheet - 96WF2961

# Superior Court of California
## County of Orange

Case Number : 96WF2961

Copy Request: 3930483

Request Type: Case Documents

Prepared for: KA

Number of documents: 1
Number of pages: 2

Case : 96WF2961 F A

Name :

| Date of Action | Seq Nbr | Code | Text |
|---|---|---|---|
| 02/20/97 | 1 | CVNTE | CLERK Docket Note for event type CERT with Notes: Note_1: *MDAN* A DO, PD. DFT PLED TO CNTS 1&2. Note_2: DFT ORD TO COMPL DIVERSION PROG. O R SIGNED.. |
| 08/20/97 | 1 | CVNTE | CLERK Docket Note for event type SENT with Notes: Note_1: *MDAN* NO APP. B/W ISS FOR DFT. BAIL SET $15,000. Note_2: O R REVK.. |
| 12/01/97 | 1 | CVNTE | CLERK Docket Note for event type FTA with Notes: Note_1: *SBAT* - FTA D-78 SENTENCING - A.DO, PD PER OCJ DEF Note_2: POSTED BAIL ON FTA CHARGE AND ORDERED TO D-5. |
| | 1 | CVNTE | CLERK Docket Note for event type FTA with Notes: Note_1: THIS DATE. B/W ISSUED FOR DEFT Note_2: BAIL SET AT $150,000. Note_3: Note_4:. |
| 12/24/97 | 1 | CVNTE | CLERK Docket Note for event type SENT with Notes: Note_1: *SBAT* - FTA SENTENCING - L.BRONSTEIN, PD Note_2: CASE TRANS TO D-78 - B/W RECALLED. |
| 01/21/98 | 1 | CVNTE | CLERK Docket Note for event type MONP with Notes: Note_1: *SBAT* - NUNC PRO TUNC M.O. OF 12-24-97. Note_2: TO ADD THE FOLLOWING ORDERS: BAIL RESET IN THE. |
| | 1 | CVNTE | CLERK Docket Note for event type MONP with Notes: Note_1: AMOUNT OF $15,000.00. ALL OTHER Note_2: ORDERS REMAIN IN FULL FORCE AND EFFECT. Note_3: Note_4:. |
| 02/02/98 | 1 | CVNTE | CLERK Docket Note for event type MONP with Notes: Note_1: *SBAT* - NUNC PRO TUNC M.O. OF 12-1-97 Note_2: THIS COURT'S ORDER OF 12-1-97 IS ORDERED. |
| | 1 | CVNTE | CLERK Docket Note for event type MONP with Notes: Note_1: VACATED IN ITS ENTIRETY AS DEFT WAS Note_2: NOT ORDERED TO APPEAR ON 12-1-97 HE WAS ORDERED Note_3: TO APPEAR ON 12-24-97. Note_4:. |
| 02/25/98 | 1 | CVNTE | CLERK Docket Note for event type FUR with Notes: Note_1: ABOW- J. BARNETT, PD- CASE ASSIGNED TO D-5 Note_2:. |
| 03/04/98 | 1 | CVNTE | CLERK Docket Note for event type FUR with Notes: Note_1: *SBAT* - LISA BRONSTEIN, PD - OFF CALENDAR Note_2:. |

Case : 96WF2961 F A

Name : ███████████

| Date of Action | Seq Nbr | Code | Text |
|---|---|---|---|
| 12/11/99 | 1 | CVCAS | CLERK Case converted. |
| 11/11/02 | 1 | CSCLS | **Case closed.** |
| 07/07/06 | 1 | CSCLS | **Case closed.** |
| 04/27/15 | 1 | CSCLS | **Case closed.** |
| 07/29/20 | 1 | FITXT | Petition for Dismissal (Pen. Code 17(b), 17(d)(2), 1203.4, 1203.4a, 1203.41, 1203.42, 1203.43, 1203.49) filed. |
| | 2 | TXRNF | Order for Dismissal received, not filed. |
| | 3 | FIMTN2 | Defense Motion to Withdraw Guilty or Nolo Contendere Plea, Enter not Guilty Plea, and Dismiss the Complaint or Information Pursuant to Penal Code Section 1203.43 filed. |
| | 4 | FIDOC | Proof of Service filed. |
| 07/30/20 | 1 | CSCLS | **Case closed.** |
| 07/31/20 | 1 | TXRFR | Case referred to Legal Research for review. |
| 08/11/20 | 1 | HHELD | Hearing held on 08/11/2020 at 12:00 AM in Department C47 for Chambers Work. |
| | 2 | OFJUD | Judicial Officer: Robert A. Knox, Judge |
| | 3 | OFJA | Clerk: A. Garcia |
| | 4 | APNCR | No Court Reporter present at proceedings. |
| | 5 | APNAP | No appearance by parties. |
| | 6 | TEXT | Having reviewed Defendant's petition for relief pursuant to Penal Code section 1203.43, the Court issues the following order: |
| | 7 | TEXT | The Court finds the defendant meets the requirements prescribed within Penal Code Section 1203.43. The Court further finds that the prior guilty plea entered on 2/20/97 as to counts 1 and 2 are constitutionally invalid pursuant to Penal Code section 1203.43(a) and the Court permits the defendant to withdraw the guilty plea and enter a plea of NOT GUILTY. The Court orders counts 1 and 2 DISMISSED pursuant to Penal Code section 1203.43(b). |
| | 8 | FIDOC | Order for Dismissal (Penal Code 17(b), 17(d)(2), 1203.4, 1203.4a, 1203.41, 1203.43, 1203.49) filed. |
| | 9 | TEXT | The Clerk of the Court is directed to serve a copy of this order on the Office of the Orange County District Attorney and on Defendant. |
| | 10 | NTCSL | Case Processing directed to send notice by letter. |
| | 11 | OFMDD | Minutes of 08/11/2020 entered on 08/12/2020. |

# MINUTES

Case : 96WF2961 F A

Name :

| Date of Action | Seq Nbr | Code | Text |
|---|---|---|---|
| 12/11/99 | 1 | CVCAS | CLERK Case converted. |
| 11/11/02 | 1 | CSCLS | Case closed. |
| 07/07/06 | 1 | CSCLS | Case closed. |
| 04/27/15 | 1 | CSCLS | Case closed. |
| 07/29/20 | 1 | FITXT | Petition for Dismissal (Pen. Code 17(b), 17(d)(2), 1203.4, 1203.4a, 1203.41, 1203.42, 1203.43, 1203.49) filed. |
| | 2 | TXRNF | Order for Dismissal received, not filed. |
| | 3 | FIMTN2 | Defense Motion to Withdraw Guilty or Nolo Contendere Plea, Enter not Guilty Plea, and Dismiss the Complaint or Information Pursuant to Penal Code Section 1203.43 filed. |
| | 4 | FIDOC | Proof of Service filed. |
| 07/30/20 | 1 | CSCLS | Case closed. |
| 07/31/20 | 1 | TXRFR | Case referred to Legal Research for review. |
| 08/11/20 | 1 | HHELD | Hearing held on 08/11/2020 at 12:00 AM in Department C47 for Chambers Work. |
| | 2 | OFJUD | Judicial Officer: Robert A. Knox, Judge |
| | 3 | OFJA | Clerk: A. Garcia |
| | 4 | APNCR | No Court Reporter present at proceedings. |
| | 5 | APNAP | No appearance by parties. |
| | 6 | TEXT | Having reviewed Defendant's petition for relief pursuant to Penal Code section 1203.43, the Court issues the following order: |
| | 7 | TEXT | The Court finds the defendant meets the requirements prescribed within Penal Code Section 1203.43. The Court further finds that the prior guilty plea entered on 2/20/97 as to counts 1 and 2 are constitutionally invalid pursuant to Penal Code section 1203.43(a) and the Court permits the defendant to withdraw the guilty plea and enter a plea of NOT GUILTY. The Court orders counts 1 and 2 DISMISSED pursuant to Penal Code section 1203.43(b). |
| | 8 | FIDOC | Order for Dismissal (Penal Code 17(b), 17(d)(2), 1203.4, 1203.4a, 1203.41, 1203.43, 1203.49) filed. |
| | 9 | TEXT | The Clerk of the Court is directed to serve a copy of this order on the Office of the Orange County District Attorney and on Defendant. |
| | 10 | NTCSL | Case Processing directed to send notice by letter. |
| | 11 | OFMDD | Minutes of 08/11/2020 entered on 08/12/2020. |

# MINUTES

Case : 96WF2961 F A

Name : ██████████

| Date of Action | Seq Nbr | Code | Text |
|---|---|---|---|
| 08/20/20 | 1 | CSCLS | Case closed. |

| ATTORNEY OR PARTY WITHOUT ATTORNEY: | STATE BAR NO.: 235438 | FOR COURT USE ONLY |
|---|---|---|
| NAME: Christopher A. Reed<br>FIRM NAME: Law Offices of Brian D. Lerner, APC<br>STREET ADDRESS: 3233 E. Broadway<br>CITY: Long Beach STATE: CA ZIP CODE: 90803<br>TELEPHONE NO.: (562) 495-0554 FAX NO.: (562) 512-2036<br>E-MAIL ADDRESS: creed@eimmigration.org<br>ATTORNEY FOR (name): | | **FILED**<br>SUPERIOR COURT OF CALIFORNIA<br>COUNTY OF ORANGE<br>CENTRAL JUSTICE CENTER<br><br>JUL 2 9 2020<br><br>DAVID H. YAMASAKI, Clerk of the Court<br>BY: D. ROSALES DEPUTY |

| PEOPLE OF THE STATE OF CALIFORNIA | | |
|---|---|---|
| v. | | |
| DEFENDANT: | DATE OF BIRTH: 03/21/1976 | |

| | CASE NUMBER:<br>96WF2961 |
|---|---|
| **PETITION FOR DISMISSAL**<br>(Pen. Code, §§ 17(b), 17(d)(2), 1203.4, 1203.4a, 1203.41, 1203.42, 1203.43, 1203.49) | FOR COURT USE ONLY<br>DATE:<br>TIME:<br>DEPARTMENT: |

1. On *(date):* , the petitioner *(the defendant in the above-entitled criminal action)* was convicted of a violation of the following offenses or was granted deferred entry of judgment for the following offenses:

| Code | Section | Type of offense (felony, misdemeanor, or infraction): | Eligible for reduction to misdemeanor under Penal Code, § 17(b) (yes or no) | Eligible for reduction to infraction under Penal Code, § 17(d)(2) (yes or no) |
|---|---|---|---|---|
| HS | 11377(a) | Felony | Yes | No |
| HS | 11364 | Misdemeanor | N/A | No |
| | | | | |
| | | | | |
| | | | | |

If additional space is needed for listing offenses, use *Attachment to Judicial Council Form* (form MC-025).

2. ☐ **Felony or misdemeanor with probation granted** *(Pen. Code, § 1203.4)*

Probation was granted on the terms and conditions stated in the docket of the above-entitled court; the petitioner is not serving a sentence for any offense, on probation for any offense, or under charge of commission of any crime, and the petitioner *(check all that apply)*

　a. ☐ has fulfilled the conditions of probation for the entire period thereof.

　b. ☐ has been discharged from probation prior to the termination of the period thereof.

　c. ☐ should be granted relief in the interests of justice. *(Please note: You may explain why granting a dismissal would be in the interests of justice. You can provide that information by writing in the space below, or by attaching a letter or other relevant documents. If you need more space for your writing, you can use the Attached Declaration (form MC-031) and attach it to this petition.)*

Form Approved for Optional Use<br>Judicial Council of California<br>CR-180 [Rev. January 1, 2019]

**PETITION FOR DISMISSAL**

Penal Code, §§ 17(b), 17(d)(2), 1203.4, 1203.4a,<br>1203.41, 1203.42, 1203.43, and 1203.49<br>www.courts.ca.gov

| PEOPLE OF THE STATE OF CALIFORNIA v. DEFENDANT: | CASE NUMBER: |
|---|---|
| ▆▆▆▆▆▆▆▆ | 96WF2961 |

3. ☐ **Misdemeanor or infraction with sentence other than probation** *(Pen. Code, § 1203.4a)*

Probation was not granted; more than one year has elapsed since the date of pronouncement of judgment. Petitioner has complied with the sentence of the court and is not serving a sentence for any offense or under charge of commission of any crime; and the petitioner *(check one):*

   a. ☐ has lived an honest and upright life since pronouncement of judgment and conformed to and obeyed the laws of the land; *or*

   b. ☐ should be granted relief in the interests of justice. *(Please note: You may explain why granting a dismissal would be in the interests of justice. You can provide that information by writing in the space below or by attaching a letter or other relevant documents. If you need more space for your writing, you can use the Attached Declaration (form MC-031) and attach it to this petition.)*

4. ☐ **Misdemeanor conviction under Penal Code section 647(b)** *(Pen. Code, § 1203.49)*

Petitioner has completed a term of probation for a conviction under Penal Code section 647(b) and should be granted relief because the petitioner can establish by clear and convincing evidence that the conviction was the result of his or her status as a victim of human trafficking.

*(Please note: You may provide evidence that the conviction was the result of your status as a victim of human trafficking. You can provide that information by writing in the space below or by attaching a letter or other relevant documents. If you need more space for your writing, you can use the Attached Declaration (form MC-031) and attach it to this petition.)*

5. ☐ **Felony county jail sentence under Penal Code section 1170(h)(5)** *(Pen. Code, § 1203.41)*

Petitioner is not under supervision under Penal Code section 1170(h)(5)(B); is not serving a sentence for, on probation for, or charged with the commission of any offense; and should be granted relief in the interests of justice, and *(check one)*

   a. ☐ more than one year has elapsed since petitioner completed the felony county jail sentence **with** a period of mandatory supervision imposed under Penal Code section 1170(h)(5)(B); *or*

   b. ☐ more than two years have elapsed since petitioner completed the felony county jail sentence **without** a period of mandatory supervision imposed under Penal Code section 1170(h)(5)(A).

   *(Please note: You may explain why granting a dismissal would be in the interests of justice. You can provide that information by writing in the space below or by attaching a letter or other relevant documents. If you need more space for your writing, you can use the Attached Declaration (form MC-031) and attach it to this petition.)*

| PEOPLE OF THE STATE OF CALIFORNIA v. DEFENDANT: | CASE NUMBER: 96WF2961 |
|---|---|

6. [ ] **Felony prison sentence that would have been eligible for a felony county jail sentence after 2011 under Penal Code section 1170(h)(5) (Pen. Code, § 1203.42)**

Petitioner is not under supervision and is not serving a sentence for, on probation for, or charged with the commission of any offense; more than two years have elapsed since petitioner completed the felony prison sentence; and petitioner should be granted relief in the interests of justice.

*(Please note: You may explain why granting a dismissal would be in the interests of justice. You can provide that information by writing in the space below or by attaching a letter or other relevant documents. If you need more space for your writing, you can use the Attached Declaration (form MC-031) and attach it to this petition.)*

7. [X] **Deferred entry of judgment (Pen. Code, § 1203.43)**
Petitioner performed satisfactorily during the period in which deferred entry of judgment was granted. The criminal charge(s) were dismissed under former Penal Code section 1000.3 on *(date):* 02/23/1999 . Furthermore *(check one)*,

    a. [X] court records are available showing the case resolution; *or*

    b. [ ] petitioner declares under penalty of perjury that the charges were dismissed after he or she completed the requirements for deferred entry of judgment. Petitioner *(check one)*
        (1) [ ] has
        (2) [ ] has not
        attached a copy of his or her state summary criminal history information.

8. Petitioner requests that the eligible felony offenses listed above be reduced to misdemeanors under Penal Code section 17(b) and eligible misdemeanor offenses be reduced to infractions under Penal Code section 17(d)(2).

9. Petitioner requests that he or she be permitted to withdraw the plea of guilty, or that the verdict or finding of guilt be set aside and a plea of not guilty be entered and the court dismiss this action under the Penal Code section(s) noted above.

I declare under penalty of perjury under the laws of the State of California that the foregoing is true and correct.

Date: 06/24/2020

▶ _____
(SIGNATURE OF PETITIONER OR ATTORNEY)

| 26702 Aracena Drive | Mission Viejo | CA | 92691 |
|---|---|---|---|
| (ADDRESS OF PETITIONER) | (CITY) | (STATE) | (ZIP CODE) |

- Jury Services
- Juvenile
- Probate/Mental Health
- Small Claims
- Traffic & Infractions
- General Info
  - ADA
  - Appearances in Court
  - Bids/Solicitations
  - Budget and Filing / Workload Information
  - Children's Chambers
  - Court Governance
  - Court Holidays
  - Court Locations, Hours & Phone Numbers
  - Community Outreach/Education
  - DUI Court
  - Employment
  - Government Claim Forms
  - Judicial Officers
  - Lawyers and Litigants
  - Media Relations
  - Online Services
  - Records
  - Temporary Judge Program

Home » Online Services » Case Access » Case Detail

- Online Services
  - Account Services
  - Cases on Calendar
  - Case Access
  - Case Index Search
  - Case Name Search
  - Civil-Reserve A Motion Date
  - Court Reporter Transcript Requests
  - eFiling
  - eJuror
  - My Court Portal-Traffic & Criminal
  - Probate Notes
  - Tentative Rulings

Case Detail - 2415369

Case Search Home

# Case Detail - 2415369

## Case Summary

**Case No. Case Category Case Level/Type Plaintiff Person/Business Name Party Role**

2415369  Criminal/Traffic Misdemeanor     People  ███████████

**Filing Date Case Status Case Status Date Destruction Date     File Location**

07/20/1998  Convicted    01/07/2007      12/19/2010      WJC - CRAC Conversion

## Case Detail

| Charge | Charge Date | Charge Dispo Date | Charge Dispo Type |
| --- | --- | --- | --- |
| VC 40508(b) | 09/29/2000 | 07/19/2001 | Dismissed |
| VC 40508(b) | 12/13/1999 | 06/30/2000 | Pled Guilty |
| VC 40508(a) | 09/30/1998 | 09/29/1999 | Pled Guilty |
| VC 22350 | 06/22/1998 | 09/29/1999 | Pled Guilty |

Back to Results   New Search

# EXHIBIT '9'

Orange County Superior Court Docket Sheet - 2438069

- Jury Services
- Juvenile
- Probate/Mental Health
- Small Claims
- Traffic & Infractions
- General Info
  - ADA
  - Appearances in Court
  - Bids/Solicitations
  - Budget and Filing / Workload Information
  - Children's Chambers
  - Court Governance
  - Court Holidays
  - Court Locations, Hours & Phone Numbers
  - Community Outreach/Education
  - DUI Court
  - Employment
  - Government Claim Forms
  - Judicial Officers
  - Lawyers and Litigants
  - Media Relations
  - Online Services
  - Records
  - Temporary Judge Program

Home » Online Services » Case Access » Case Detail

- Online Services
  - Account Services
  - Cases on Calendar
  - Case Access
  - Case Index Search
  - Case Name Search
  - Civil-Reserve A Motion Date
  - Court Reporter Transcript Requests
  - eFiling
  - eJuror
  - My Court Portal-Traffic & Criminal
  - Probate Notes
  - Tentative Rulings

Case Detail - 2438069

Case Search Home

## Case Detail - 2438069

### Case Summary

**Case No. Case Category Case Level/Type Plaintiff Person/Business Name Party Role**

2438069  Criminal/Traffic Misdemeanor    People    ███████████

**Filing Date Case Status Case Status Date Destruction Date      File Location**

12/17/1998  Convicted    01/07/2007      12/19/2010      WJC - CRAC Conversion

## Case Detail

| Charge | Charge Date | Charge Dispo Date | Charge Dispo Type |
| --- | --- | --- | --- |
| VC 40508(b) | 07/31/2000 | 07/19/2001 | Dismissed |
| VC 40508(b) | 10/15/1999 | 06/30/2000 | Pled Guilty |
| VC 40508(a) | 01/22/1999 | 09/29/1999 | Pled Guilty |
| VC 4454(a) | 12/11/1998 | 09/29/1999 | Pled Guilty |
| VC 27315(d) | 12/11/1998 | 09/29/1999 | Pled Guilty |

Back to Results    New Search

© 2014 Superior Court of Orange County
Locations Telephone Numbers Employment Sitemap RSS Privacy Policy Webmaster

Orange County Superior Court Docket Sheet - 400031

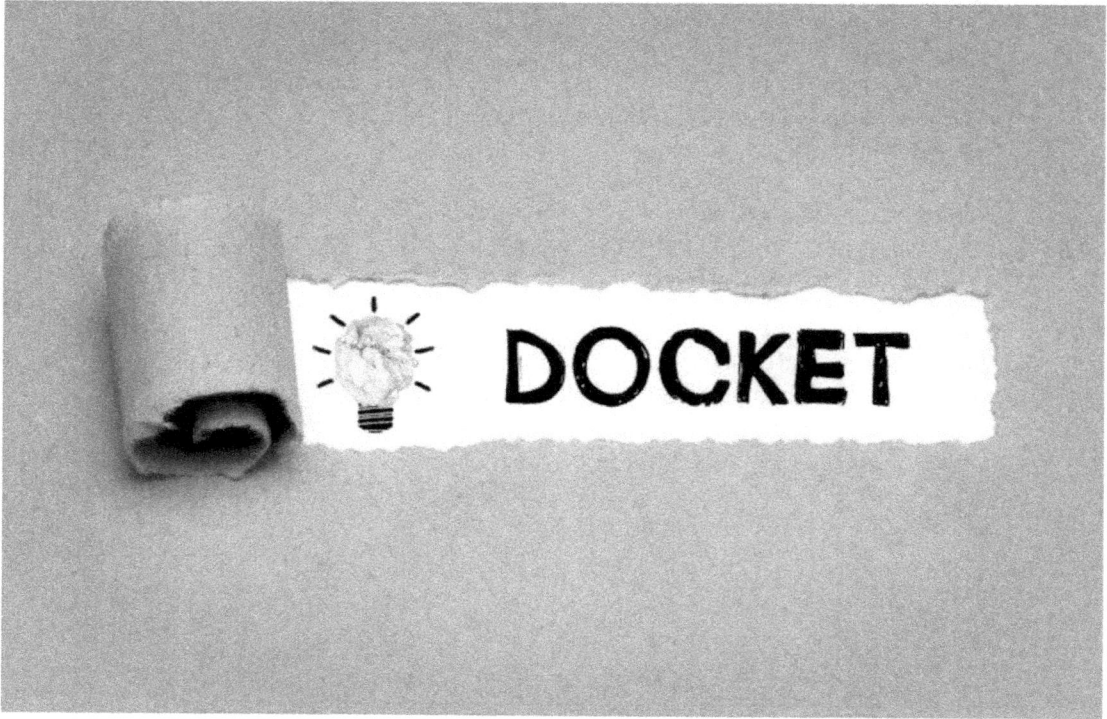

- o Jury Services
- o Juvenile
- o Probate/Mental Health
- o Small Claims
- o Traffic & Infractions
- General Info
  - o ADA
  - o Appearances in Court
  - o Bids/Solicitations
  - o Budget and Filing / Workload Information
  - o Children's Chambers
  - o Court Governance
  - o Court Holidays
  - o Court Locations, Hours & Phone Numbers
  - o Community Outreach/Education
  - o DUI Court
  - o Employment
  - o Government Claim Forms
  - o Judicial Officers
  - o Lawyers and Litigants
  - o Media Relations
  - o Online Services
  - o Records
  - o Temporary Judge Program

Home » Online Services » Case Access » Case Detail

- Online Services
  - o Account Services
  - o Cases on Calendar
  - o Case Access
  - o Case Index Search
  - o Case Name Search
  - o Civil-Reserve A Motion Date
  - o Court Reporter Transcript Requests
  - o eFiling
  - o eJuror
  - o My Court Portal-Traffic & Criminal
  - o Probate Notes
  - o Tentative Rulings

Case Detail - 400031

Case Search Home

# Case Detail - 400031

## Case Summary

Case No. Case Category Case Level/Type Plaintiff Person/Business Name Party Role

400031   Criminal/Traffic Misdemeanor    People   ███████████

**Filing Date Case Status Case Status Date Destruction Date    File Location**
05/10/1999  Convicted   01/07/2007      12/18/2010      HJC - CRAC Conversion

## Case Detail

| Charge | Charge Date | Charge Dispo Date | Charge Dispo Type |
| --- | --- | --- | --- |
| VC 40508(b) | 02/14/2000 | 06/27/2000 | Pled Guilty |
| VC 40508(a) | 06/16/1999 | 01/12/2000 | Pled Guilty |
| VC 12951(a) | 05/01/1999 | 01/12/2000 | Pled Guilty |

© 2014 Superior Court of Orange County
Locations Telephone Numbers Employment Sitemap RSS Privacy Policy Webmaster

EXHIBIT '11'

Orange County Superior Court Docket Sheet - 417974

- ○ Jury Services
- ○ Juvenile
- ○ Probate/Mental Health
- ○ Small Claims
- ○ Traffic & Infractions
- General Info
  - ○ ADA
  - ○ Appearances in Court
  - ○ Bids/Solicitations
  - ○ Budget and Filing / Workload Information
  - ○ Children's Chambers
  - ○ Court Governance
  - ○ Court Holidays
  - ○ Court Locations, Hours & Phone Numbers
  - ○ Community Outreach/Education
  - ○ DUI Court
  - ○ Employment
  - ○ Government Claim Forms
  - ○ Judicial Officers
  - ○ Lawyers and Litigants
  - ○ Media Relations
  - ○ Online Services
  - ○ Records
  - ○ Temporary Judge Program

Home » Online Services » Case Access » Case Detail

- Online Services
  - ○ Account Services
  - ○ Cases on Calendar
  - ○ Case Access
  - ○ Case Index Search
  - ○ Case Name Search
  - ○ Civil-Reserve A Motion Date
  - ○ Court Reporter Transcript Requests
  - ○ eFiling
  - ○ eJuror
  - ○ My Court Portal-Traffic & Criminal
  - ○ Probate Notes
  - ○ Tentative Rulings

Case Detail - 417974

Case Search Home

## Case Detail - 417974

### Case Summary

**Case No. Case Category Case Level/Type Plaintiff Person/Business Name Party Role**

417974   Criminal/Traffic Misdemeanor     People ███████████

**Filing Date Case Status Case Status Date Destruction Date     File Location**
06/28/1999 Closed        01/07/2007      12/19/2010      HJC - CRAC Conversion

## Case Detail

| Charge | Charge Date | Charge Dispo Date | Charge Dispo Type |
|---|---|---|---|
| VC 40508(b) | 02/14/2000 | 06/27/2000 | Pled Guilty |
| VC 40508(a) | 07/21/1999 | 01/12/2000 | Pled Guilty |
| VC 14601.1(a) | 06/01/1999 | 01/12/2000 | Pled Guilty |

Back to Results   New Search

EXHIBIT '12'

Orange County Superior Court Docket Sheet - 99HM07501

- o Jury Services
- o Juvenile
- o Probate/Mental Health
- o Small Claims
- o Traffic & Infractions
- General Info
  - o ADA
  - o Appearances in Court
  - o Bids/Solicitations
  - o Budget and Filing / Workload Information
  - o Children's Chambers
  - o Court Governance
  - o Court Holidays
  - o Court Locations, Hours & Phone Numbers
  - o Community Outreach/Education
  - o DUI Court
  - o Employment
  - o Government Claim Forms
  - o Judicial Officers
  - o Lawyers and Litigants
  - o Media Relations
  - o Online Services
  - o Records
  - o Temporary Judge Program

Home » Online Services » Case Access » Case Detail

- Online Services
  - o Account Services
  - o Cases on Calendar
  - o Case Access
  - o Case Index Search
  - o Case Name Search
  - o Civil-Reserve A Motion Date
  - o Court Reporter Transcript Requests
  - o eFiling
  - o eJuror
  - o My Court Portal-Traffic & Criminal
  - o Probate Notes
  - o Tentative Rulings

Case Detail - 99HM07501

Case Search Home

# Case Detail - 99HM07501

## Case Summary

Case No.   Case Category Case Level/Type Plaintiff Person/Business Name Party Role

99HM07501 Criminal/Traffic Misdemeanor    People ███████████

**Filing Date Case Status Case Status Date Destruction Date    File Location**
11/24/1999 Closed        01/03/2007     12/13/2010      HJC - CRAC Conversion

## Case Detail

| Charge | Charge Date | Charge Dispo Date | Charge Dispo Type |
| --- | --- | --- | --- |
| VC 40508(b) | 08/28/2000 | 01/30/2001 | Dismissed |
| VC 12500(a) | 10/29/1999 | 07/28/2000 | Pled Guilty |
| VC 27315(d) | 10/29/1999 | 07/28/2000 | Pled Guilty |
| VC 14601.1(a) | 10/29/1999 | 07/28/2000 | Pled Guilty |
| VC 14601(a) | 10/29/1999 | 07/28/2000 | Pled Guilty |

Back to Results   New Search

© 2014 Superior Court of Orange County
Locations Telephone Numbers Employment Sitemap RSS Privacy Policy Webmaster

Orange County Superior Court Docket Sheet - LJ55294

- Jury Services
- Juvenile
- Probate/Mental Health
- Small Claims
- Traffic & Infractions
- General Info
  - ADA
  - Appearances in Court
  - Bids/Solicitations
  - Budget and Filing / Workload Information
  - Children's Chambers
  - Court Governance
  - Court Holidays
  - Court Locations, Hours & Phone Numbers
  - Community Outreach/Education
  - DUI Court
  - Employment
  - Government Claim Forms
  - Judicial Officers
  - Lawyers and Litigants
  - Media Relations
  - Online Services
  - Records
  - Temporary Judge Program

Home » Online Services » Case Access » Case Detail

- Online Services
  - Account Services
  - Cases on Calendar
  - Case Access
  - Case Index Search
  - Case Name Search
  - Civil-Reserve A Motion Date
  - Court Reporter Transcript Requests
  - eFiling
  - eJuror
  - My Court Portal-Traffic & Criminal
  - Probate Notes
  - Tentative Rulings

Case Detail - LJ55294

Case Search Home

# Case Detail - LJ55294

## Case Summary

**Case No. Case Category Case Level/Type Plaintiff Person/Business Name Party Role**

LJ55294  Criminal/Traffic Misdemeanor    People ████████████

**Filing Date Case Status Case Status Date Destruction Date    File Location**

03/02/2000  Closed      01/03/2007      12/13/2010      WJC - CRAC Conversion

## Case Detail

| Charge | Charge Date | Charge Dispo Date | Charge Dispo Type |
|---|---|---|---|
| VC 40508(b) | 08/21/2000 | 07/19/2001 | Dismissed |
| VC 40508(a) | 03/30/2000 | 07/20/2000 | Pled Guilty |
| VC 22349(a) | 02/09/2000 | 07/20/2000 | Pled Guilty |
| VC 16028(a) | 02/09/2000 | 07/20/2000 | Dismissed - Proof of Correction |
| VC 12500(a) | 02/09/2000 | 07/20/2000 | Pled Guilty |

Back to Results   New Search

EXHIBIT '14'

Orange County Superior Court Docket Sheet - X007620

Home » Online Services » Case Access » Case Detail

Case Detail - X007620

Case Search Home

# Case Detail - X007620

## Case Summary

**Case No. Case Category Case Level/Type Plaintiff Person/Business Name Party Role**

X007620 Criminal/Traffic Misdemeanor    People  ████████████

**Filing Date Case Status Case Status Date Destruction Date    File Location**

10/16/2001 Closed    01/04/2007    12/18/2010    HJC - CRAC Conversion

## Case Detail

| Charge | Charge Date | Charge Dispo Date | Charge Dispo Type |
|---|---|---|---|
| VC 40508(a) | 10/31/2001 | 04/23/2002 | Pled Guilty |
| VC 12951(a) | 10/06/2001 | 04/23/2002 | Dismissed |
| VC 22350 | 10/06/2001 | 08/10/2002 | Bail Forfeiture |

Back to Results   New Search

# Superior Court of California
## County of Orange

Case Number : 03SF0869

Copy Request: 3930486

Request Type: Case Documents

Prepared for: KA

Number of documents: 1

Number of pages: 17

# MINUTES

Case : 03SF0869

Name :

12/14/2018 15:29:27 PM

| Date of Action | Text |
|---|---|
| 12/09/2003 | Original Complaint filed on 12/09/2003 by Orange County District Attorney. |
| 12/09/2003 | FELONY charge of 496(a) PC filed as count 1. Date of violation: 08/26/2003. |
| 12/09/2003 | MISDEMEANOR charge of 530.5(d) PC filed as count 2. Date of violation: 08/26/2003. |
| 12/09/2003 | MISDEMEANOR charge of 530.5(d) PC filed as count 3. Date of violation: 08/26/2003. |
| 12/09/2003 | MISDEMEANOR charge of 530.5(d) PC filed as count 4. Date of violation: 08/26/2003. |
| 12/09/2003 | Declaration/Affidavit in Support of Arrest filed. |
| 12/09/2003 | Felony Warrant of Arrest requested. |
| 12/09/2003 | Warrant of Arrest warrant signed by Matthew S. Anderson and issued for defendant. Bail set at $25, 000.00, Mandatory Appearance. |
| 12/12/2003 | Warrant File Number 02786796 sent from AWSS for Warrant # 2069255. |
| 12/16/2003 | Hearing set on 12/16/2003 at 02:00 PM in Department S2. |
| 12/16/2003 | Hearing held on 12/16/2003 at 02:00:00 PM in Department S2 for Hearing. |
| 12/16/2003 | Officiating Judge: Matthew S. Anderson, Judge |
| 12/16/2003 | Clerk: P. Rossner |
| 12/16/2003 | Bailiff: W. T. Hoffman |
| 12/16/2003 | Court Reporter: Kristy Damron |
| 12/16/2003 | People represented by Mike Jacobs, Deputy District Attorney, present. |
| 12/16/2003 | Mark S. Devore, Retained Attorney, makes a special appearance for Paul S. Meyer. Defendant present. |
| 12/16/2003 | Warrant issued on 12/09/2003 ordered recalled for defendant. |
| 12/16/2003 | Fingerprint card is received and filed. |
| 12/16/2003 | Copy of complaint given to Defense Attorney. |
| 12/16/2003 | Defendant waives reading and advisement of the Original Complaint. |
| 12/16/2003 | Arraignment set on 12/23/2003 at 08:30 AM in Department S2. |
| 12/16/2003 | Defendant and Counsel ordered to return. |
| 12/16/2003 | Court orders defendant released on own recognizance. |
| 12/16/2003 | Own Release Recognizance filed. |
| 12/23/2003 | Hearing held on 12/23/2003 at 08:30:00 AM in Department S2 for Arraignment. |
| 12/23/2003 | Officiating Judge: Matthew S. Anderson, Judge |
| 12/23/2003 | Clerk: K. Heaney |
| 12/23/2003 | Bailiff: W. T. Hoffman |
| 12/23/2003 | Court Reporter: Kristy Damron |
| 12/23/2003 | People represented by Constance Smith, Deputy District Attorney, present. |
| 12/23/2003 | Robert Goode, Retained Attorney, makes a special appearance for Paul S. Meyer. Defendant present. |
| 12/23/2003 | Defendant taken into custody. |
| 12/23/2003 | Copy of Original Complaint given to defendant. |
| 12/23/2003 | Defendant advised of legal and constitutional rights. |
| 12/23/2003 | To the Original Complaint defendant pleads NOT GUILTY to all counts. |
| 12/23/2003 | Defendant waives reading and advisement of the Original Complaint. |
| 12/23/2003 | Preliminary Hearing set on 01/06/2004 at 08:30 AM in Department S2. |

# MINUTES

Case : 03SF0869

Name : ▮▮▮▮▮▮▮▮▮▮▮▮                                      12/14/2018 15:29:27 PM

| Date of Action | Text |
|---|---|
| 12/23/2003 | Defendant and Counsel ordered to return. |
| 12/23/2003 | Defendant remanded to the custody of the Sheriff. |
| 12/23/2003 | Court orders bail set in the amount of $15, 000.00. |
| 12/23/2003 | Notice to Sheriff issued. |
| 12/23/2003 | Later same day bond posted over the counter for defendant's release. |
| 12/23/2003 | Bail Bond Number S25-00753551 posted in the amount of $15000.00 by DFS of SENEC. |
| 12/23/2003 | Surety Bond # S25-00753551 filed. |
| 12/23/2003 | Bail posted in Clerk's Office. Defendant to be released. Notice to Sheriff issued. |
| 01/06/2004 | Hearing held on 01/06/2004 at 08:30:00 AM in Department S2 for Preliminary Hearing. |
| 01/06/2004 | Officiating Judge: Luis A. Rodriguez, Judge |
| 01/06/2004 | Judge Rodriguez presiding for Judge Anderson |
| 01/06/2004 | Clerk: P. Rossner |
| 01/06/2004 | Bailiff: W. T. Hoffman |
| 01/06/2004 | Court Reporter: Kristy Damron |
| 01/06/2004 | People represented by Tammy Jacobs, Deputy District Attorney, present. |
| 01/06/2004 | Defendant present in Court with counsel Paul S. Meyer, Retained Attorney. |
| 01/06/2004 | Case called. People answer not ready. Defense answers not ready. |
| 01/06/2004 | Court finds good cause to continue Preliminary hearing over the objections of co-defendant Ryan Walker |
| 01/06/2004 | Preliminary Hearing set on 01/20/2004 at 08:30 AM in Department S2. |
| 01/06/2004 | Defendant and Counsel ordered to return. |
| 01/06/2004 | Present bail deemed sufficient and continued. |
| 01/20/2004 | Hearing held on 01/20/2004 at 08:30:00 AM in Department S2 for Preliminary Hearing. |
| 01/20/2004 | Officiating Judge: Brett London, Judge |
| 01/20/2004 | Clerk: K. Heaney |
| 01/20/2004 | Bailiff: W. T. Hoffman |
| 01/20/2004 | Court Reporter: Kristy Damron |
| 01/20/2004 | Judge London presiding for Judge Anderson |
| 01/20/2004 | People represented by Mike Jacobs, Deputy District Attorney, present. |
| 01/20/2004 | Defendant present in Court with counsel Paul S. Meyer, Retained Attorney. |
| 01/20/2004 | Defendant's motion to WITHDRAW NOT GUILTY PLEA to count(s) 1 granted. |
| 01/20/2004 | Court finds defendant intelligently and voluntarily waives legal and constitutional rights to jury trial, confront and examine witnesses, and to remain silent. |
| 01/20/2004 | To the Original Complaint defendant pleads GUILTY as to count(s) 1. |
| 01/20/2004 | Defendant's written waiver of legal and constitutional rights for guilty plea received and ordered filed. |
| 01/20/2004 | Court finds factual basis and accepts plea. |
| 01/20/2004 | Defendant advised of the possible consequences of plea affecting deportation and citizenship. |
| 01/20/2004 | Defendant advised of maximum possible sentence. |

# MINUTES

Case : 03SF0869

Name : ███████████

12/14/2018 15:29:27 PM

| Date of Action | Text |
|---|---|
| 01/20/2004 | Defendant advised of consequences of violating probation and parole. |
| 01/20/2004 | This constitutes a prior conviction. |
| 01/20/2004 | Counsel joins in waivers, pleas, and admissions. |
| 01/20/2004 | Defendant waives arraignment for sentencing. |
| 01/20/2004 | Defendant requests immediate sentencing. |
| 01/20/2004 | Probation report waived. |
| 01/20/2004 | Defendant waives statutory time for Sentencing. |
| 01/20/2004 | Count(s) 2, 3, 4 DISMISSED - Plea negotiation. |
| 01/20/2004 | No legal cause why judgment should not be pronounced and defendant having Pled Guilty to count(s) 1, Imposition of sentence is suspended and defendant is placed on 3 Years FORMAL PROBATION on the following terms and conditions: |
| 01/20/2004 | Serve 30 Days  Orange County Jail as to count(s) 1. |
| 01/20/2004 | Credit for time served: 3 actual, 0 conduct, totaling 3 days. |
| 01/20/2004 | Court grants jail stay until 02/27/2004 at 07:00 PM,  Orange County Jail. Defendant to report as ordered. |
| 01/20/2004 | JAIL sentence of 30 Days to be served as 10 WEEKENDS from Friday at 07:00 PM to Sunday at 07:00 PM commencing 02/27/2004 as to count(s) 1. Defendant ordered to pay for weekend jail commitment. |
| 01/20/2004 | Pay $200.00 Restitution Fine pursuant to Penal Code 1202.4 or Penal Code 1202.4(b). |
| 01/20/2004 | Pay the costs of probation based on the ability to pay as directed by the Probation Officer. |
| 01/20/2004 | Use no unauthorized drugs, narcotics, or controlled substances. Submit to drug or narcotic testing as directed by Probation Officer or Police Officer. |
| 01/20/2004 | Submit your person and property including any residence, premises, container, or vehicle under your control to search and seizure at any time of the day or night by any law enforcement or probation officer with or without a warrant, and with or without reasonable cause or reasonable suspicion. |
| 01/20/2004 | Cooperate with Probation Officer in any plan for psychiatric, psychological, alcohol and/or drug treatment, or counseling. |
| 01/20/2004 | Seek training, schooling, or employment and maintain residence as approved by Probation Department. |
| 01/20/2004 | Defendant provided a copy of "Prohibited Persons Notice Form and Power of Attorney for Firearms and Disposal" pursuant to Penal Code 12021(d)(2). |
| 01/20/2004 | Do not own, use, or possess any type of dangerous or deadly weapon. |
| 01/20/2004 | Pay $20.00 for Security Fee pursuant to Penal Code 1465.8. |
| 01/20/2004 | Obey all laws, orders, rules, and regulations of the Court, Jail, and Probation. |
| 01/20/2004 | Do not associate with anyone disapproved of by your Probation Officer. |
| 01/20/2004 | Violate no law. |
| 01/20/2004 | Do not have any contact with Ryan Walker directly, indirectly, or through a third party except by an Attorney of Record. |
| 01/20/2004 | Defendant accepts terms and conditions of probation. |
| 01/20/2004 | All fees payable through the Probation Department. |
| 01/20/2004 | Defendant to report to Probation Officer forthwith. |
| 01/20/2004 | Notice to Sheriff issued. |

# MINUTES

Case : 03SF0869

Name : Ashaary, Kiarash                                    12/14/2018 15:29:27 PM

| Date of Action | Text |
|---|---|
| 01/20/2004 | Court orders bail bond # S25-00753551 exonerated. |
| 02/26/2004 | DOJ Initial Abstract sent. |
| 03/10/2004 | Submitted to court services for bond review. rc. |
| 08/04/2004 | Jail notice of failure to complete filed. |
| 08/04/2004 | Deft. not accepted for commitment forwarded to West Justice Center from Harbor Justice Center - Laguna Niguel Facility. |
| 08/13/2004 | Defendant failed to report to the Orange County Jail. Notice filed. |
| 08/13/2004 | Probation ordered revoked based on the following: Defendant failed to comply with Jail. |
| 08/13/2004 | Probation Violation warrant ordered issued for defendant. Bail set at $0.00, Mandatory Appearance. |
| 08/13/2004 | Probation Violation warrant signed by Thomas J. Borris and issued for defendant. Bail set at $0.00, Mandatory Appearance. |
| 08/17/2004 | Warrant File Number 02842430 sent from AWSS for Warrant # 2128807. |
| 08/27/2004 | Warrant 02842430 for Kiarash Ashaary DEFENDANT served by Laguna Beach Police Department on 08/27/2004. |
| 08/30/2004 | Warrant status reactivated by Sheriff through Central Warrant Repository Interface. |
| 08/30/2004 | Warrant 02842430 for Kiarash Ashaary DEFENDANT served by Orange County Sheriff Department on 08/29/2004. |
| 09/02/2004 | Probation Violation re: Arraignment - In Custody set on 09/02/2004 at 02:00 PM in Department S2. |
| 09/02/2004 | Hearing held on 09/02/2004 at 02:00:00 PM in Department S2 for Probation Violation Arraignment - In Custody. |
| 09/02/2004 | Officiating Judge: Matthew S. Anderson, Judge |
| 09/02/2004 | Clerk: K. Heaney |
| 09/02/2004 | Bailiff: W. T. Hoffman |
| 09/02/2004 | Court Reporter: Starr Armijo |
| 09/02/2004 | People represented by Anne Selin, Deputy District Attorney, present. |
| 09/02/2004 | Defendant present in Court with counsel James G. Merwin, Public Defender. |
| 09/02/2004 | Warrant issued on 08/13/2004 ordered recalled for defendant. |
| 09/02/2004 | Probation Violation re: Arraignment set on 09/08/2004 at 08:30 AM in Department H2. |
| 09/02/2004 | Defendant and Counsel ordered to return. |
| 09/02/2004 | Defendant remanded to the custody of the Sheriff. |
| 09/02/2004 | Court orders bail set at NO BAIL. |
| 09/02/2004 | Notice to Sheriff issued. |
| 09/02/2004 | Keep with companion cases(s) 04hf1326. |
| 09/02/2004 | Action taken without file |
| 09/08/2004 | Hearing held on 09/08/2004 at 08:30:00 AM in Department H2 for Probation Violation Arraignment. |
| 09/08/2004 | Officiating Judge: Craig E. Robison, Judge |
| 09/08/2004 | Clerk: L. K. Mc Donald |
| 09/08/2004 | Bailiff: D. Cheli |
| 09/08/2004 | Court Reporter: Karen Lee |

SUPERIOR COURT OF CALIFORNIA, COUNTY OF ORANGE

# MINUTES

Case : 03SF0869

Name : ███████████                                          12/14/2018 15:29:27 PM

| Date of Action | Text |
| --- | --- |
| 09/08/2004 | People represented by Yvette Patko, Deputy District Attorney, present. |
| 09/08/2004 | Defendant not present in Court represented by Michael Mc Clellan, Public Defender. |
| 09/08/2004 | Defendant remains in holding cell, not brought into courtroom. |
| 09/08/2004 | Probation Violation re: Arraignment continued to 09/13/2004 at 08:30 AM in Department H2 by stipulation of all parties. |
| 09/08/2004 | Current bail set for defendant to remain. |
| 09/08/2004 | Notice to Sheriff issued. |
| 09/08/2004 | Keep with companion cases(s) 04HF1326, 04HM01441 & 02HM02571. |
| 09/13/2004 | Hearing held on 09/13/2004 at 08:30:00 AM in Department H2 for Probation Violation Arraignment. |
| 09/13/2004 | Officiating Judge: Thomas Rees, Commissioner |
| 09/13/2004 | Clerk: R. M. Hume |
| 09/13/2004 | Bailiff:. Present |
| 09/13/2004 | Court Reporter: Karen Lee |
| 09/13/2004 | People represented by Yvette Patko, Deputy District Attorney, present. |
| 09/13/2004 | Defendant not present in Court represented by Michael Mc Clellan, Public Defender. |
| 09/13/2004 | Defendant remains in holding cell, not brought into courtroom. |
| 09/13/2004 | Probation Violation re: Arraignment continued to 09/15/2004 at 09:00 AM in Department H2 by stipulation of all parties. |
| 09/13/2004 | Current bail set for defendant to remain. |
| 09/13/2004 | Notice to Sheriff issued. |
| 09/13/2004 | Keep with companion cases(s) 04HF1326. |
| 09/15/2004 | Hearing held on 09/15/2004 at 09:00:00 AM in Department H2 for Probation Violation Arraignment. |
| 09/15/2004 | Officiating Judge: Craig E. Robison, Judge |
| 09/15/2004 | Clerk: L. K. Mc Donald |
| 09/15/2004 | Bailiff: D. Cheli |
| 09/15/2004 | Court Reporter: Karen Lee |
| 09/15/2004 | People represented by Yvette Patko, Deputy District Attorney, present. |
| 09/15/2004 | Defendant present in Court with counsel Michael Mc Clellan, Public Defender. |
| 09/15/2004 | Probation Violation re: Arraignment continued to 09/17/2004 at 08:30 AM in Department H2 at request of Defense. |
| 09/15/2004 | Defendant ordered to appear. |
| 09/15/2004 | Current bail set for defendant to remain. |
| 09/15/2004 | Defendant remanded to the custody of the Sheriff. |
| 09/15/2004 | Notice to Sheriff issued. |
| 09/15/2004 | Keep with companion cases(s) 04HF1326, 04HM01441, 02HM02571. |
| 09/17/2004 | Hearing held on 09/17/2004 at 08:30:00 AM in Department H2 for Probation Violation Arraignment. |
| 09/17/2004 | Officiating Judge: Craig E. Robison, Judge |
| 09/17/2004 | Clerk: L. K. Mc Donald |
| 09/17/2004 | Bailiff: D. Cheli |

# MINUTES

Case : 03SF0869

Name : ██████████                                        12/14/2018 15:29:27 PM

| Date of Action | Text |
|---|---|
| 09/17/2004 | Court Reporter: Karen Lee |
| 09/17/2004 | People represented by Sandra Nassar, Deputy District Attorney, present. |
| 09/17/2004 | Defendant present in Court with counsel Michael Mc Clellan, Public Defender. |
| 09/17/2004 | Robert M Brodney, Retained Attorney, substituting in as Attorney of Record. |
| 09/17/2004 | Michael Mc Clellan relieved as Counsel of Record. |
| 09/17/2004 | Defendant present in Court with counsel Robert M Brodney, Retained Attorney. |
| 09/17/2004 | Probation Violation re: Arraignment continued to 10/22/2004 at 08:30 AM in Department H2 at request of Defense. |
| 09/17/2004 | Probation Violation re: Arraignment vacated for 10/22/2004 at 08:30 AM in H2. (Entered NUNC_PRO_TUNC on 09/23/04) |
| 09/17/2004 | Probation Violation re: Arraignment continued to 10/20/2004 at 08:30 AM in Department H2 at request of Defense. (Entered NUNC_PRO_TUNC on 09/23/04) |
| 09/17/2004 | Defendant ordered to appear. |
| 09/17/2004 | Current bail set for defendant to remain. |
| 09/17/2004 | Defendant remanded to the custody of the Sheriff. |
| 09/17/2004 | Notice to Sheriff issued. |
| 09/17/2004 | Notice to Sheriff issued. (Entered NUNC_PRO_TUNC on 09/23/04) |
| 09/17/2004 | Keep with companion cases(s) 04HF1326, 04HM01441, 02HM02571. |
| 09/17/2004 | Minute Order reprinted for 09/17/2004. |
| 09/23/2004 | Case calendared on 09/23/04 at 10:00 AM in H2 for HRG. |
| 09/23/2004 | Hearing held on 09/23/2004 at 10:00:00 AM in Department H2 for Hearing. |
| 09/23/2004 | Officiating Judge: Craig E. Robison, Judge |
| 09/23/2004 | Clerk: L. K. Mc Donald |
| 09/23/2004 | Bailiff: D. Cheli |
| 09/23/2004 | Court Reporter: Karen Lee |
| 09/23/2004 | People represented by Joe Williams, Deputy District Attorney, present. |
| 09/23/2004 | Defendant not present in Court represented by Robert M Brodney, Retained Attorney. |
| 09/23/2004 | Nunc Pro Tunc entry(s) made on this date for 09/17/2004. |
| 09/23/2004 | Order to allow visitation for interview purposes signed and filed. |
| 09/23/2004 | (Order filed in case number 04HF1326) |
| 09/23/2004 | Probation Violation re: Arraignment for 10/20/2004 at 08:30 AM in H2 to remain. |
| 10/20/2004 | Hearing held on 10/20/2004 at 08:30:00 AM in Department H2 for Probation Violation Arraignment. |
| 10/20/2004 | Officiating Judge: Craig E. Robison, Judge |
| 10/20/2004 | Clerk: L. K. Mc Donald |
| 10/20/2004 | Bailiff: D. Cheli |
| 10/20/2004 | Court Reporter: Karen Lee |
| 10/20/2004 | People represented by Yvette Patko, Deputy District Attorney, present. |
| 10/20/2004 | Defendant present in Court with counsel Brodney, Robert M, Retained Attorney. |
| 10/20/2004 | Probation Violation re: Arraignment continued to 11/15/2004 at 08:30 AM in Department H2 at request of Defense. |

# MINUTES

Case : 03SF0869

Name : ███████████████

12/14/2018 15:29:27 PM

| Date of Action | Text |
|---|---|
| 10/20/2004 | Defendant ordered to appear. |
| 10/20/2004 | Current bail set for defendant to remain. |
| 10/20/2004 | Defendant remanded to the custody of the Sheriff. |
| 10/20/2004 | Notice to Sheriff issued. |
| 10/20/2004 | Keep with companion cases(s) 04HF1326, 04HM01441, 02HM02571. |
| 11/15/2004 | Hearing held on 11/15/2004 at 08:30:00 AM in Department H2 for Probation Violation Arraignment. |
| 11/15/2004 | Officiating Judge: Craig E. Robison, Judge |
| 11/15/2004 | Clerk: L. K. Mc Donald |
| 11/15/2004 | Bailiff: D. Cheli |
| 11/15/2004 | Court Reporter: Tina O'Rourke |
| 11/15/2004 | People represented by Yvette Patko, Deputy District Attorney, present. |
| 11/15/2004 | Defendant present in Court with counsel Brodney, Robert M, Retained Attorney. |
| 11/15/2004 | Probation Violation re: Arraignment continued to 12/02/2004 at 08:30 AM in Department H2 at request of Defense. |
| 11/15/2004 | Defendant ordered to appear. |
| 11/15/2004 | Current bail set for defendant to remain. |
| 11/15/2004 | Defendant remanded to the custody of the Sheriff. |
| 11/15/2004 | Notice to Sheriff issued. |
| 11/15/2004 | Keep with companion cases(s) 04HF1326, 04HM01441, 02HM02571. |
| 12/02/2004 | Hearing held on 12/02/2004 at 08:30:00 AM in Department H2 for Probation Violation Arraignment. |
| 12/02/2004 | Officiating Judge: Craig E. Robison, Judge |
| 12/02/2004 | Clerk: L. K. Mc Donald |
| 12/02/2004 | Bailiff: D. Cheli |
| 12/02/2004 | Court Reporter: Karen Lee |
| 12/02/2004 | Joe Williams made a special appearance for District Attorney Yvette Patko. |
| 12/02/2004 | Defendant present in Court with counsel Brodney, Robert M, Retained Attorney. |
| 12/02/2004 | Probation Violation re: Arraignment continued to 12/23/2004 at 08:30 AM in Department H2 at request of Defense. |
| 12/02/2004 | Defendant ordered to appear. |
| 12/02/2004 | Current bail set for defendant to remain. |
| 12/02/2004 | Defendant remanded to the custody of the Sheriff. |
| 12/02/2004 | Notice to Sheriff issued. |
| 12/02/2004 | Keep with companion cases(s) 04HF1326, 04HM01441, 02HM02571. |
| 12/23/2004 | Hearing held on 12/23/2004 at 08:30:00 AM in Department H2 for Probation Violation Arraignment. |
| 12/23/2004 | Officiating Judge: James Odriozola, Commissioner |
| 12/23/2004 | Clerk: A. T. Akahoshi |
| 12/23/2004 | Bailiff: L. Trebil |
| 12/23/2004 | Court Reporter: Karen Lee |
| 12/23/2004 | People represented by Yvette Patko, Deputy District Attorney, present. |

# MINUTES

Case : 03SF0869

Name : ▮▮▮▮▮▮▮▮▮                                                    12/14/2018 15:29:27 PM

| Date of Action | Text |
|---|---|
| 12/23/2004 | Defendant advised of legal and constitutional rights. |
| 12/23/2004 | Defendant waives right to probation hearing. Defendant admits violation of probation. |
| 12/23/2004 | Court finds defendant in violation of probation. |
| 12/23/2004 | Court orders probation reinstated and modified as follows: |
| 12/23/2004 | Court orders jail weekend sentence vacated. Balance of original 30 Day(s) sentence imposed on 01/20/2004 now reimposed as to count(s) 1. |
| 12/23/2004 | Court orders JAIL imposed on 12/23/2004 VACATED as to count(s) 1. |
| 12/23/2004 | Serve 180 Day(s) Orange County Jail as to count(s) 1. |
| 12/23/2004 | 180 days Jail sentenced on 12/23/2004 and stayed as to count(s) 1 stayed pending completion of 180 days at River Community Facility in Los Angeles. |
| 12/23/2004 | 180 days OCJ stayed pending completion of 180 days at River Community Facility in Los Angeles |
| 12/23/2004 | Defendant released on this case only. Release issued. |
| 12/23/2004 | Notice to Sheriff issued. |
| 02/18/2005 | Case calendared on 02/18/05 at 09:00 AM in H2 for PV. |
| 02/18/2005 | Probation Violation vacated for 02/18/2005 at 09:00 AM in H2. |
| 02/18/2005 | Motion re: Modification of Probation set on 02/18/2005 at 09:30 AM in Department H2. |
| 02/18/2005 | Hearing held on 02/18/2005 at 09:30:00 AM in Department H2 for Motion Modification of Probation. |
| 02/18/2005 | Officiating Judge: Craig E. Robison, Judge |
| 02/18/2005 | Clerk: L. K. Mc Donald |
| 02/18/2005 | Bailiff: D. Cheli |
| 02/18/2005 | Court Reporter: Karen Lee |
| 02/18/2005 | People represented by Clarissa Stone, Deputy District Attorney, present. |
| 02/18/2005 | Defendant present in Court with counsel Brodney, Robert M, Retained Attorney. |
| 02/18/2005 | Correspondence from Cornerstone Program filed. |
| 02/18/2005 | Motion by Defense to change program from "River Community Facility" to "Cornerstone Program" for service of 180 days in lieu of 180 days OCJ |
| 02/18/2005 | Motion granted. |
| 02/18/2005 | Probation modified as follows: |
| 02/18/2005 | Defendant may serve 180 days in Cornerstone Program in lieu of 180 days OCJ. Any time completed in River Community Facility may be credited towards 180 day sentence. Defendant to complete a total of 180 days in a program |
| 02/18/2005 | 180 days Jail sentenced on 12/23/2004 and stayed as to count(s) 1 further stayed pending completion of 180 days total in River Community Facility and/or Cornerstone Program. |
| 02/18/2005 | All terms and conditions of probation are to remain the same. |
| 05/07/2005 | DOJ Subsequent Abstract sent. |
| 09/22/2005 | Hearing held on 09/22/2005 at 08:30 AM in Department C5 for Chambers Work. |
| 09/22/2005 | Officiating Judge: Richard F. Toohey, Judge |
| 09/22/2005 | Clerk: M. Alcaraz |
| 09/22/2005 | No Court Reporter present at proceedings. |
| 09/22/2005 | No appearances |

# MINUTES

Case : 03SF0869

Name : ████████████

12/14/2018 15:29:27 PM

| Date of Action | Text |
|---|---|
| 09/22/2005 | Petition for Warrant of Arrest signed and filed. |
| 09/22/2005 | Probation ordered revoked as to count(s) 1. |
| 09/22/2005 | Bench warrant ordered issued for defendant. Bail set at $0.00, NO BAIL. |
| 09/27/2005 | Bench warrant signed by Richard F. Toohey and issued for defendant. Bail set at $0.00, NO BAIL. |
| 09/28/2005 | Warrant File Number 02924707 sent from AWSS for Warrant # 2216359. |
| 02/08/2006 | Warrant 02924707 for Kiarash Ashaary DEFENDANT served by Irvine Police Department on 02/08/2006. |
| 02/09/2006 | Probation Violation re: Arraignment - In Custody set on 02/09/2006 at 09:00 AM in Department C5. |
| 02/09/2006 | Hearing held on 02/09/2006 at 09:00:00 AM in Department C5 for Probation Violation Arraignment - In Custody. |
| 02/09/2006 | # 101 on calendar. |
| 02/09/2006 | Officiating Judge: Kazuharu Makino, Judge |
| 02/09/2006 | Clerk: L. Torres |
| 02/09/2006 | Bailiff: R. P. Holt |
| 02/09/2006 | Court Reporter: Caryl Axton |
| 02/09/2006 | Warrant issued on 09/27/2005 ordered recalled for defendant. |
| 02/09/2006 | Defendant present in Court with counsel James Steinberg, Public Defender. |
| 02/09/2006 | People represented by Gary Logalbo, Deputy District Attorney, present. |
| 02/09/2006 | Probation Violation re: Arraignment - In Custody continued to 02/23/2006 at 09:00 AM in Department C5 by stipulation of all parties. |
| 02/09/2006 | Defendant ordered to appear. |
| 02/09/2006 | Court orders bail set at NO BAIL. |
| 02/09/2006 | Defendant remanded to the custody of the Sheriff. |
| 02/09/2006 | Notice to Sheriff issued. |
| 02/09/2006 | Minutes entered by S. Young. |
| 02/23/2006 | Hearing held on 02/23/2006 at 09:00:00 AM in Department C5 for Probation Violation Arraignment - In Custody. |
| 02/23/2006 | Officiating Judge: Kazuharu Makino, Judge |
| 02/23/2006 | Clerk: L. Torres |
| 02/23/2006 | Bailiff: R. P. Holt |
| 02/23/2006 | Court Reporter: Colleen Flynn |
| 02/23/2006 | # 18 on calendar. |
| 02/23/2006 | Defendant present in Court with counsel Brodney, Robert M, Retained Attorney. |
| 02/23/2006 | People represented by Gary Logalbo, Deputy District Attorney, present. |
| 02/23/2006 | Robert M Brodney, Retained Attorney, substituting in as Attorney of Record. |
| 02/23/2006 | James Steinberg relieved as Counsel of Record. |
| 02/23/2006 | Probation Violation re: Arraignment - In Custody continued to 03/23/2006 at 09:00 AM in Department C5 at request of Defense. |
| 02/23/2006 | Defendant ordered to return. |
| 02/23/2006 | Defendant remanded to the custody of the Sheriff. |

# MINUTES

Case : 03SF0869

Name : ▮▮▮▮▮▮▮▮▮

12/14/2018 15:29:27 PM

| Date of Action | Text |
|---|---|
| 02/23/2006 | Current bail set for defendant to remain. |
| 02/23/2006 | Notice to Sheriff issued. |
| 02/23/2006 | Keep with companion cases(s) 04HF1326. |
| 02/23/2006 | Minutes entered by C. Anderson. |
| 03/23/2006 | Hearing held on 03/23/2006 at 09:00:00 AM in Department C5 for Probation Violation Arraignment - In Custody. |
| 03/23/2006 | Officiating Judge: Kazuharu Makino, Judge |
| 03/23/2006 | Clerk: L. Torres |
| 03/23/2006 | Bailiff: R. P. Holt |
| 03/23/2006 | Court Reporter: Colleen Flynn |
| 03/23/2006 | # 22 on calendar. |
| 03/23/2006 | Defendant present in Court with counsel Brodney, Robert M, Retained Attorney. |
| 03/23/2006 | People represented by Andrew Haughton, Deputy District Attorney, present. |
| 03/23/2006 | Defendant waives statutory time for Probation Violation. |
| 03/23/2006 | Counsel joins in waivers. |
| 03/23/2006 | Probation Violation re: Arraignment - In Custody continued to 04/10/2006 at 09:00 AM in Department C5 at request of Defense. |
| 03/23/2006 | Defendant ordered to return. |
| 03/23/2006 | Defendant remanded to the custody of the Sheriff. |
| 03/23/2006 | Current bail set for defendant to remain. |
| 03/23/2006 | Notice to Sheriff issued. |
| 03/23/2006 | Keep with companion cases(s) 04HF1326. |
| 03/23/2006 | Minutes entered by C. Anderson. |
| 04/10/2006 | Hearing held on 04/10/2006 at 09:00:00 AM in Department C5 for Probation Violation Arraignment - In Custody. |
| 04/10/2006 | Officiating Judge: Kazuharu Makino, Judge |
| 04/10/2006 | Clerk: L. Torres |
| 04/10/2006 | Bailiff: C. J. Thurber |
| 04/10/2006 | Court Reporter: Colleen Flynn |
| 04/10/2006 | # 12 on calendar. |
| 04/10/2006 | Defendant present in Court with counsel Brodney, Robert M, Retained Attorney. |
| 04/10/2006 | People represented by Daniel Wagner, Deputy District Attorney, present. |
| 04/10/2006 | Probation Violation re: Arraignment - In Custody continued to 05/25/2006 at 09:00 AM in Department C5 at request of Defense. |
| 04/10/2006 | Defendant ordered to return. |
| 04/10/2006 | Defendant remanded to the custody of the Sheriff. |
| 04/10/2006 | Current bail set for defendant to remain. |
| 04/10/2006 | Notice to Sheriff issued. |
| 04/10/2006 | Keep with companion cases(s) 04HF1326. |
| 04/10/2006 | Minutes entered by C. Anderson. |
| 05/25/2006 | Hearing held on 05/25/2006 at 09:00:00 AM in Department C5 for Probation Violation Arraignment - In Custody. |

# MINUTES

Case : 03SF0869

Name [REDACTED]                                           12/14/2018 15:29:27 PM

| Date of Action | Text |
| --- | --- |
| 05/25/2006 | Officiating Judge: Kazuharu Makino, Judge |
| 05/25/2006 | Clerk: L. Torres |
| 05/25/2006 | Bailiff: C. J. Thurber |
| 05/25/2006 | Court Reporter: Shelley Hill |
| 05/25/2006 | # 6 on calendar. |
| 05/25/2006 | Defendant present in Court with counsel Brodney, Robert M, Retained Attorney. |
| 05/25/2006 | People represented by Andre Manssourian, Deputy District Attorney, present. |
| 05/25/2006 | Defendant advised of legal and constitutional rights. |
| 05/25/2006 | Defendant waives right to probation hearing. Defendant admits violation of probation as to count(s) 1. |
| 05/25/2006 | Court finds defendant in violation of probation. |
| 05/25/2006 | Probation report waived. |
| 05/25/2006 | Defendant waives arraignment for sentencing. |
| 05/25/2006 | Defendant requests immediate sentencing. |
| 05/25/2006 | Counsel joins in waivers and admissions. |
| 05/25/2006 | Court orders probation reinstated and modified as to count(s) 1 as follows: |
| 05/25/2006 | Serve 160 Day(s) Orange County Jail as to count(s) 1. |
| 05/25/2006 | Credit for time served: 107 actual, 53 conduct, totaling 160 days. |
| 05/25/2006 | Defendant to report to Probation Officer within 72 hours of release. |
| 05/25/2006 | Defendant remanded to the custody of the Sheriff. |
| 05/25/2006 | Notice to Sheriff issued. |
| 05/25/2006 | Keep with companion cases(s) 04HF1326. |
| 05/25/2006 | Minutes entered by C. Anderson. |
| 05/29/2006 | DOJ Subsequent Abstract sent. |
| 11/22/2006 | Probation Violation re: Arraignment set on 11/27/2006 at 09:00 AM in Department C55. |
| 11/22/2006 | Defendant's release status updated to reflect: In Custody. |
| 11/22/2006 | Probation Violation Petition dated 11/21/2006 filed. |
| 11/22/2006 | Hearing held on 11/22/2006 at 09:00:00 AM in Department H2 for Probation Violation Arraignment. |
| 11/22/2006 | Officiating Judge: Peter J. Polos, Judge |
| 11/22/2006 | Clerk: C. B. Henderson |
| 11/22/2006 | Bailiff: J. Winovich |
| 11/22/2006 | Court Reporter: Marcia Gahring |
| 11/22/2006 | People represented by Matthew Zandi, Deputy District Attorney, present. |
| 11/22/2006 | Defendant present in Court with counsel Robert M Brodney, Retained Attorney. |
| 11/22/2006 | Probation Violation re: Arraignment vacated for 11/27/2006 at 09:00 AM in C55. |
| 11/22/2006 | Probation ordered revoked as to count(s) 1. |
| 11/22/2006 | Probation Violation re: Arraignment set on 01/09/2007 at 08:30 AM in Department H2. |
| 11/22/2006 | Defendant ordered to appear. |
| 11/22/2006 | Court orders bail set in the amount of $10, 000.00. |

# MINUTES

Case : 03SF0869

Name : Ashaary, Kiarash

12/14/2018 15:29:27 PM

| Date of Action | Text |
|---|---|
| 11/22/2006 | Defendant remanded to the custody of the Sheriff. |
| 11/22/2006 | Notice to Sheriff issued. |
| 11/22/2006 | Minutes done without case. Case ordered. |
| 11/22/2006 | Keep with companion cases(s) 06HF2202. |
| 11/30/2006 | Surety Bond # S10 01125675 filed. |
| 11/30/2006 | OCJ bond receipt# S250725 filed. |
| 12/01/2006 | Bail Bond Number S10 01125675 posted in the amount of $10000.00 by GOLDB of SENEC. |
| 12/06/2006 | Do not transport defendant to Dept. C55 on 12-07-06. Defendant is set for Probation Violation in Dept. H2 on 01-09-07. |
| 12/06/2006 | Notice to Sheriff issued. |
| 12/06/2006 | Probation Violation Petition dated 12/06/2006 filed. |
| 12/12/2006 | Certified Copy of prior packet forwarded to Orange County District Attorney's Office, N. Adams. |
| 01/08/2007 | Do not defendant to Dept. C55 on 01-09-07. Defendant is set for Probation Violation in Dept. H2 on 01-09-07. |
| 01/08/2007 | Notice to Sheriff issued. |
| 01/09/2007 | Hearing held on 01/09/2007 at 08:30:00 AM in Department H2 for Probation Violation Arraignment. |
| 01/09/2007 | Officiating Judge: Peter J. Polos, Judge |
| 01/09/2007 | Clerk: M. Johnson |
| 01/09/2007 | Bailiff: L. Martinez |
| 01/09/2007 | Court Reporter: Marcia Gahring |
| 01/09/2007 | People represented by Matthew Zandi, Deputy District Attorney, present. |
| 01/09/2007 | Defendant not present in Court represented by Robert M Brodney, Retained Attorney. |
| 01/09/2007 | Defendant inadvertanly brought to Central Justice Center |
| 01/09/2007 | Court reporter waived by all parties. |
| 01/09/2007 | Probation Violation re: Arraignment continued to 01/12/2007 at 08:30 AM in Department H2 at request of Defense. |
| 01/09/2007 | Keep with companion cases(s) 07HF0020, 06HF2202. |
| 01/09/2007 | Notice to Sheriff issued. |
| 01/12/2007 | Hearing held on 01/12/2007 at 08:30:00 AM in Department H2 for Probation Violation Arraignment. |
| 01/12/2007 | Officiating Judge: Peter J. Polos, Judge |
| 01/12/2007 | Clerk: M. Johnson |
| 01/12/2007 | Bailiff: J. Winovich |
| 01/12/2007 | Court Reporter: Marcia Gahring |
| 01/12/2007 | People represented by George W. McFetridge Jr., Deputy District Attorney, present. |
| 01/12/2007 | Defendant present in Court with counsel Brodney, Robert M, Retained Attorney. |
| 01/12/2007 | Probation Violation re: Arraignment continued to 02/15/2007 at 08:30 AM in Department H2 by stipulation of all parties. |
| 01/12/2007 | Defendant waives statutory time for Hearing. |
| 01/12/2007 | Present bail deemed sufficient and continued. |

# MINUTES

Case : 03SF0869

Name : ███████████████

12/14/2018 15:29:27 PM

| Date of Action | Text |
|---|---|
| 01/12/2007 | Court notes bond has been posted on this case |
| 01/12/2007 | Defendant released on this case only. Release issued. |
| 01/12/2007 | Notice to Sheriff issued. |
| 01/12/2007 | Keep with companion cases(s) 06HF2202 & 07HF0020. |
| 01/12/2007 | Minutes entered by R. Hume. |
| 02/15/2007 | Hearing held on 02/15/2007 at 08:30:00 AM in Department H2 for Probation Violation Arraignment. |
| 02/15/2007 | Officiating Judge: Peter J. Polos, Judge |
| 02/15/2007 | Clerk: T. Hauck |
| 02/15/2007 | Bailiff: J. Winovich |
| 02/15/2007 | Court Reporter: Marcia Gahring |
| 02/15/2007 | People represented by George W. McFetridge Jr., Deputy District Attorney, present. |
| 02/15/2007 | Susan L. Angell makes a special appearance for Robert M Brodney, Retained Attorney. Defendant present. |
| 02/15/2007 | Probation Violation re: Arraignment continued to 03/27/2007 at 08:30 AM in Department H2 at request of Defense. |
| 02/15/2007 | Defendant waives statutory time for Hearing. |
| 02/15/2007 | Defendant ordered to appear. |
| 02/15/2007 | Present bail deemed sufficient and continued. |
| 02/15/2007 | Keep with companion cases(s) 07HF0020, 06HF2202. |
| 03/27/2007 | Hearing held on 03/27/2007 at 08:30:00 AM in Department H2 for Probation Violation Arraignment. |
| 03/27/2007 | Officiating Judge: Peter J. Polos, Judge |
| 03/27/2007 | Clerk: K. Reinke |
| 03/27/2007 | Bailiff: J. Winovich |
| 03/27/2007 | Court Reporter: Marcia Gahring |
| 03/27/2007 | People represented by Nikki Chambers, Deputy District Attorney, present. |
| 03/27/2007 | Defendant present in Court with counsel Brodney, Robert M, Retained Attorney. |
| 03/27/2007 | Probation Violation re: Arraignment set on 05/07/2007 at 08:30 AM in Department H2. |
| 03/27/2007 | Defendant waives statutory time for Hearing. |
| 03/27/2007 | Counsel joins in waivers. |
| 03/27/2007 | Defendant ordered to return. |
| 03/27/2007 | Current bail set for defendant to remain. |
| 03/27/2007 | Defendant remanded to the custody of the Sheriff. |
| 03/27/2007 | Notice to Sheriff issued. |
| 03/27/2007 | Keep with companion cases(s) 06HF2202 and 07HF0020. |
| 03/27/2007 | Correction: (Entered NUNC_PRO_TUNC on 04/03/07) |
| 03/27/2007 | Defendant released on this case only. Release issued. (Entered NUNC_PRO_TUNC on 04/03/07) |
| 03/27/2007 | Notice to Sheriff issued. |
| 03/27/2007 | Notice to Sheriff issued. |
| 04/03/2007 | Nunc Pro Tunc entry(s) made on this date for 03/27/2007. |

# MINUTES

Case : 03SF0869

Name : ██████████████                                    12/14/2018 15:29:27 PM

| Date of Action | Text |
|---|---|
| 05/07/2007 | Hearing held on 05/07/2007 at 08:30:00 AM in Department H2 for Probation Violation Arraignment. |
| 05/07/2007 | Officiating Judge: Peter J. Polos, Judge |
| 05/07/2007 | Clerk: C. B. Henderson |
| 05/07/2007 | Bailiff: J. Winovich |
| 05/07/2007 | Court Reporter: Marcia Gahring |
| 05/07/2007 | People represented by George W. McFetridge Jr., Deputy District Attorney, present. |
| 05/07/2007 | Brian Cretney makes a special appearance for Robert M Brodney, Retained Attorney. Defendant present. |
| 05/07/2007 | Probation Violation re: Arraignment set on 05/21/2007 at 08:30 AM in Department H2. |
| 05/07/2007 | Defendant ordered to appear. |
| 05/07/2007 | Present bail deemed sufficient and continued. |
| 05/07/2007 | Keep with companion cases(s) 06HF2202 and 07HF0020. |
| 05/21/2007 | Hearing held on 05/21/2007 at 08:30:00 AM in Department H2 for Probation Violation Arraignment. |
| 05/21/2007 | Officiating Judge: Kelly MacEachern, Judge |
| 05/21/2007 | Clerk: C. B. Henderson |
| 05/21/2007 | Bailiff: J. Winovich |
| 05/21/2007 | Court Reporter: Marcia Gahring |
| 05/21/2007 | People represented by George W. McFetridge Jr., Deputy District Attorney, present. |
| 05/21/2007 | Lloyd Freeberg, Retained Attorney, substituting in as Attorney of Record. |
| 05/21/2007 | Robert M Brodney relieved as Counsel of Record. |
| 05/21/2007 | Defendant present in Court with counsel Lloyd Freeberg, Retained Attorney. |
| 05/21/2007 | Probation Violation re: Arraignment set on 06/07/2007 at 08:30 AM in Department H2. |
| 05/21/2007 | Defendant ordered to appear. |
| 05/21/2007 | Present bail deemed sufficient and continued. |
| 05/21/2007 | Keep with companion cases(s) 06HF2202 and 07HF0020. |
| 06/07/2007 | Hearing held on 06/07/2007 at 08:30:00 AM in Department H2 for Probation Violation Arraignment. |
| 06/07/2007 | Officiating Judge: Peter J. Polos, Judge |
| 06/07/2007 | Clerk: T. Hauck |
| 06/07/2007 | Bailiff: J. Winovich |
| 06/07/2007 | Court Reporter: Marcia Gahring |
| 06/07/2007 | People represented by Chris Kralick, Deputy District Attorney, present. |
| 06/07/2007 | Martin Joseph Heneghan makes a special appearance for Lloyd Freeberg, Retained Attorney. Defendant present. |
| 06/07/2007 | Probation Violation re: Arraignment set on 06/28/2007 at 08:30 AM in Department H2. |
| 06/07/2007 | Defendant ordered to appear. |
| 06/07/2007 | Present bail deemed sufficient and continued. |
| 06/07/2007 | Keep with companion cases(s) 07HF0020, 06HF2202. |

# MINUTES

Case : 03SF0869

Name :  ███████████                                              12/14/2018 15:29:27 PM

| Date of Action | Text |
|---|---|
| 06/28/2007 | Hearing held on 06/28/2007 at 08:30:00 AM in Department H2 for Probation Violation Arraignment. |
| 06/28/2007 | Officiating Judge: Peter J. Polos, Judge |
| 06/28/2007 | Clerk: C. B. Henderson |
| 06/28/2007 | Bailiff: P. Ada |
| 06/28/2007 | Court Reporter: Marcia Gahring |
| 06/28/2007 | People represented by George W. McFetridge Jr., Deputy District Attorney, present. |
| 06/28/2007 | James Sweeney makes a special appearance for Lloyd Freeberg, Retained Attorney. Defendant present. |
| 06/28/2007 | Probation Violation re: Arraignment set on 08/01/2007 at 08:30 AM in Department H2. |
| 06/28/2007 | Defendant ordered to appear. |
| 06/28/2007 | Present bail deemed sufficient and continued. |
| 06/28/2007 | Keep with companion cases(s) 07HF0020 and 06HF2202. |
| 08/01/2007 | Hearing held on 08/01/2007 at 08:30:00 AM in Department H2 for Probation Violation Arraignment. |
| 08/01/2007 | Officiating Judge: Kelly MacEachern, Judge |
| 08/01/2007 | Clerk: T. Hauck |
| 08/01/2007 | Bailiff: L. Martinez |
| 08/01/2007 | Court Reporter: Lori Shepherd |
| 08/01/2007 | People represented by George W. McFetridge Jr., Deputy District Attorney, present. |
| 08/01/2007 | Defendant present in Court with counsel Freeberg, Lloyd, Retained Attorney. |
| 08/01/2007 | Defendant denies violation of probation as to count(s) 1. |
| 08/01/2007 | Probation Violation re: Disposition and Reset set on 10/04/2007 at 08:30 AM in Department H2. |
| 08/01/2007 | Defendant waives statutory time for Hearing. |
| 08/01/2007 | Counsel joins in waivers. |
| 08/01/2007 | Defendant ordered to appear. |
| 08/01/2007 | Present bail deemed sufficient and continued. |
| 08/01/2007 | Keep with companion cases(s) 07HF0020, 06HF2202. |
| 10/04/2007 | Hearing held on 10/04/2007 at 08:30:00 AM in Department H2 for Probation Violation Disposition and Reset. |
| 10/04/2007 | Officiating Judge: James Odriozola, Commissioner |
| 10/04/2007 | Clerk: C. Le |
| 10/04/2007 | Bailiff:. Present |
| 10/04/2007 | Court Reporter: Michelle Lott-Megenhofer |
| 10/04/2007 | Minutes entered by s. Bartush. |
| 10/04/2007 | People represented by George W. McFetridge Jr., Deputy District Attorney, present. |
| 10/04/2007 | Defendant present in Court with counsel Lloyd Freeberg, Retained Attorney. |
| 10/04/2007 | Probation Violation re: Disposition and Reset set on 11/06/2007 at 08:30 AM in Department H2. |
| 10/04/2007 | Defendant waives statutory time for Probation Violation. |

# MINUTES

Case : 03SF0869

Name : ▓▓▓▓▓▓▓▓▓                                          12/14/2018 15:29:27 PM

| Date of Action | Text |
|---|---|
| 10/04/2007 | Present bail deemed sufficient and continued. |
| 10/04/2007 | Keep with companion cases(s) 06HF2202 07HF0020. |
| 11/06/2007 | Hearing held on 11/06/2007 at 08:30:00 AM in Department H2 for Probation Violation Disposition and Reset. |
| 11/06/2007 | Officiating Judge: Gregory W. Jones, Commissioner |
| 11/06/2007 | Clerk: M. Johnson |
| 11/06/2007 | Bailiff: I. Hamdallah |
| 11/06/2007 | Court Reporter: Karen Puckett |
| 11/06/2007 | People represented by George W. McFetridge Jr., Deputy District Attorney, present. |
| 11/06/2007 | Defendant present in Court with counsel Freeberg, Lloyd, Retained Attorney. |
| 11/06/2007 | Probation Violation re: Disposition and Reset continued to 11/29/2007 at 08:30 AM in Department H2 at request of Defense. |
| 11/06/2007 | Defendant waives statutory time for Hearing. |
| 11/06/2007 | Counsel joins in waivers. |
| 11/06/2007 | Defendant ordered to return. |
| 11/06/2007 | Present bail deemed sufficient and continued. |
| 11/29/2007 | Hearing held on 11/29/2007 at 08:30:00 AM in Department H2 for Probation Violation Disposition and Reset. |
| 11/29/2007 | Officiating Judge: James Odriozola, Commissioner |
| 11/29/2007 | Clerk: K. Reinke |
| 11/29/2007 | Bailiff: I. Hamdallah |
| 11/29/2007 | Court Reporter: Roxanne Drake |
| 11/29/2007 | People represented by George W. McFetridge Jr., Deputy District Attorney, present. |
| 11/29/2007 | Defendant present in Court with counsel Freeberg, Lloyd, Retained Attorney. |
| 11/29/2007 | Probation Violation re: Disposition and Reset set on 12/11/2007 at 08:30 AM in Department H2. |
| 11/29/2007 | Defendant waives statutory time for Hearing. |
| 11/29/2007 | Defendant ordered to return. |
| 11/29/2007 | Present bail deemed sufficient and continued. |
| 12/11/2007 | Hearing held on 12/11/2007 at 08:30:00 AM in Department H2 for Probation Violation Disposition and Reset. |
| 12/11/2007 | Officiating Judge: Gregory W. Jones, Commissioner |
| 12/11/2007 | Clerk: K. Reinke |
| 12/11/2007 | Bailiff: B. Cate |
| 12/11/2007 | Court Reporter: Tina O'Rourke |
| 12/11/2007 | People represented by George W. McFetridge Jr., Deputy District Attorney, present. |
| 12/11/2007 | Douglas Myers makes a special appearance for Lloyd Freeberg, Retained Attorney. Defendant present. |
| 12/11/2007 | Defendant advised of and waives the following: |
| 12/11/2007 | - The right to confront and cross-examine witnesses. |
| 12/11/2007 | - The right against self incrimination. |
| 12/11/2007 | Defendant waives the right to subpoena and present evidence. |

# MINUTES

Case : 03SF0869

Name :　███████████

12/14/2018 15:29:27 PM

| Date of Action | Text |
|---|---|
| 12/11/2007 | Defendant waives right to probation hearing. Defendant admits violation of probation as to count(s) 1. |
| 12/11/2007 | Court finds defendant in violation of probation. |
| 12/11/2007 | Court orders probation terminated as to count(s) 1. |
| 12/11/2007 | Court orders bail bond # S10 01125675 exonerated. |
| 12/15/2007 | DOJ Subsequent Abstract sent. |
| 12/17/2007 | Case closed. |
| 03/14/2015 | Case closed. |
| 03/18/2015 | Case closed. |
| 11/30/2018 | At the request of Defense Counsel, case calendared on 11/30/18 at 08:30 AM in C53 for HRG. |
| 11/30/2018 | Hearing held on 11/30/2018 at 08:30:00 AM in Department C53 for Hearing. |
| 11/30/2018 | Judicial Officer: Gary M Pohlson, Judge |
| 11/30/2018 | Clerk: N. Robles |
| 11/30/2018 | Bailiff: E. F. Richardson |
| 11/30/2018 | Court Reporter: Shelley Hill |
| 11/30/2018 | People represented by George William McFetridge Jr, Deputy District Attorney, present. |
| 11/30/2018 | Defendant not present in Court represented by Saif Rahman, Retained Attorney. |
| 11/30/2018 | Defense Motion to Withdraw Plea Pursuant to Penal Code 1473.7 filed. |
| 11/30/2018 | Court read and considered Petition for Relief Under Penal Code 1473.7. |
| 11/30/2018 | People submit(s). |
| 11/30/2018 | Motion granted. |
| 11/30/2018 | Court finds the defendant was not advised of their immigration consequences and grants the motion pursuant to Penal Code 1473.7. The defendant withdraws his guilty plea(s). People state they are unable to proceed at this time. Defense requests the Court dismiss this case in the furtherance of justice. The Court orders this case dismissed pursuant to Penal Code 1385. |
| 11/30/2018 | Defendant's motion to WITHDRAW GUILTY PLEA to count(s) 1 granted. |
| 11/30/2018 | Case dismissed - pursuant to Penal Code 1385 - Furtherance of justice. |
| 11/30/2018 | Order Vacating Conviction Under Penal Code 1473.7 signed and filed. |
| 11/30/2018 | Minutes of 11/30/2018 entered on 12/03/2018. |
| 12/05/2018 | Deleted DD1 - Abstract of Conviction abstract from case. |
| 12/06/2018 | Case closed. |

EXHIBIT '16'

Orange County Superior Court Docket Sheet - 04HM01441

# Superior Court of California
## County of Orange

Case Number : 04HM01441

Copy Request: 3930489

Request Type: Case Documents

Prepared for: KA

Number of documents: 1

Number of pages: 7

SUPERIOR COURT OF CALIFORNIA, COUNTY OF ORANGE

# MINUTES

Case : 04HM01441

Name : ▮▮▮▮▮▮▮▮▮

12/14/2018 15:31:09 PM

| Date of Action | Text |
|---|---|
| 02/18/2004 | Original Complaint filed on 02/18/2004 by Orange County District Attorney. |
| 02/18/2004 | Name filed: Ashaary, Kiarash |
| 02/18/2004 | MISDEMEANOR charge of 459-460(b) PC filed as count 1. Date of violation: 01/21/2004. |
| 02/18/2004 | MISDEMEANOR charge of 470(d) PC filed as count 2. Date of violation: 01/21/2004. |
| 02/18/2004 | MISDEMEANOR charge of 476 PC filed as count 3. Date of violation: 01/21/2004. |
| 02/18/2004 | Declaration/Affidavit in Support of Arrest filed. |
| 02/18/2004 | Misdemeanor Warrant of Arrest requested. |
| 02/24/2004 | Warrant of Arrest warrant signed by Carlton P. Biggs and issued for defendant. Bail set at $7, 500.00, Mandatory Appearance. |
| 02/26/2004 | Warrant File Number 02804098 sent from AWSS for Warrant # 2086829. |
| 02/26/2004 | Case calendared on 02/26/04 at 2:30 PM in H8 for ARGN. |
| 02/26/2004 | Hearing held on 02/26/2004 at 02:30:00 PM in Department H8 for Arraignment. |
| 02/26/2004 | Officiating Judge: Craig E. Robison, Judge |
| 02/26/2004 | Clerk: T. Ngo |
| 02/26/2004 | Bailiff: D. Cheli |
| 02/26/2004 | Court Reporter: None |
| 02/26/2004 | Warrant issued on 02/24/2004 ordered recalled for defendant. |
| 02/26/2004 | District Attorney waives appearance. |
| 02/26/2004 | Defendant not present in Court represented by Paul S. Meyer, Retained Attorney. |
| 02/26/2004 | Defendant waives reading and advisement of the Original Complaint. |
| 02/26/2004 | To the Original Complaint defendant pleads NOT GUILTY to all counts. |
| 02/26/2004 | Pre Trial set on 03/11/2004 at 08:30 AM in Department H1. |
| 02/26/2004 | Defendant waives statutory time for Jury Trial. |
| 02/26/2004 | Court orders defendant released on own recognizance. |
| 02/26/2004 | Defendant released O.R. through attorney |
| 03/11/2004 | Hearing held on 03/11/2004 at 08:30:00 AM in Department H1 for Pre Trial. |
| 03/11/2004 | Officiating Judge: Frances Munoz, Judge |
| 03/11/2004 | Clerk: J. Appleby |
| 03/11/2004 | Defendant not present in Court represented by Paul S. Meyer, Retained Attorney. |
| 03/11/2004 | People represented by Jason Trumpler, Deputy District Attorney, present. |
| 03/11/2004 | Pre Trial continued to 04/22/2004 at 08:30 AM in Department H1 at request of Defense. |
| 03/11/2004 | Defendant waives statutory time for Jury Trial. |
| 03/11/2004 | Request for continuance filed. |
| 03/11/2004 | Keep with companion cases(s) 02HM02571. |
| 03/11/2004 | Minutes of J. Appleby entered by A. Fikes on 03/12/2004. |
| 04/22/2004 | Hearing held on 04/22/2004 at 08:30:00 AM in Department H1 for Pre Trial. |
| 04/22/2004 | Officiating Judge: Frances Munoz, Judge |
| 04/22/2004 | Clerk: J. Appleby |
| 04/22/2004 | Defendant not present in Court represented by Paul S. Meyer, Retained Attorney. |

# MINUTES

Case : 04HM01441

Name ▆▆▆▆▆▆▆▆                                                    12/14/2018 15:31:09 PM

| Date of Action | Text |
| --- | --- |
| 04/22/2004 | People represented by Cynthia Nichols, Deputy District Attorney, present. |
| 04/22/2004 | Request for continuance filed. |
| 04/22/2004 | Pre Trial set on 05/20/2004 at 08:30 AM in Department H1. |
| 04/22/2004 | Defendant waives statutory time for Jury Trial. |
| 04/22/2004 | Court orders defendant released on own recognizance. |
| 04/22/2004 | Keep with companion cases(s) 02HM02571. |
| 04/22/2004 | Minutes of J. appleby entered by L. Ansley on 04/23/2004. |
| 05/20/2004 | Hearing held on 05/20/2004 at 08:30:00 AM in Department H1 for Pre Trial. |
| 05/20/2004 | Officiating Judge: Frances Munoz, Judge |
| 05/20/2004 | Clerk: T. Hauck |
| 05/20/2004 | Bailiff:. Present |
| 05/20/2004 | Court Reporter: None |
| 05/20/2004 | Caroline Smith made a special appearance for District Attorney Jason Trumpler. |
| 05/20/2004 | Defendant not present in Court represented by Paul S. Meyer, Retained Attorney. |
| 05/20/2004 | Original Complaint amended by interlineation to add COUNT 4, 484/488 PC, MISDEMEANOR, date of violation 01/21/2004. |
| 05/20/2004 | Original Complaint amended by interlineation to add COUNT 5, 496.1 PC, MISDEMEANOR, date of violation 01/21/2004. |
| 05/20/2004 | District Attorney states that count 5 should be PC 490.1 "Infraction" |
| 05/20/2004 | To the Original Complaint count 5 amended by interlineation to read 490.1 PC, INFRACTION. Date of violation: 01/21/2004. |
| 05/20/2004 | Defendant waives reading and advisement of the Original Complaint. |
| 05/20/2004 | To the Original Complaint defendant pleads GUILTY as to count(s) 4, 5. |
| 05/20/2004 | Court finds factual basis and accepts plea. |
| 05/20/2004 | Count(s) 1, 2, 3 DISMISSED - Motion of People. |
| 05/20/2004 | Court finds defendant intelligently and voluntarily waives legal and constitutional rights to jury trial, confront and examine witnesses, and to remain silent. |
| 05/20/2004 | Defendant's written waiver of legal and constitutional rights for guilty plea received and ordered filed. |
| 05/20/2004 | Notarized Tahl |
| 05/20/2004 | Defendant waives statutory time for Sentencing. |
| 05/20/2004 | No legal cause why judgment should not be pronounced and defendant having Pled Guilty to count(s) 4, Imposition of sentence is suspended and defendant is placed on 3 Years INFORMAL PROBATION on the following terms and conditions: |
| 05/20/2004 | No legal cause why judgment should not be pronounced and defendant having Pled Guilty to count(s) 5, Imposition of sentence is suspended and defendant is placed on 3 Years INFORMAL PROBATION in addition to the existing probation on count(s) 4 on the following terms and conditions: |
| 05/20/2004 | Violate no law. |
| 05/20/2004 | Pay $10.00 Local Crime Prevention Fund pursuant to Penal Code 1202.5. |
| 05/20/2004 | Pay $100.00 Restitution Fine pursuant to Penal Code 1202.4 or Penal Code 1202.4(b). |
| 05/20/2004 | Payment of fee(s) stayed to 08/20/2004. |

# MINUTES

Case : 04HM01441

Name :  ▮▮▮▮▮▮▮▮

12/14/2018 15:31:09 PM

| Date of Action | Text |
|---|---|
| 05/20/2004 | Submit your person and property including any residence, premises, container, or vehicle under your control to search and seizure at any time of the day or night by any law enforcement or probation officer with or without a warrant, and with or without reasonable cause or reasonable suspicion. |
| 05/20/2004 | Pay restitution in the amount as determined and directed by Victim Witness as to count(s) 4. |
| 05/20/2004 | Court orders 10% interest of judgment from date of loss. |
| 05/20/2004 | The restitution ordered on 05/20/2004 is deemed a civil judgment pursuant to Penal Code Section 1214(b) as to count(s) 4. |
| 05/20/2004 | Defendant advised of the right to have the amount of restitution determined by a Judicial Bench Officer after a formal hearing. |
| 05/20/2004 | Pay $50.00 to the Victim Witness Emergency Fund as to count(s) 4. |
| 05/20/2004 | Payment to Victim Witness Emergency Fund stayed to 08/20/2004 for proof. |
| 05/20/2004 | Upon successful completion of 1 year probation the People will dismiss Count 4 and defendant will be sentenced solely on count 5 |
| 05/20/2004 | Defendant accepts terms and conditions of probation. |
| 05/29/2004 | DOJ Initial Abstract sent. |
| 06/07/2004 | Case calendared on 06/14/04 at 1:30 PM in H1 for PV. |
| 06/14/2004 | Hearing held on 06/14/2004 at 01:30:00 PM in Department H1 for Probation Violation. |
| 06/14/2004 | Officiating Judge: Frances Munoz, Judge |
| 06/14/2004 | Clerk: T. Hauck |
| 06/14/2004 | Bailiff:. Present |
| 06/14/2004 | Court Reporter: None |
| 06/14/2004 | No action taken. |
| 06/14/2004 | Minutes of T. Hauck entered by J. Barrera. |
| 08/09/2004 | Remittance from receipt # 3607257 received in the amount of $ 148.50. |
| 08/09/2004 | Payment to Victim Witness Emergency Fund proof filed. |
| 09/01/2004 | Case calendared on 09/01/04 at 1:30 PM in H2 for PV ARRIC. |
| 09/01/2004 | Hearing held on 09/01/2004 at 01:30:00 PM in Department H2 for Probation Violation Arraignment - In Custody. |
| 09/01/2004 | Officiating Judge: Craig E. Robison, Judge |
| 09/01/2004 | Clerk: L. K. Mc Donald |
| 09/01/2004 | Bailiff: G. J. Van Patten |
| 09/01/2004 | Court Reporter: Karen Lee |
| 09/01/2004 | People represented by Yvette Patko, Deputy District Attorney, present. |
| 09/01/2004 | Defendant present in Court in propria persona. |
| 09/01/2004 | Court appoints Public Defender to represent Defendant. |
| 09/01/2004 | Defendant present in Court with counsel Michael Mc Clellan, Public Defender. |
| 09/01/2004 | Copy of Petition for Arraignment on Probation Violation given to defense attorney. |
| 09/01/2004 | Court orders probation revoked. |
| 09/01/2004 | Probation Violation re: Arraignment set on 09/08/2004 at 08:30 AM in Department H2. |
| 09/01/2004 | Defendant ordered to appear. |
| 09/01/2004 | Court orders bail set in the amount of $10, 000.00. |

# MINUTES

Case : 04HM01441

Name :  ▇▇▇▇▇▇▇▇▇                                         12/14/2018 15:31:09 PM

| Date of Action | Text |
|---|---|
| 09/01/2004 | Defendant remanded to the custody of the Sheriff. |
| 09/01/2004 | Notice to Sheriff issued. |
| 09/01/2004 | Keep with companion cases(s) 04HF1326, 02HM02571. |
| 09/08/2004 | Hearing held on 09/08/2004 at 08:30:00 AM in Department H2 for Probation Violation Arraignment. |
| 09/08/2004 | Officiating Judge: Craig E. Robison, Judge |
| 09/08/2004 | Clerk: L. K. Mc Donald |
| 09/08/2004 | Bailiff: D. Cheli |
| 09/08/2004 | Court Reporter: Karen Lee |
| 09/08/2004 | People represented by Yvette Patko, Deputy District Attorney, present. |
| 09/08/2004 | Defendant not present in Court represented by Michael Mc Clellan, Public Defender. |
| 09/08/2004 | Defendant remains in holding cell, not brought into courtroom. |
| 09/08/2004 | Probation Violation re: Arraignment continued to 09/13/2004 at 08:30 AM in Department H2 by stipulation of all parties. |
| 09/08/2004 | Current bail set for defendant to remain. |
| 09/08/2004 | Notice to Sheriff issued. |
| 09/08/2004 | Keep with companion cases(s) 04HF1326, 03SF0869 & 02HM02571. |
| 09/13/2004 | Hearing held on 09/13/2004 at 08:30:00 AM in Department H2 for Probation Violation Arraignment. |
| 09/13/2004 | Officiating Judge: Thomas Rees, Commissioner |
| 09/13/2004 | Clerk: R. M. Hume |
| 09/13/2004 | Bailiff:. Present |
| 09/13/2004 | Court Reporter: Karen Lee |
| 09/13/2004 | People represented by Yvette Patko, Deputy District Attorney, present. |
| 09/13/2004 | Defendant not present in Court represented by Michael Mc Clellan, Public Defender. |
| 09/13/2004 | Defendant remains in holding cell, not brought into courtroom. |
| 09/13/2004 | Probation Violation re: Arraignment continued to 09/15/2004 at 09:00 AM in Department H2 by stipulation of all parties. |
| 09/13/2004 | Current bail set for defendant to remain. |
| 09/13/2004 | Notice to Sheriff issued. |
| 09/13/2004 | Keep with companion cases(s) 04HF1326. |
| 09/15/2004 | Hearing held on 09/15/2004 at 09:00:00 AM in Department H2 for Probation Violation Arraignment. |
| 09/15/2004 | Officiating Judge: Craig E. Robison, Judge |
| 09/15/2004 | Clerk: L. K. Mc Donald |
| 09/15/2004 | Bailiff: D. Cheli |
| 09/15/2004 | Court Reporter: Karen Lee |
| 09/15/2004 | People represented by Yvette Patko, Deputy District Attorney, present. |
| 09/15/2004 | Defendant present in Court with counsel Michael Mc Clellan, Public Defender. |
| 09/15/2004 | Probation Violation re: Arraignment continued to 09/17/2004 at 08:30 AM in Department H2 at request of Defense. |
| 09/15/2004 | Defendant ordered to appear. |

# MINUTES

Case : 04HM01441

Name : ██████████                                                      12/14/2018 15:31:09 PM

| Date of Action | Text |
| --- | --- |
| 09/15/2004 | Current bail set for defendant to remain. |
| 09/15/2004 | Defendant remanded to the custody of the Sheriff. |
| 09/15/2004 | Notice to Sheriff issued. |
| 09/15/2004 | Keep with companion cases(s) 04HF1326, 03SF0869, 02HM02571. |
| 09/17/2004 | Hearing held on 09/17/2004 at 08:30:00 AM in Department H2 for Probation Violation Arraignment. |
| 09/17/2004 | Officiating Judge: Craig E. Robison, Judge |
| 09/17/2004 | Clerk: L. K. Mc Donald |
| 09/17/2004 | Bailiff: D. Cheli |
| 09/17/2004 | Court Reporter: Karen Lee |
| 09/17/2004 | People represented by Sandra Nassar, Deputy District Attorney, present. |
| 09/17/2004 | Defendant present in Court with counsel Michael Mc Clellan, Public Defender. |
| 09/17/2004 | Robert M Brodney, Retained Attorney, substituting in as Attorney of Record. |
| 09/17/2004 | Michael Mc Clellan relieved as Counsel of Record. |
| 09/17/2004 | Defendant present in Court with counsel Robert M Brodney, Retained Attorney. |
| 09/17/2004 | Probation Violation re: Arraignment continued to 10/20/2004 at 08:30 AM in Department H2 at request of Defense. |
| 09/17/2004 | Defendant ordered to appear. |
| 09/17/2004 | Current bail set for defendant to remain. |
| 09/17/2004 | Defendant remanded to the custody of the Sheriff. |
| 09/17/2004 | Notice to Sheriff issued. |
| 09/17/2004 | Keep with companion cases(s) 04HF1326, 03SF0869, 02HM02571. |
| 09/23/2004 | Case calendared on 09/23/04 at 10:00 AM in H2 for HRG. |
| 09/23/2004 | Hearing held on 09/23/2004 at 10:00:00 AM in Department H2 for Hearing. |
| 09/23/2004 | Officiating Judge: Craig E. Robison, Judge |
| 09/23/2004 | Clerk: L. K. Mc Donald |
| 09/23/2004 | Bailiff: D. Cheli |
| 09/23/2004 | Court Reporter: Karen Lee |
| 09/23/2004 | People represented by Joe Williams, Deputy District Attorney, present. |
| 09/23/2004 | Defendant not present in Court represented by Robert M Brodney, Retained Attorney. |
| 09/23/2004 | Order to allow visitation for interview purposes signed and filed. |
| 09/23/2004 | (Order filed in case number 04HF1326) |
| 09/23/2004 | Probation Violation re: Arraignment for 10/20/2004 at 08:30 AM in H2 to remain. |
| 10/20/2004 | Hearing held on 10/20/2004 at 08:30:00 AM in Department H2 for Probation Violation Arraignment. |
| 10/20/2004 | Officiating Judge: Craig E. Robison, Judge |
| 10/20/2004 | Clerk: L. K. Mc Donald |
| 10/20/2004 | Bailiff: D. Cheli |
| 10/20/2004 | Court Reporter: Karen Lee |
| 10/20/2004 | People represented by Yvette Patko, Deputy District Attorney, present. |
| 10/20/2004 | Defendant present in Court with counsel Brodney, Robert M, Retained Attorney. |

# MINUTES

Case : 04HM01441

Name : ███████████                                  12/14/2018 15:31:09 PM

| Date of Action | Text |
|---|---|
| 10/20/2004 | Probation Violation re: Arraignment continued to 11/15/2004 at 08:30 AM in Department H2 at request of Defense. |
| 10/20/2004 | Defendant ordered to appear. |
| 10/20/2004 | Current bail set for defendant to remain. |
| 10/20/2004 | Defendant remanded to the custody of the Sheriff. |
| 10/20/2004 | Notice to Sheriff issued. |
| 10/20/2004 | Keep with companion cases(s) 04HF1326, 03SF0869, 02HM02571. |
| 11/15/2004 | Hearing held on 11/15/2004 at 08:30:00 AM in Department H2 for Probation Violation Arraignment. |
| 11/15/2004 | Officiating Judge: Craig E. Robison, Judge |
| 11/15/2004 | Clerk: L. K. Mc Donald |
| 11/15/2004 | Bailiff: D. Cheli |
| 11/15/2004 | Court Reporter: Tina O'Rourke |
| 11/15/2004 | People represented by Yvette Patko, Deputy District Attorney, present. |
| 11/15/2004 | Defendant present in Court with counsel Brodney, Robert M, Retained Attorney. |
| 11/15/2004 | Probation Violation re: Arraignment continued to 12/02/2004 at 08:30 AM in Department H2 at request of Defense. |
| 11/15/2004 | Defendant ordered to appear. |
| 11/15/2004 | Current bail set for defendant to remain. |
| 11/15/2004 | Defendant remanded to the custody of the Sheriff. |
| 11/15/2004 | Notice to Sheriff issued. |
| 11/15/2004 | Keep with companion cases(s) 04HF1326, 03SF0869, 02HM02571. |
| 12/02/2004 | Hearing held on 12/02/2004 at 08:30:00 AM in Department H2 for Probation Violation Arraignment. |
| 12/02/2004 | Officiating Judge: Craig E. Robison, Judge |
| 12/02/2004 | Clerk: L. K. Mc Donald |
| 12/02/2004 | Bailiff: D. Cheli |
| 12/02/2004 | Court Reporter: Karen Lee |
| 12/02/2004 | Joe Williams made a special appearance for District Attorney Yvette Patko. |
| 12/02/2004 | Defendant present in Court with counsel Brodney, Robert M, Retained Attorney. |
| 12/02/2004 | Probation Violation re: Arraignment continued to 12/23/2004 at 08:30 AM in Department H2 at request of Defense. |
| 12/02/2004 | Defendant ordered to appear. |
| 12/02/2004 | Current bail set for defendant to remain. |
| 12/02/2004 | Defendant remanded to the custody of the Sheriff. |
| 12/02/2004 | Notice to Sheriff issued. |
| 12/02/2004 | Keep with companion cases(s) 04HF1326, 03SF0869, 02HM02571. |
| 12/23/2004 | Hearing held on 12/23/2004 at 08:30:00 AM in Department H2 for Probation Violation Arraignment. |
| 12/23/2004 | Officiating Judge: James Odriozola, Commissioner |
| 12/23/2004 | Clerk: A. T. Akahoshi |
| 12/23/2004 | Bailiff: L. Trebil |

# MINUTES

Case : 04HM01441

Name :

12/14/2018 15:31:09 PM

| Date of Action | Text |
|---|---|
| 12/23/2004 | Court Reporter: Karen Lee |
| 12/23/2004 | People represented by Yvette Patko, Deputy District Attorney, present. |
| 12/23/2004 | Defendant present in Court with counsel Robert M Brodney, Retained Attorney. |
| 12/23/2004 | Defendant advised of legal and constitutional rights. |
| 12/23/2004 | Defendant waives right to probation hearing. Defendant admits violation of probation. |
| 12/23/2004 | Court finds defendant in violation of probation. |
| 12/23/2004 | Court orders probation reinstated. |
| 12/23/2004 | Court orders probation terminated as to count(s) 5. |
| 12/23/2004 | Defendant released on this case only. Release issued. |
| 12/23/2004 | Notice to Sheriff issued. |
| 05/07/2005 | DOJ Subsequent Abstract sent. |
| 08/26/2011 | Certified Copy of Complaint, Minute Order, Minutes, Tahl Form, Probation Order mailed to US District Court, Southern District of Texas, Probation Office Attn: Leticia Hernandez, Probatio Officer Asst.. |
| 11/30/2018 | At the request of Defense Counsel, case calendared on 11/30/18 at 08:30 AM in C53 for PET. |
| 11/30/2018 | Hearing held on 11/30/2018 at 08:30:00 AM in Department C53 for Petition. |
| 11/30/2018 | Judicial Officer: Gary M Pohlson, Judge |
| 11/30/2018 | Clerk: N. Robles |
| 11/30/2018 | Bailiff: E. F. Richardson |
| 11/30/2018 | Court Reporter: Shelley Hill |
| 11/30/2018 | People represented by George William McFetridge Jr, Deputy District Attorney, present. |
| 11/30/2018 | Defendant not present in Court represented by Saif Rahman, Retained Attorney. |
| 11/30/2018 | Defense Motion to Withdraw Plea Pursuant to Penal Code 1473.7 filed. |
| 11/30/2018 | Court read and considered Petition for Relief Under Penal Code 1473.7. |
| 11/30/2018 | People submit(s). |
| 11/30/2018 | Motion granted. |
| 11/30/2018 | Court finds the defendant was not advised of their immigration consequences and grants the motion pursuant to Penal Code 1473.7. The defendant withdraws his guilty plea(s). People state they are unable to proceed at this time. Defense requests the Court dismiss this case in the furtherance of justice. The Court orders this case dismissed pursuant to Penal Code 1385. |
| 11/30/2018 | Defendant's motion to WITHDRAW GUILTY PLEA to count(s) 4, 5 granted. |
| 11/30/2018 | Case dismissed - pursuant to Penal Code 1385 - Furtherance of justice. |
| 11/30/2018 | Order Vacating Conviction Under Penal Code 1473.7 signed and filed. |
| 11/30/2018 | Minutes of 11/30/2018 entered on 12/03/2018. |
| 12/03/2018 | DOJ Correction Abstract sent. |
| 12/05/2018 | Deleted DD1 - Abstract of Conviction abstract from case. |

Orange County Superior Court Docket Sheet - 04HM01441

# Superior Court of California
## County of Orange

Case Number : 04HF1326

Copy Request: 3930494

Request Type: Case Documents

Prepared for: KA

Number of documents: 1

Number of pages: 11

# MINUTES

Case : 04HF1326

Name :

12/14/2018 15:32:17 PM

| Date of Action | Text |
|---|---|
| 09/01/2004 | Original Complaint filed on 09/01/2004 by Orange County District Attorney. |
| 09/01/2004 | FELONY charge of 496(a) PC filed as count 1. Date of violation: 08/27/2004. |
| 09/01/2004 | FELONY charge of 11377(a) HS filed as count 2. Date of violation: 08/27/2004. |
| 09/01/2004 | MISDEMEANOR charge of 11364 HS filed as count 3. Date of violation: 08/27/2004. |
| 09/01/2004 | MISDEMEANOR charge of 530.5(a) PC filed as count 4. Date of violation: 08/27/2004. |
| 09/01/2004 | Case calendared on 09/01/04 at 1:30 PM in H2 for ARGN. |
| 09/01/2004 | Declaration/Affidavit in Support of Arrest filed. |
| 09/01/2004 | Hearing held on 09/01/2004 at 01:30:00 PM in Department H2 for Arraignment. |
| 09/01/2004 | Officiating Judge: Craig E. Robison, Judge |
| 09/01/2004 | Clerk: L. K. Mc Donald |
| 09/01/2004 | Bailiff: G. J. Van Patten |
| 09/01/2004 | Court Reporter: Karen Lee |
| 09/01/2004 | People represented by Yvette Patko, Deputy District Attorney, present. |
| 09/01/2004 | Defendant present in Court in propria persona. |
| 09/01/2004 | Defendant states true name and date of birth are correct as shown on the complaint. |
| 09/01/2004 | Court appoints Public Defender to represent Defendant. |
| 09/01/2004 | Defendant present in Court with counsel Michael Mc Clellan, Public Defender. |
| 09/01/2004 | Counsel acknowledges receipt of the complaint. |
| 09/01/2004 | Defendant waives reading and advisement of the Original Complaint. |
| 09/01/2004 | To the Original Complaint defendant pleads NOT GUILTY to all counts. |
| 09/01/2004 | Pre Trial set on 09/08/2004 at 08:30 AM in Department H2. |
| 09/01/2004 | Preliminary Hearing set on 09/15/2004 at 08:30 AM in Department H2. |
| 09/01/2004 | Defendant ordered to appear. |
| 09/01/2004 | Court orders bail set in the amount of $25, 000.00. |
| 09/01/2004 | Defendant remanded to the custody of the Sheriff. |
| 09/01/2004 | Notice to Sheriff issued. |
| 09/01/2004 | Fingerprint card is received and filed. |
| 09/01/2004 | Keep with companion cases(s) 04HM01441, 02HM02571. |
| 09/08/2004 | Hearing held on 09/08/2004 at 08:30:00 AM in Department H2 for Pre Trial. |
| 09/08/2004 | Officiating Judge: Craig E. Robison, Judge |
| 09/08/2004 | Clerk: L. K. Mc Donald |
| 09/08/2004 | Bailiff: D. Cheli |
| 09/08/2004 | Court Reporter: Karen Lee |
| 09/08/2004 | People represented by Yvette Patko, Deputy District Attorney, present. |
| 09/08/2004 | Defendant not present in Court represented by Michael Mc Clellan, Public Defender. |
| 09/08/2004 | Defendant remains in holding cell, not brought into courtroom. |
| 09/08/2004 | Pre Trial continued to 09/13/2004 at 08:30 AM in Department H2 by stipulation of all parties. |
| 09/08/2004 | Preliminary Hearing for 09/15/2004 08:30 AM in H2 to remain. |
| 09/08/2004 | Current bail set for defendant to remain. |
| 09/08/2004 | Notice to Sheriff issued. |

# MINUTES

Case : 04HF1326

Name :  ▮▮▮▮▮▮▮▮▮▮

12/14/2018 15:32:17 PM

| Date of Action | Text |
|---|---|
| 09/08/2004 | Keep with companion cases(s) 04HM01441, 02HM02571 & 03SF0869. |
| 09/13/2004 | Hearing held on 09/13/2004 at 08:30:00 AM in Department H2 for Pre Trial. |
| 09/13/2004 | Officiating Judge: Thomas Rees, Commissioner |
| 09/13/2004 | Clerk: R. M. Hume |
| 09/13/2004 | Bailiff:. Present |
| 09/13/2004 | Court Reporter: Karen Lee |
| 09/13/2004 | People represented by Yvette Patko, Deputy District Attorney, present. |
| 09/13/2004 | Defendant not present in Court represented by Michael Mc Clellan, Public Defender. |
| 09/13/2004 | Defendant remains in holding cell, not brought into courtroom. |
| 09/13/2004 | Pretrial off calendar, Preliminary Hearing set on 09/15/2004 at 08:30 AM in H2 to remain. |
| 09/13/2004 | Current bail set for defendant to remain. |
| 09/13/2004 | Notice to Sheriff issued. |
| 09/13/2004 | Keep with companion cases(s) 03SF0869, 04HM01441 & 02HM02571. |
| 09/15/2004 | Hearing held on 09/15/2004 at 08:30:00 AM in Department H2 for Preliminary Hearing. |
| 09/15/2004 | Officiating Judge: Craig E. Robison, Judge |
| 09/15/2004 | Clerk: L. K. Mc Donald |
| 09/15/2004 | Bailiff: D. Cheli |
| 09/15/2004 | Court Reporter: Karen Lee |
| 09/15/2004 | People represented by Yvette Patko, Deputy District Attorney, present. |
| 09/15/2004 | Defendant present in Court with counsel Michael Mc Clellan, Public Defender. |
| 09/15/2004 | First Amended Complaint filed by Orange County District Attorney. |
| 09/15/2004 | To the First Amended Complaint count 1 now reads 496(a) PC, FELONY. Date of violation: 05/01/2004. |
| 09/15/2004 | To the First Amended Complaint count 4 now reads 530.5(a) PC, FELONY. Date of violation: 05/01/2004. |
| 09/15/2004 | First Amended Complaint now charges COUNT 5, 496(a) PC, FELONY, date of violation 07/12/2004. |
| 09/15/2004 | First Amended Complaint now charges COUNT 6, 530.5(a) PC, FELONY, date of violation 07/12/2004. |
| 09/15/2004 | First Amended Complaint now charges COUNT 7, 496(a) PC, FELONY, date of violation 08/22/2004. |
| 09/15/2004 | First Amended Complaint now charges COUNT 8, 530.5(a) PC, FELONY, date of violation 08/22/2004. |
| 09/15/2004 | First Amended Complaint now charges COUNT 9, 496(a) PC, FELONY, date of violation 07/15/2004. |
| 09/15/2004 | First Amended Complaint now charges COUNT 10, 530.5(a) PC, FELONY, date of violation 07/15/2004. |
| 09/15/2004 | First Amended Complaint now charges COUNT 11, 496(a) PC, FELONY, date of violation 08/27/2004. |
| 09/15/2004 | First Amended Complaint now charges COUNT 12, 530.5(a) PC, FELONY, date of violation 08/27/2004. |
| 09/15/2004 | First Amended Complaint now charges COUNT 13, 496(a) PC, FELONY, date of violation 08/27/2004. |

# MINUTES

Case : 04HF1326

Name :

12/14/2018 15:32:17 PM

| Date of Action | Text |
|---|---|
| 09/15/2004 | First Amended Complaint now charges COUNT 14, 530.5(a) PC, FELONY, date of violation 08/27/2004. |
| 09/15/2004 | First Amended Complaint now charges COUNT 15, 496(a) PC, FELONY, date of violation 08/27/2004. |
| 09/15/2004 | First Amended Complaint now charges COUNT 16, 530.5(a) PC, FELONY, date of violation 08/27/2004. |
| 09/15/2004 | First Amended Complaint now charges COUNT 17, 496(a) PC, FELONY, date of violation 08/27/2004. |
| 09/15/2004 | First Amended Complaint now charges COUNT 18, 530.5(a) PC, FELONY, date of violation 08/27/2004. |
| 09/15/2004 | First Amended Complaint now charges COUNT 19, 496(a) PC, FELONY, date of violation 08/27/2004. |
| 09/15/2004 | First Amended Complaint now charges COUNT 20, 530.5(a) PC, FELONY, date of violation 08/27/2004. |
| 09/15/2004 | First Amended Complaint now charges COUNT 21, 496(a) PC, FELONY, date of violation 08/27/2004. |
| 09/15/2004 | First Amended Complaint now charges COUNT 22, 530.5(a) PC, FELONY, date of violation 08/27/2004. |
| 09/15/2004 | Counsel acknowledges receipt of the complaint. |
| 09/15/2004 | Defendant waives reading and advisement of the First Amended Complaint. |
| 09/15/2004 | Arraignment set on 09/17/2004 at 08:30 AM in Department H2. |
| 09/15/2004 | re: arraignment on 1st amended complaint |
| 09/15/2004 | Defendant waives the right to be arraigned today. |
| 09/15/2004 | Court finds the defendant understandingly, knowingly, and voluntarily waives the right to a Preliminary Hearing within 10 court days of arraignment. |
| 09/15/2004 | Counsel joins in waivers. |
| 09/15/2004 | Defendant ordered to appear. |
| 09/15/2004 | Current bail set for defendant to remain. |
| 09/15/2004 | Defendant remanded to the custody of the Sheriff. |
| 09/15/2004 | Notice to Sheriff issued. |
| 09/15/2004 | Keep with companion cases(s) 03SF0869, 04HM01441, 02HM02571. |
| 09/17/2004 | Hearing held on 09/17/2004 at 08:30:00 AM in Department H2 for Arraignment. |
| 09/17/2004 | Officiating Judge: Craig E. Robison, Judge |
| 09/17/2004 | Clerk: L. K. Mc Donald |
| 09/17/2004 | Bailiff: D. Cheli |
| 09/17/2004 | Court Reporter: Karen Lee |
| 09/17/2004 | People represented by Sandra Nassar, Deputy District Attorney, present. |
| 09/17/2004 | Defendant present in Court with counsel Michael Mc Clellan, Public Defender. |
| 09/17/2004 | Robert M Brodney, Retained Attorney, substituting in as Attorney of Record. |
| 09/17/2004 | Michael Mc Clellan relieved as Counsel of Record. |
| 09/17/2004 | Defendant present in Court with counsel Brodney, Robert M, Retained Attorney. |
| 09/17/2004 | Counsel acknowledges receipt of the complaint. |
| 09/17/2004 | Defendant waives reading and advisement of the First Amended Complaint. |

# MINUTES

Case : 04HF1326

Name : ██████████

| Date of Action | Text |
|---|---|
| 09/17/2004 | To the First Amended Complaint defendant pleads NOT GUILTY to all counts. |
| 09/17/2004 | Pre Trial set on 10/20/2004 at 08:30 AM in Department H2. |
| 09/17/2004 | Preliminary Hearing set on 11/09/2004 at 08:30 AM in Department H2. |
| 09/17/2004 | Court finds the defendant understandingly, knowingly, and voluntarily waives the right to a Preliminary Hearing within 10 court days/60 calendar days of arraignment. |
| 09/17/2004 | Counsel joins in waivers. |
| 09/17/2004 | Defendant ordered to appear. |
| 09/17/2004 | Current bail set for defendant to remain. |
| 09/17/2004 | Defendant remanded to the custody of the Sheriff. |
| 09/17/2004 | Notice to Sheriff issued. |
| 09/17/2004 | Keep with companion cases(s) 03SF0869, 04HM01441, 02HM02571. |
| 09/23/2004 | Case calendared on 09/23/04 at 10:00 AM in H2 for HRG. |
| 09/23/2004 | Hearing held on 09/23/2004 at 10:00:00 AM in Department H2 for Hearing. |
| 09/23/2004 | Officiating Judge: Craig E. Robison, Judge |
| 09/23/2004 | Clerk: L. K. Mc Donald |
| 09/23/2004 | Bailiff: D. Cheli |
| 09/23/2004 | Court Reporter: Karen Lee |
| 09/23/2004 | People represented by Joe Williams, Deputy District Attorney, present. |
| 09/23/2004 | Defendant not present in Court represented by Robert M Brodney, Retained Attorney. |
| 09/23/2004 | Order to allow visitation for interview purposes signed and filed. |
| 09/23/2004 | (Order filed in case number 04HF1326) |
| 09/23/2004 | Pre Trial for 10/20/2004 08:30 AM in H2 to remain. |
| 09/23/2004 | Preliminary Hearing for 11/09/2004 08:30 AM in H2 to remain. |
| 09/23/2004 | Certified Copy of order given to counsel. |
| 09/23/2004 | Certified Copy of Order forwarded to OCJ. |
| 10/20/2004 | Hearing held on 10/20/2004 at 08:30:00 AM in Department H2 for Pre Trial. |
| 10/20/2004 | Officiating Judge: Craig E. Robison, Judge |
| 10/20/2004 | Clerk: L. K. Mc Donald |
| 10/20/2004 | Bailiff: D. Cheli |
| 10/20/2004 | Court Reporter: Karen Lee |
| 10/20/2004 | People represented by Yvette Patko, Deputy District Attorney, present. |
| 10/20/2004 | Defendant present in Court with counsel Brodney, Robert M, Retained Attorney. |
| 10/20/2004 | Preliminary Hearing vacated for 11/09/2004 at 08:30 AM in H2. |
| 10/20/2004 | Pre Trial continued to 11/15/2004 at 08:30 AM in Department H2 at request of Defense. |
| 10/20/2004 | Court finds the defendant understandingly, knowingly, and voluntarily waives the right to a Preliminary Hearing within 60 calendar days of arraignment. |
| 10/20/2004 | Counsel joins in waivers. |
| 10/20/2004 | Defendant ordered to appear. |
| 10/20/2004 | Current bail set for defendant to remain. |
| 10/20/2004 | Defendant remanded to the custody of the Sheriff. |

SUPERIOR COURT OF CALIFORNIA, COUNTY OF ORANGE

# MINUTES

Case : 04HF1326

Name :

| Date of Action | Text |
| --- | --- |
| 10/20/2004 | Notice to Sheriff issued. |
| 10/20/2004 | Keep with companion cases(s) 03SF0869, 04HM01441, 02HM02571. |
| 11/15/2004 | Hearing held on 11/15/2004 at 08:30:00 AM in Department H2 for Pre Trial. |
| 11/15/2004 | Officiating Judge: Craig E. Robison, Judge |
| 11/15/2004 | Clerk: L. K. Mc Donald |
| 11/15/2004 | Bailiff: D. Cheli |
| 11/15/2004 | Court Reporter: Tina O'Rourke |
| 11/15/2004 | People represented by Yvette Patko, Deputy District Attorney, present. |
| 11/15/2004 | Defendant present in Court with counsel Brodney, Robert M, Retained Attorney. |
| 11/15/2004 | Pre Trial continued to 12/02/2004 at 08:30 AM in Department H2 at request of Defense. |
| 11/15/2004 | Court finds the defendant understandingly, knowingly, and voluntarily waives the right to a Preliminary Hearing within 60 calendar days of arraignment. |
| 11/15/2004 | Counsel joins in waivers. |
| 11/15/2004 | Defendant ordered to appear. |
| 11/15/2004 | Current bail set for defendant to remain. |
| 11/15/2004 | Defendant remanded to the custody of the Sheriff. |
| 11/15/2004 | Notice to Sheriff issued. |
| 11/15/2004 | Keep with companion cases(s) 03SF0869, 04HM01441, 02HM02571. |
| 12/02/2004 | Hearing held on 12/02/2004 at 08:30:00 AM in Department H2 for Pre Trial. |
| 12/02/2004 | Officiating Judge: Craig E. Robison, Judge |
| 12/02/2004 | Clerk: L. K. Mc Donald |
| 12/02/2004 | Bailiff: D. Cheli |
| 12/02/2004 | Court Reporter: Karen Lee |
| 12/02/2004 | Joe Williams made a special appearance for District Attorney Yvette Patko. |
| 12/02/2004 | Defendant present in Court with counsel Brodney, Robert M, Retained Attorney. |
| 12/02/2004 | Defendant advised of legal and constitutional rights. |
| 12/02/2004 | Defendant advised of the possible consequences of plea affecting deportation and citizenship. |
| 12/02/2004 | Defendant advised of maximum possible sentence. |
| 12/02/2004 | Defendant advised of consequences of violating probation and parole. |
| 12/02/2004 | Defendant's motion to WITHDRAW NOT GUILTY PLEA to count(s) 2, 4, 6, 8, 10, 11, 14, 16, 17, 20, 22 granted. |
| 12/02/2004 | To the First Amended Complaint defendant pleads GUILTY as to count(s) 2, 4, 6, 8, 10, 11, 14, 16, 17, 20, 22. |
| 12/02/2004 | Court finds defendant intelligently and voluntarily waives legal and constitutional rights to jury trial, confront and examine witnesses, and to remain silent. |
| 12/02/2004 | Court finds factual basis and accepts plea. |
| 12/02/2004 | Defendant's written waiver of legal and constitutional rights for guilty plea received and ordered filed. |
| 12/02/2004 | Sentencing set on 12/23/2004 at 08:30 AM in Department H2. |
| 12/02/2004 | Defendant waives statutory time for Sentencing. |

| Date of Action | Text |
|---|---|
| 12/02/2004 | Counsel joins in waivers. |
| 12/02/2004 | If restitution is paid in full by 12/23/2004, then defendant to receive probation sentence. If not, defendant to receive State Prison sentence) |
| 12/02/2004 | Defendant ordered to appear. |
| 12/02/2004 | Current bail set for defendant to remain. |
| 12/02/2004 | Defendant remanded to the custody of the Sheriff. |
| 12/02/2004 | Notice to Sheriff issued. |
| 12/02/2004 | Keep with companion cases(s) 03SF1326, 04HM01441, 02HM02571. |
| 12/23/2004 | Hearing held on 12/23/2004 at 08:30:00 AM in Department H2 for Sentencing. |
| 12/23/2004 | Officiating Judge: James Odriozola, Commissioner |
| 12/23/2004 | Clerk: A. T. Akahoshi |
| 12/23/2004 | Bailiff: L. Trebil |
| 12/23/2004 | Court Reporter: Karen Lee |
| 12/23/2004 | People represented by Yvette Patko, Deputy District Attorney, present. |
| 12/23/2004 | Defendant present in Court with counsel Robert M Brodney, Retained Attorney. |
| 12/23/2004 | All Parties being advised of their right to have this matter heard by a Judge of the court have stipulated that the matter be heard by Commissioner James Odriozola. |
| 12/23/2004 | Defendant waives arraignment for sentencing. |
| 12/23/2004 | Defendant applies for probation. |
| 12/23/2004 | Probation report waived. |
| 12/23/2004 | Count(s) 1, 3, 5, 7, 9, 12, 13, 15, 18, 19, 21 DISMISSED - Motion of People. |
| 12/23/2004 | No legal cause why judgment should not be pronounced and defendant having Pled Guilty to count(s) 2, 4, 6, 8, 10, 11, 14, 16, 17, 20, 22, Imposition of sentence is suspended and defendant is placed on 3 Years FORMAL PROBATION on the following terms and conditions: |
| 12/23/2004 | Serve 180 Day(s) Orange County Jail as to count(s) 2, 4, 6, 8, 10, 11, 14, 16, 17, 20, 22. |
| 12/23/2004 | Credit for time served: 119 actual, 60 conduct, totaling 179 days. |
| 12/23/2004 | Pay $200.00 Restitution Fine pursuant to Penal Code 1202.4 or Penal Code 1202.4(b). |
| 12/23/2004 | Defendant is ordered to make restitution on dismissed count(s) 1, 3, 5, 7, 9, 12, 13, 15, 18, 19, 21 pursuant to Harvey Waiver. |
| 12/23/2004 | Pay restitution in the amount as determined and directed by Probation Officer as to count(s) 2, 4, 6, 8, 10, 11, 14, 16, 17, 20, 22. |
| 12/23/2004 | Defendant advised of the right to have the amount of restitution determined by a Judicial Bench Officer after a formal hearing. |
| 12/23/2004 | Court orders 10% interest of judgment from date of loss. |
| 12/23/2004 | The restitution ordered on 12/23/2004 is deemed a civil judgment pursuant to Penal Code Section 1214(b) as to count(s) 2, 4, 6, 8, 10, 11, 14, 16, 17, 20, 22. |
| 12/23/2004 | Register pursuant to Health & Safety Code 11590. |
| 12/23/2004 | Pay $50.00 Controlled Substance Lab FEE pursuant to Health and Safety Code Section 11372.5. |
| 12/23/2004 | All fees payable through the Probation Department. |

# MINUTES

Case : 04HF1326

Name : ████████████                                    12/14/2018 15:32:17 PM

| Date of Action | Text |
|---|---|
| 12/23/2004 | Use no unauthorized drugs, narcotics, or controlled substances. Submit to drug or narcotic testing as directed by Probation Officer or Police Officer. |
| 12/23/2004 | Submit your person and property including any residence, premises, container, or vehicle under your control to search and seizure at any time of the day or night by any law enforcement or probation officer with or without a warrant, and with or without reasonable cause or reasonable suspicion. |
| 12/23/2004 | Cooperate with Probation Officer in any plan for psychiatric, psychological, alcohol and/or drug treatment, or counseling. |
| 12/23/2004 | Have no blank checks in possession, nor write any portion of any checks, nor have checking account, nor use or possess credit cards or open credit accounts unless approved by Probation. |
| 12/23/2004 | Seek training, schooling, or employment and maintain residence as approved by Probation Department. |
| 12/23/2004 | Do not associate with anyone disapproved of by your Probation Officer. |
| 12/23/2004 | Do not own, use, or possess any type of dangerous or deadly weapon. |
| 12/23/2004 | Defendant provided a copy of "Prohibited Persons Notice Form and Power of Attorney for Firearms and Disposal" pursuant to Penal Code 12021(d)(2). |
| 12/23/2004 | Obey all laws, orders, rules, and regulations of the Court, Jail, and Probation. |
| 12/23/2004 | Violate no law. |
| 12/23/2004 | Do not have any contact with Gregory Kaltenbach, Candace Wengert, Donald Seward, Donna Colema, John Richmond, Judith Brown Gibbs, Mildred Wynne, Douglas Mahaffey, Shirley Smith, Liliuana Nuila and Meghan McClain directly, indirectly, or through a third party except by an Attorney of Record. |
| 12/23/2004 | Defendant accepts terms and conditions of probation. |
| 12/23/2004 | All terms and conditions to be directed and monitored through the Probation Department. |
| 12/23/2004 | Defendant to report to Probation Office upon release from custody by Monday, December 27, 2004, at 5:00 p.m. |
| 12/23/2004 | Pay the costs of probation based on the ability to pay as directed by the Probation Officer. |
| 12/23/2004 | Defendant remanded to the custody of the Sheriff. |
| 12/23/2004 | Notice to Sheriff issued. |
| 12/23/2004 | Probation Order printed. |
| 12/27/2004 | DD1-GJZ sent to DMV. Return Code: 800 |
| 12/31/2004 | DOJ Initial Abstract sent. |
| 02/18/2005 | Case calendared on 02/18/05 at 08:30 AM in H2 for MTN MOP. |
| 02/18/2005 | MTN MOP set on 02/18/05 at 08:30 AM in H2 has been cancelled. |
| 09/22/2005 | Hearing held on 09/22/2005 at 08:30 AM in Department C5 for Chambers Work. |
| 09/22/2005 | Officiating Judge: Richard F. Toohey, Judge |
| 09/22/2005 | Clerk: M. Alcaraz |
| 09/22/2005 | No Court Reporter present at proceedings. |
| 09/22/2005 | No appearance |
| 09/22/2005 | Petition for Warrant of Arrest signed and filed. |
| 09/22/2005 | Probation ordered revoked as to count(s) 2, 4, 6, 8, 10, 11, 14, 16, 17, 20, 22. |
| 09/22/2005 | Bench warrant ordered issued for defendant. Bail set at $0.00, NO BAIL. |

# MINUTES

Case : 04HF1326

Name :  ███████████

12/14/2018 15:32:17 PM

| Date of Action | Text |
|---|---|
| 09/27/2005 | Bench warrant signed by Richard F. Toohey and issued for defendant. Bail set at $0.00, NO BAIL. |
| 09/28/2005 | Warrant File Number 02924708 sent from AWSS for Warrant # 2216368. |
| 02/08/2006 | Warrant 02924708 for Kiarash Ashaary DEFENDANT served by Irvine Police Department on 02/08/2006. |
| 02/09/2006 | Probation Violation re: Arraignment - In Custody set on 02/09/2006 at 09:00 AM in Department C5. |
| 02/09/2006 | Hearing held on 02/09/2006 at 09:00:00 AM in Department C5 for Probation Violation Arraignment - In Custody. |
| 02/09/2006 | # 103 on calendar. |
| 02/09/2006 | Officiating Judge: Kazuharu Makino, Judge |
| 02/09/2006 | Clerk: L. Torres |
| 02/09/2006 | Bailiff: R. P. Holt |
| 02/09/2006 | Court Reporter: Caryl Axton |
| 02/09/2006 | Warrant issued on 09/27/2005 ordered recalled for defendant. |
| 02/09/2006 | Defendant present in Court with counsel James Steinberg, Public Defender. |
| 02/09/2006 | People represented by Gary Logalbo, Deputy District Attorney, present. |
| 02/09/2006 | Probation Violation re: Arraignment - In Custody continued to 02/23/2006 at 09:00 AM in Department C5 by stipulation of all parties. |
| 02/09/2006 | Defendant ordered to appear. |
| 02/09/2006 | Court orders bail set at NO BAIL. |
| 02/09/2006 | Defendant remanded to the custody of the Sheriff. |
| 02/09/2006 | Notice to Sheriff issued. |
| 02/09/2006 | Minutes entered by S. Young. |
| 02/23/2006 | Hearing held on 02/23/2006 at 09:00:00 AM in Department C5 for Probation Violation Arraignment - In Custody. |
| 02/23/2006 | Officiating Judge: Kazuharu Makino, Judge |
| 02/23/2006 | Clerk: L. Torres |
| 02/23/2006 | Bailiff: R. P. Holt |
| 02/23/2006 | Court Reporter: Colleen Flynn |
| 02/23/2006 | # 30 on calendar. |
| 02/23/2006 | Defendant present in Court with counsel Brodney, Robert M, Retained Attorney. |
| 02/23/2006 | People represented by Gary Logalbo, Deputy District Attorney, present. |
| 02/23/2006 | Robert M Brodney, Retained Attorney, substituting in as Attorney of Record. |
| 02/23/2006 | James Steinberg relieved as Counsel of Record. |
| 02/23/2006 | Probation Violation re: Arraignment - In Custody continued to 03/23/2006 at 09:00 AM in Department C5 at request of Defense. |
| 02/23/2006 | Defendant ordered to return. |
| 02/23/2006 | Defendant remanded to the custody of the Sheriff. |
| 02/23/2006 | Current bail set for defendant to remain. |
| 02/23/2006 | Notice to Sheriff issued. |
| 02/23/2006 | Keep with companion cases(s) 03SF0869. |

# MINUTES

Case : 04HF1326

Name :  ▮▮▮▮▮▮▮▮▮                                    12/14/2018 15:32:17 PM

| Date of Action | Text |
|---|---|
| 02/23/2006 | Minutes entered by C. Anderson. |
| 03/23/2006 | Hearing held on 03/23/2006 at 09:00:00 AM in Department C5 for Probation Violation Arraignment - In Custody. |
| 03/23/2006 | Officiating Judge: Kazuharu Makino, Judge |
| 03/23/2006 | Clerk: L. Torres |
| 03/23/2006 | Bailiff: R. P. Holt |
| 03/23/2006 | Court Reporter: Colleen Flynn |
| 03/23/2006 | # 29 on calendar. |
| 03/23/2006 | Defendant present in Court with counsel Brodney, Robert M, Retained Attorney. |
| 03/23/2006 | People represented by Andrew Haughton, Deputy District Attorney, present. |
| 03/23/2006 | Defendant waives statutory time for Probation Violation. |
| 03/23/2006 | Counsel joins in waivers. |
| 03/23/2006 | Probation Violation re: Arraignment - In Custody continued to 04/10/2006 at 09:00 AM in Department C5 at request of Defense. |
| 03/23/2006 | Defendant ordered to return. |
| 03/23/2006 | Defendant remanded to the custody of the Sheriff. |
| 03/23/2006 | Current bail set for defendant to remain. |
| 03/23/2006 | Notice to Sheriff issued. |
| 03/23/2006 | Keep with companion cases(s) 03SF0869. |
| 03/23/2006 | Minutes entered by C. Anderson. |
| 04/10/2006 | Hearing held on 04/10/2006 at 09:00:00 AM in Department C5 for Probation Violation Arraignment - In Custody. |
| 04/10/2006 | Officiating Judge: Kazuharu Makino, Judge |
| 04/10/2006 | Clerk: L. Torres |
| 04/10/2006 | Bailiff: C. J. Thurber |
| 04/10/2006 | Court Reporter: Colleen Flynn |
| 04/10/2006 | # 22 on calendar. |
| 04/10/2006 | Defendant present in Court with counsel Brodney, Robert M, Retained Attorney. |
| 04/10/2006 | People represented by Daniel Wagner, Deputy District Attorney, present. |
| 04/10/2006 | Probation Violation re: Arraignment - In Custody continued to 05/25/2006 at 09:00 AM in Department C5 at request of Defense. |
| 04/10/2006 | Defendant ordered to return. |
| 04/10/2006 | Defendant remanded to the custody of the Sheriff. |
| 04/10/2006 | Current bail set for defendant to remain. |
| 04/10/2006 | Notice to Sheriff issued. |
| 04/10/2006 | Keep with companion cases(s) 03SF0869. |
| 04/10/2006 | Minutes entered by C. Anderson. |
| 05/25/2006 | Hearing held on 05/25/2006 at 09:00:00 AM in Department C5 for Probation Violation Arraignment - In Custody. |
| 05/25/2006 | Officiating Judge: Kazuharu Makino, Judge |
| 05/25/2006 | Clerk: L. Torres |
| 05/25/2006 | Bailiff: C. J. Thurber |

SUPERIOR COURT OF CALIFORNIA, COUNTY OF ORANGE

# MINUTES

Case : 04HF1326

Name : ████████████

12/14/2018 15:32:17 PM

| Date of Action | Text |
|---|---|
| 05/25/2006 | Court Reporter: Shelley Hill |
| 05/25/2006 | # 15 on calendar. |
| 05/25/2006 | Defendant present in Court with counsel Brodney, Robert M, Retained Attorney. |
| 05/25/2006 | People represented by Andre Manssourian, Deputy District Attorney, present. |
| 05/25/2006 | Defendant advised of legal and constitutional rights. |
| 05/25/2006 | Defendant waives right to probation hearing. Defendant admits violation of probation as to count(s) 2, 4, 6, 8, 10, 11, 14, 16, 17, 20, 22. |
| 05/25/2006 | Court finds defendant in violation of probation. |
| 05/25/2006 | Probation report waived. |
| 05/25/2006 | Defendant waives arraignment for sentencing. |
| 05/25/2006 | Defendant requests immediate sentencing. |
| 05/25/2006 | Counsel joins in waivers and admissions. |
| 05/25/2006 | Court orders probation reinstated and modified as to count(s) 2, 4, 6, 8, 10, 11, 14, 16, 17, 20, 22 as follows: |
| 05/25/2006 | Court orders probation terminated as to count(s) 2, 4, 6, 8, 10, 11, 14, 16, 17, 20, 22. |
| 05/25/2006 | Defendant released on this case only. Release issued. |
| 05/25/2006 | Notice to Sheriff issued. |
| 05/25/2006 | Minutes entered by C. Anderson. |
| 05/29/2006 | DOJ Subsequent Abstract sent. |
| 12/08/2006 | Certified Copy of prior packet forwarded to Orange County District Attorney's Office, N. Adams. |
| 09/28/2007 | Transferred from: Ashaary, Kiarash |
| 09/20/2008 | Case closed. |
| 11/30/2018 | At the request of Defense Counsel, case calendared on 11/30/18 at 08:30 AM in C53 for PET. |
| 11/30/2018 | Hearing held on 11/30/2018 at 08:30:00 AM in Department C53 for Petition. |
| 11/30/2018 | Judicial Officer: Gary M Pohlson, Judge |
| 11/30/2018 | Clerk: N. Robles |
| 11/30/2018 | Bailiff: E. F. Richardson |
| 11/30/2018 | Court Reporter: Shelley Hill |
| 11/30/2018 | People represented by George William McFetridge Jr, Deputy District Attorney, present. |
| 11/30/2018 | Defendant not present in Court represented by Saif Rahman, Retained Attorney. |
| 11/30/2018 | Defense Motion to Withdraw Plea Pursuant to Penal Code 1473.7 filed. |
| 11/30/2018 | Court read and considered Petition for Relief Under Penal Code 1473.7. |
| 11/30/2018 | People submit(s). |
| 11/30/2018 | Motion granted. |
| 11/30/2018 | Court finds the defendant was not advised of their immigration consequences and grants the motion pursuant to Penal Code 1473.7. The defendant withdraws his guilty plea(s). People state they are unable to proceed at this time. Defense requests the Court dismiss this case in the furtherance of justice. The Court orders this case dismissed pursuant to Penal Code 1385. |

SUPERIOR COURT OF CALIFORNIA, COUNTY OF ORANGE

# MINUTES

Case : 04HF1326

Name ███████████

12/14/2018 15:32:17 PM

| Date of Action | Text |
| --- | --- |
| 11/30/2018 | Defendant's motion to WITHDRAW GUILTY PLEA to count(s) 2, 4, 6, 8, 10, 11, 14, 16, 17, 20, 22 granted. |
| 11/30/2018 | Case dismissed - pursuant to Penal Code 1385 - Furtherance of justice. |
| 11/30/2018 | Order Vacating Conviction Under Penal Code 1473.7 signed and filed. |
| 11/30/2018 | Minutes of 11/30/2018 entered on 12/03/2018. |
| 12/03/2018 | DOJ Correction Abstract sent. |
| 12/05/2018 | Deleted DD1 - Abstract of Conviction abstract from case. |
| 12/06/2018 | Case closed. |

Orange County Superior Court Docket Sheet - 85932VK

- Jury Services
- Juvenile
- Probate/Mental Health
- Small Claims
- Traffic & Infractions
- General Info
  - ADA
  - Appearances in Court
  - Bids/Solicitations
  - Budget and Filing / Workload Information
  - Children's Chambers
  - Court Governance
  - Court Holidays
  - Court Locations, Hours & Phone Numbers
  - Community Outreach/Education
  - DUI Court
  - Employment
  - Government Claim Forms
  - Judicial Officers
  - Lawyers and Litigants
  - Media Relations
  - Online Services
  - Records
  - Temporary Judge Program

Home » Online Services » Case Access » Case Detail

- Online Services
  - Account Services
  - Cases on Calendar
  - Case Access
  - Case Index Search
  - Case Name Search
  - Civil-Reserve A Motion Date
  - Court Reporter Transcript Requests
  - eFiling
  - eJuror
  - My Court Portal-Traffic & Criminal
  - Probate Notes
  - Tentative Rulings

Case Detail - 85932VK

Case Search Home

# Case Detail - 85932VK

## Case Summary

**Case No. Case Category Case Level/Type Plaintiff Person/Business Name Party Role**

85932VK Criminal/Traffic Infraction        People    ████████████

**Filing Date Case Status Case Status Date Destruction Date File Location**
04/15/2005  Closed        12/31/2006        09/28/2012

## Case Detail

| Charge | Charge Date | Charge Dispo Date | Charge Dispo Type |
|---|---|---|---|
| VC 27315(d) | 04/15/2005 | 10/06/2006 | Pled Guilty |
| VC 16028(a) | 04/15/2005 | 10/06/2006 | Dismissed - Proof of Correction |

Orange County Superior Court Docket Sheet - 06HF2202

# Superior Court of California
## County of Orange

Case Number : 06HF2202

Copy Request: 3993154

Request Type: Case Documents

Prepared for: KA

Number of documents: 1
Number of pages: 29

# MINUTES

Case : 06HF2202

Name :█████████

02/01/2019 10:01:46 AM

| Date of Action | Text |
|---|---|
| 11/07/2006 | Original Complaint filed on 11/07/2006 by Orange County District Attorney. |
| 11/07/2006 | Name filed: Ashaary, Kiarash |
| 11/07/2006 | FELONY charge of 530.5(a) PC filed as count 1. Date of violation: 12/26/2005. |
| 11/07/2006 | FELONY charge of 530.5(a) PC filed as count 2. Date of violation: 01/30/2006. |
| 11/07/2006 | FELONY charge of 530.5(a) PC filed as count 3. Date of violation: 02/05/2006. |
| 11/07/2006 | FELONY charge of 530.5(a) PC filed as count 4. Date of violation: 01/28/2006. |
| 11/07/2006 | FELONY charge of 530.5(a) PC filed as count 5. Date of violation: 01/24/2006. |
| 11/07/2006 | FELONY charge of 530.5(a) PC filed as count 6. Date of violation: 01/25/2006. |
| 11/07/2006 | FELONY charge of 530.5(a) PC filed as count 7. Date of violation: 12/06/2005. |
| 11/07/2006 | FELONY charge of 530.5(a) PC filed as count 8. Date of violation: 01/04/2006. |
| 11/07/2006 | FELONY charge of 530.5(a) PC filed as count 9. Date of violation: 11/27/2005. |
| 11/07/2006 | FELONY charge of 530.5(a) PC filed as count 10. Date of violation: 02/02/2006. |
| 11/07/2006 | FELONY charge of 530.5(a) PC filed as count 11. Date of violation: 02/08/2006. |
| 11/07/2006 | FELONY charge of 530.5(a) PC filed as count 12. Date of violation: 10/27/2005. |
| 11/07/2006 | FELONY charge of 459-460(b) PC filed as count 13. Date of violation: 10/17/2005. |
| 11/07/2006 | FELONY charge of 115(a) PC filed as count 14. Date of violation: 02/08/2006. |
| 11/07/2006 | FELONY charge of 470a PC filed as count 15. Date of violation: 02/08/2006. |
| 11/07/2006 | FELONY charge of 470b PC filed as count 16. Date of violation: 02/08/2006. |
| 11/07/2006 | MISDEMEANOR charge of 529.5(a) PC filed as count 17. Date of violation: 02/08/2006. |
| 11/07/2006 | FELONY charge of 475(b) PC filed as count 18. Date of violation: 02/08/2006. |
| 11/07/2006 | FELONY charge of 476 PC filed as count 19. Date of violation: 10/24/2005. |
| 11/07/2006 | 529.5(d) PC added as other allegation as to count 17. |
| 11/07/2006 | 13202.5(a) VC added as other allegation as to count 17. |
| 11/07/2006 | Declaration/Affidavit in Support of Arrest filed. |
| 11/07/2006 | Police/Arrest Report filed. |
| 11/07/2006 | Request for booking fees received. |
| 11/07/2006 | Felony Warrant of Arrest requested. |
| 11/07/2006 | Warrant of Arrest warrant signed by Peter J. Polos and issued for defendant. Bail set at $100, 000.00, Mandatory Appearance. |
| 11/07/2006 | Warrant faxed to Central Warrant Repository (CWR). |
| 11/07/2006 | Warrant File Number 03006452 sent from AWSS for Warrant # 2303379. |
| 11/20/2006 | Warrant 03006452 for Kiarash Ashaary DEFENDANT served by Irvine Police Department on 11/20/2006. |
| 11/22/2006 | Case calendared on 11/22/06 at 1:30 PM in H2 for ARGN IC. |
| 11/22/2006 | Hearing held on 11/22/2006 at 01:30:00 PM in Department H2 for Arraignment In Custody. |
| 11/22/2006 | Officiating Judge: Peter J. Polos, Judge |
| 11/22/2006 | Clerk: C. B. Henderson |
| 11/22/2006 | Bailiff: J. Winovich |
| 11/22/2006 | Court Reporter: Marcia Gahring |
| 11/22/2006 | Warrant issued on 11/07/2006 ordered recalled for defendant. |

SUPERIOR COURT OF CALIFORNIA, COUNTY OF ORANGE

# MINUTES

Case : 06HF2202

Name : █████████

02/01/2019 10:01:46 AM

| Date of Action | Text |
|---|---|
| 11/22/2006 | People represented by Matthew Zandi, Deputy District Attorney, present. |
| 11/22/2006 | Defendant present in Court with counsel Robert M Brodney, Retained Attorney. |
| 11/22/2006 | Defendant states true name and date of birth are correct as shown on the complaint. |
| 11/22/2006 | Counsel acknowledges receipt of the complaint. |
| 11/22/2006 | Defendant waives reading and advisement of the Original Complaint. |
| 11/22/2006 | To the Original Complaint defendant pleads NOT GUILTY to all counts. |
| 11/22/2006 | Defendant denies allegations. |
| 11/22/2006 | Pre Trial set on 01/09/2007 at 08:30 AM in Department H2. |
| 11/22/2006 | Preliminary Hearing set on 01/17/2007 at 08:30 AM in Department H2. |
| 11/22/2006 | Court finds the defendant understandingly, knowingly, and voluntarily waives the right to a Preliminary Hearing within 10 court days/60 calendar days of arraignment. |
| 11/22/2006 | Counsel joins in waivers. |
| 11/22/2006 | Motion by Defense for bail reduction |
| 11/22/2006 | Motion granted. |
| 11/22/2006 | Court orders bail set in the amount of $40, 000.00. |
| 11/22/2006 | Defendant remanded to the custody of the Sheriff. |
| 11/22/2006 | Notice to Sheriff issued. |
| 11/22/2006 | Fingerprint card is received and filed. |
| 11/30/2006 | Surety Bond # S100-01136444 filed. |
| 12/01/2006 | Bail Bond Number S100-01136444 posted in the amount of $40000.00 by GOLDB of SENEC. |
| 01/09/2007 | Hearing held on 01/09/2007 at 08:30:00 AM in Department H2 for Pre Trial. |
| 01/09/2007 | Officiating Judge: Peter J. Polos, Judge |
| 01/09/2007 | Clerk: M. Johnson |
| 01/09/2007 | Bailiff: L. Martinez |
| 01/09/2007 | Court Reporter: Marcia Gahring |
| 01/09/2007 | People represented by Matthew Zandi, Deputy District Attorney, present. |
| 01/09/2007 | Defendant not present in Court represented by Robert M Brodney, Retained Attorney. |
| 01/09/2007 | Defendant inadvertanly brought to Central Justice Center |
| 01/09/2007 | Court reporter waived by all parties. |
| 01/09/2007 | Pre Trial continued to 01/12/2007 at 08:30 AM in Department H2 at request of Defense. |
| 01/09/2007 | Present bail deemed sufficient and continued. |
| 01/09/2007 | Keep with companion cases(s) 07HF0020, 03SF0869. |
| 01/12/2007 | Hearing held on 01/12/2007 at 08:30:00 AM in Department H2 for Pre Trial. |
| 01/12/2007 | Officiating Judge: Peter J. Polos, Judge |
| 01/12/2007 | Clerk: M. Johnson |
| 01/12/2007 | Bailiff: J. Winovich |
| 01/12/2007 | Court Reporter: Marcia Gahring |
| 01/12/2007 | People represented by George W. McFetridge Jr., Deputy District Attorney, present. |
| 01/12/2007 | Defendant present in Court with counsel Brodney, Robert M, Retained Attorney. |

# MINUTES

Case : 06HF2202

Name : ████████████

02/01/2019 10:01:46 AM

| Date of Action | Text |
|---|---|
| 01/12/2007 | Preliminary Hearing vacated for 01/17/2007 at 08:30 AM in H2. |
| 01/12/2007 | Pre Trial continued to 02/15/2007 at 08:30 AM in Department H2 by stipulation of all parties. |
| 01/12/2007 | Defendant waives statutory time for Preliminary Hearing. |
| 01/12/2007 | Present bail deemed sufficient and continued. |
| 01/12/2007 | Keep with companion cases(s) 07HF0020 & 03SF0869. |
| 01/12/2007 | Minutes entered by R. Hume. |
| 02/15/2007 | Hearing held on 02/15/2007 at 08:30:00 AM in Department H2 for Pre Trial. |
| 02/15/2007 | Officiating Judge: Peter J. Polos, Judge |
| 02/15/2007 | Clerk: T. Hauck |
| 02/15/2007 | Bailiff: J. Winovich |
| 02/15/2007 | Court Reporter: Marcia Gahring |
| 02/15/2007 | People represented by George W. McFetridge Jr., Deputy District Attorney, present. |
| 02/15/2007 | Susan L. Angell makes a special appearance for Robert M Brodney, Retained Attorney. Defendant present. |
| 02/15/2007 | Pre Trial continued to 03/27/2007 at 08:30 AM in Department H2 at request of Defense. |
| 02/15/2007 | Court finds the defendant understandingly, knowingly, and voluntarily waives the right to a Preliminary Hearing within 60 calendar days of arraignment. |
| 02/15/2007 | Counsel joins in waivers. |
| 02/15/2007 | Defendant ordered to appear. |
| 02/15/2007 | Current bail set for defendant to remain. |
| 02/15/2007 | Keep with companion cases(s) 07HF0020, 03SF0869. |
| 03/27/2007 | Hearing held on 03/27/2007 at 08:30:00 AM in Department H2 for Pre Trial. |
| 03/27/2007 | Officiating Judge: Peter J. Polos, Judge |
| 03/27/2007 | Clerk: K. Reinke |
| 03/27/2007 | Bailiff: J. Winovich |
| 03/27/2007 | Court Reporter: Marcia Gahring |
| 03/27/2007 | People represented by George W. McFetridge Jr., Deputy District Attorney, present. |
| 03/27/2007 | Defendant present in Court with counsel Brodney, Robert M, Retained Attorney. |
| 03/27/2007 | Pre Trial set on 05/07/2007 at 08:30 AM in Department H2. |
| 03/27/2007 | Defendant waives statutory time for Preliminary Hearing. |
| 03/27/2007 | Counsel joins in waivers. |
| 03/27/2007 | Defendant ordered to return. |
| 03/27/2007 | Current bail set for defendant to remain. |
| 03/27/2007 | Defendant remanded to the custody of the Sheriff. |
| 03/27/2007 | Notice to Sheriff issued. |
| 03/27/2007 | Keep with companion cases(s) 03SF0869 and 07HF0020. |
| 03/27/2007 | Correction: (Entered NUNC_PRO_TUNC on 04/03/07) |
| 03/27/2007 | Defendant released on this case only. Release issued. (Entered NUNC_PRO_TUNC on 04/03/07) |
| 03/27/2007 | Notice to Sheriff issued. (Entered NUNC_PRO_TUNC on 04/03/07) |

# MINUTES

Case : 06HF2202

Name : ▓▓▓▓▓▓▓▓                                   02/01/2019 10:01:46 AM

| Date of Action | Text |
| --- | --- |
| 04/03/2007 | Nunc Pro Tunc entry(s) made on this date for 03/27/2007. |
| 05/07/2007 | Hearing held on 05/07/2007 at 08:30:00 AM in Department H2 for Pre Trial. |
| 05/07/2007 | Officiating Judge: Peter J. Polos, Judge |
| 05/07/2007 | Clerk: C. B. Henderson |
| 05/07/2007 | Bailiff: J. Winovich |
| 05/07/2007 | Court Reporter: Marcia Gahring |
| 05/07/2007 | People represented by George W. McFetridge Jr., Deputy District Attorney, present. |
| 05/07/2007 | Brian Cretney makes a special appearance for Robert M Brodney, Retained Attorney. Defendant present. |
| 05/07/2007 | First Amended Complaint filed by Orange County District Attorney. |
| 05/07/2007 | First Amended Complaint now charges COUNT 20, 529(3) PC, FELONY, date of violation 02/08/2006. |
| 05/07/2007 | First Amended Complaint now charges COUNT 21, 496(a) PC, FELONY, date of violation 02/08/2006. |
| 05/07/2007 | First Amended Complaint now charges COUNT 22, 530.5(a) PC, FELONY, date of violation 01/30/2006. |
| 05/07/2007 | First Amended Complaint now charges COUNT 23, 530.5(a) PC, FELONY, date of violation 02/08/2006. |
| 05/07/2007 | First Amended Complaint now charges COUNT 24, 470(d) PC, FELONY, date of violation 02/07/2006. |
| 05/07/2007 | First Amended Complaint now charges COUNT 25, 496(a) PC, FELONY, date of violation 02/08/2006. |
| 05/07/2007 | First Amended Complaint now charges COUNT 26, 11377(a) HS, FELONY, date of violation 02/08/2006. |
| 05/07/2007 | First Amended Complaint now charges COUNT 27, 496(a) PC, FELONY, date of violation 02/08/2006. |
| 05/07/2007 | First Amended Complaint now charges COUNT 28, 459-460(b) PC, FELONY, date of violation 02/07/2006. |
| 05/07/2007 | First Amended Complaint now charges COUNT 29, 476 PC, FELONY, date of violation 02/07/2006. |
| 05/07/2007 | First Amended Complaint now charges COUNT 30, 459-460(b) PC, FELONY, date of violation 02/06/2006. |
| 05/07/2007 | First Amended Complaint now charges COUNT 31, 476 PC, FELONY, date of violation 02/06/2006. |
| 05/07/2007 | First Amended Complaint now charges COUNT 32, 459-460(b) PC, FELONY, date of violation 02/07/2006. |
| 05/07/2007 | First Amended Complaint now charges COUNT 33, 476 PC, FELONY, date of violation 02/07/2006. |
| 05/07/2007 | First Amended Complaint now charges COUNT 34, 459-460(b) PC, FELONY, date of violation 02/07/2006. |
| 05/07/2007 | First Amended Complaint now charges COUNT 35, 476 PC, FELONY, date of violation 02/07/2006. |
| 05/07/2007 | First Amended Complaint now charges COUNT 36, 459-460(b) PC, FELONY, date of violation 02/07/2006. |
| 05/07/2007 | First Amended Complaint now charges COUNT 37, 476 PC, FELONY, date of violation 02/07/2006. |

# MINUTES

Case : 06HF2202

Name : ▇▇▇▇▇▇▇▇▇

02/01/2019 10:01:46 AM

| Date of Action | Text |
| --- | --- |
| 05/07/2007 | First Amended Complaint now charges COUNT 38, 459-460(b) PC, FELONY, date of violation 02/06/2006. |
| 05/07/2007 | First Amended Complaint now charges COUNT 39, 476 PC, FELONY, date of violation 02/06/2006. |
| 05/07/2007 | First Amended Complaint now charges COUNT 40, 459-460(b) PC, FELONY, date of violation 02/07/2006. |
| 05/07/2007 | First Amended Complaint now charges COUNT 41, 476 PC, FELONY, date of violation 02/07/2006. |
| 05/07/2007 | First Amended Complaint now charges COUNT 42, 459-460(b) PC, FELONY, date of violation 12/10/2005. |
| 05/07/2007 | First Amended Complaint now charges COUNT 43, 476 PC, FELONY, date of violation 12/10/2005. |
| 05/07/2007 | First Amended Complaint now charges COUNT 44, 459-460(b) PC, FELONY, date of violation 11/21/2005. |
| 05/07/2007 | First Amended Complaint now charges COUNT 45, 476 PC, FELONY, date of violation 11/21/2005. |
| 05/07/2007 | First Amended Complaint now charges COUNT 46, 459-460(b) PC, FELONY, date of violation 12/19/2005. |
| 05/07/2007 | First Amended Complaint now charges COUNT 47, 476 PC, FELONY, date of violation 12/19/2005. |
| 05/07/2007 | First Amended Complaint now charges COUNT 48, 459-460(b) PC, FELONY, date of violation 12/24/2005. |
| 05/07/2007 | First Amended Complaint now charges COUNT 49, 476 PC, FELONY, date of violation 12/24/2005. |
| 05/07/2007 | First Amended Complaint now charges COUNT 50, 459-460(b) PC, FELONY, date of violation 12/11/2005. |
| 05/07/2007 | First Amended Complaint now charges COUNT 51, 476 PC, FELONY, date of violation 12/11/2005. |
| 05/07/2007 | First Amended Complaint now charges COUNT 52, 459-460(b) PC, FELONY, date of violation 02/06/2006. |
| 05/07/2007 | First Amended Complaint now charges COUNT 53, 476 PC, FELONY, date of violation 02/06/2006. |
| 05/07/2007 | First Amended Complaint now charges COUNT 54, 459-460(b) PC, FELONY, date of violation 01/25/2006. |
| 05/07/2007 | First Amended Complaint now charges COUNT 55, 476 PC, FELONY, date of violation 01/25/2006. |
| 05/07/2007 | First Amended Complaint now charges COUNT 56, 496(a) PC, FELONY, date of violation 02/08/2006. |
| 05/07/2007 | First Amended Complaint now charges COUNT 57, 496(a) PC, FELONY, date of violation 02/08/2006. |
| 05/07/2007 | First Amended Complaint now charges COUNT 58, 496(a) PC, FELONY, date of violation 02/08/2006. |
| 05/07/2007 | First Amended Complaint now charges COUNT 59, 496(a) PC, FELONY, date of violation 02/08/2006. |
| 05/07/2007 | First Amended Complaint now charges COUNT 60, 496(a) PC, FELONY, date of violation 01/30/2006. |
| 05/07/2007 | Copy of First Amended Complaint given to counsel. |

# MINUTES

Case : 06HF2202

Name : ▮▮▮▮▮▮▮▮                                          02/01/2019 10:01:46 AM

| Date of Action | Text |
|---|---|
| 05/07/2007 | Counsel acknowledges receipt of the complaint. |
| 05/07/2007 | Defendant waives reading and advisement of the First Amended Complaint. |
| 05/07/2007 | To the First Amended Complaint defendant pleads NOT GUILTY to all counts. |
| 05/07/2007 | Defense reserves all motions. |
| 05/07/2007 | Pre Trial set on 05/21/2007 at 08:30 AM in Department H2. |
| 05/07/2007 | Preliminary Hearing set on 06/05/2007 at 08:30 AM in Department H2. |
| 05/07/2007 | Court finds the defendant understandingly, knowingly, and voluntarily waives the right to a Preliminary Hearing within 10 court days of arraignment. |
| 05/07/2007 | Counsel joins in waivers. |
| 05/07/2007 | Defendant ordered to appear. |
| 05/07/2007 | Present bail deemed sufficient and continued. |
| 05/07/2007 | Keep with companion cases(s) 07HF0020 and 03SF0869. |
| 05/21/2007 | Hearing held on 05/21/2007 at 08:30:00 AM in Department H2 for Pre Trial. |
| 05/21/2007 | Officiating Judge: Kelly MacEachern, Judge |
| 05/21/2007 | Clerk: C. B. Henderson |
| 05/21/2007 | Bailiff: J. Winovich |
| 05/21/2007 | Court Reporter: Marcia Gahring |
| 05/21/2007 | People represented by George W. McFetridge Jr., Deputy District Attorney, present. |
| 05/21/2007 | Lloyd Freeberg, Retained Attorney, substituting in as Attorney of Record. |
| 05/21/2007 | Robert M Brodney relieved as Counsel of Record. |
| 05/21/2007 | Defendant present in Court with counsel Lloyd Freeberg, Retained Attorney. |
| 05/21/2007 | Pre Trial set on 06/07/2007 at 08:30 AM in Department H2. |
| 05/21/2007 | Preliminary Hearing set on 06/28/2007 at 08:30 AM in Department H2. |
| 05/21/2007 | Defendant waives statutory time for Preliminary Hearing. |
| 05/21/2007 | Defendant ordered to appear. |
| 05/21/2007 | Present bail deemed sufficient and continued. |
| 05/21/2007 | Keep with companion cases(s) 03SF0869 and 07HF0020. |
| 05/22/2007 | PH set on 06/05/07 at 08:30 AM in H2 has been cancelled. |
| 06/07/2007 | Hearing held on 06/07/2007 at 08:30:00 AM in Department H2 for Pre Trial. |
| 06/07/2007 | Officiating Judge: Peter J. Polos, Judge |
| 06/07/2007 | Clerk: T. Hauck |
| 06/07/2007 | Bailiff: J. Winovich |
| 06/07/2007 | Court Reporter: Marcia Gahring |
| 06/07/2007 | People represented by George W. McFetridge Jr., Deputy District Attorney, present. |
| 06/07/2007 | Martin Joseph Heneghan makes a special appearance for Lloyd Freeberg, Retained Attorney. Defendant present. |
| 06/07/2007 | Pretrial off calendar, Preliminary Hearing set on 06/28/2007 at 08:30 AM in H2 to remain. |
| 06/07/2007 | Defendant ordered to appear. |
| 06/07/2007 | Present bail deemed sufficient and continued. |
| 06/07/2007 | Keep with companion cases(s) 07HF0020, 03SF0869. |

# MINUTES

Case : 06HF2202

Name : ████████████

02/01/2019 10:01:46 AM

| Date of Action | Text |
|---|---|
| 06/28/2007 | Hearing held on 06/28/2007 at 08:30:00 AM in Department H2 for Preliminary Hearing. |
| 06/28/2007 | Officiating Judge: Peter J. Polos, Judge |
| 06/28/2007 | Clerk: C. B. Henderson |
| 06/28/2007 | Bailiff: P. Ada |
| 06/28/2007 | Court Reporter: Marcia Gahring |
| 06/28/2007 | People represented by George W. McFetridge Jr., Deputy District Attorney, present. |
| 06/28/2007 | James Sweeney makes a special appearance for Lloyd Freeberg, Retained Attorney. Defendant present. |
| 06/28/2007 | Pre Trial set on 08/01/2007 at 08:30 AM in Department H2. |
| 06/28/2007 | Defendant waives reasonable time. (Entered NUNC_PRO_TUNC on 07/02/07) |
| 06/28/2007 | Defendant ordered to appear. |
| 06/28/2007 | Present bail deemed sufficient and continued. |
| 06/28/2007 | Keep with companion cases(s) 07HF0020 and 03SF0869. |
| 07/02/2007 | Nunc Pro Tunc entry(s) made on this date for 06/28/2007. |
| 08/01/2007 | Hearing held on 08/01/2007 at 08:30:00 AM in Department H2 for Pre Trial. |
| 08/01/2007 | Officiating Judge: Kelly MacEachern, Judge |
| 08/01/2007 | Clerk: T. Hauck |
| 08/01/2007 | Bailiff: L. Martinez |
| 08/01/2007 | Court Reporter: Lori Shepherd |
| 08/01/2007 | People represented by George W. McFetridge Jr., Deputy District Attorney, present. |
| 08/01/2007 | Defendant present in Court with counsel Freeberg, Lloyd, Retained Attorney. |
| 08/01/2007 | Pre Trial set on 10/04/2007 at 08:30 AM in Department H2. |
| 08/01/2007 | Probation Department ordered to prepare a Pre-Plea report to be made available to court and counsel 5 days prior to Sentencing. |
| 08/01/2007 | Defendant is ordered to pay for probation report as determined by the Probation Department. |
| 08/01/2007 | Defendant waives statutory time for Preliminary Hearing. |
| 08/01/2007 | Counsel joins in waivers. |
| 08/01/2007 | Defendant ordered to appear. |
| 08/01/2007 | Present bail deemed sufficient and continued. |
| 08/01/2007 | Keep with companion cases(s) 07HF0020, 03SF0869. |
| 10/04/2007 | Hearing held on 10/04/2007 at 08:30:00 AM in Department H2 for Pre Trial. |
| 10/04/2007 | Officiating Judge: James Odriozola, Commissioner |
| 10/04/2007 | Clerk: C. Le |
| 10/04/2007 | Bailiff:. Present |
| 10/04/2007 | Court Reporter: Michelle Lott-Megenhofer |
| 10/04/2007 | Minutes entered by S. Bartush. |
| 10/04/2007 | People represented by George W. McFetridge Jr., Deputy District Attorney, present. |
| 10/04/2007 | Defendant present in Court with counsel Lloyd Freeberg, Retained Attorney. |
| 10/04/2007 | Pre Trial set on 11/06/2007 at 08:30 AM in Department H2. |
| 10/04/2007 | Defendant waives statutory time for Preliminary Hearing. |

# MINUTES

Case : 06HF2202

Name : ▮▮▮▮▮▮▮▮▮▮

02/01/2019 10:01:46 AM

| Date of Action | Text |
|---|---|
| 10/04/2007 | Present bail deemed sufficient and continued. |
| 10/04/2007 | Keep with companion cases(s) 07HF0020. |
| 10/04/2007 | Pre plea filed. |
| 11/06/2007 | Hearing held on 11/06/2007 at 08:30:00 AM in Department H2 for Pre Trial. |
| 11/06/2007 | Officiating Judge: Gregory W. Jones, Commissioner |
| 11/06/2007 | Clerk: M. Johnson |
| 11/06/2007 | Bailiff: I. Hamdallah |
| 11/06/2007 | Court Reporter: Karen Puckett |
| 11/06/2007 | People represented by George W. McFetridge Jr., Deputy District Attorney, present. |
| 11/06/2007 | Defendant present in Court with counsel Freeberg, Lloyd, Retained Attorney. |
| 11/06/2007 | Pre Trial continued to 11/29/2007 at 08:30 AM in Department H2 at request of Defense. |
| 11/06/2007 | Court finds the defendant understandingly, knowingly, and voluntarily waives the right to a Preliminary Hearing within 60 calendar days of arraignment. |
| 11/06/2007 | Counsel joins in waivers. |
| 11/06/2007 | Defendant ordered to return. |
| 11/06/2007 | Present bail deemed sufficient and continued. |
| 11/29/2007 | Hearing held on 11/29/2007 at 08:30:00 AM in Department H2 for Pre Trial. |
| 11/29/2007 | Officiating Judge: James Odriozola, Commissioner |
| 11/29/2007 | Clerk: K. Reinke |
| 11/29/2007 | Bailiff: I. Hamdallah |
| 11/29/2007 | Court Reporter: Roxanne Drake |
| 11/29/2007 | People represented by George W. McFetridge Jr., Deputy District Attorney, present. |
| 11/29/2007 | Defendant present in Court with counsel Freeberg, Lloyd, Retained Attorney. |
| 11/29/2007 | Pre Trial set on 12/11/2007 at 08:30 AM in Department H2. |
| 11/29/2007 | Defendant waives reasonable time. |
| 11/29/2007 | Counsel joins in waivers. |
| 11/29/2007 | Present bail deemed sufficient and continued. |
| 11/29/2007 | Release status of defendant entered in error. Correct release status should reflect: Released on Bond. |
| 12/11/2007 | Hearing held on 12/11/2007 at 08:30:00 AM in Department H2 for Pre Trial. |
| 12/11/2007 | Officiating Judge: Gregory W. Jones, Commissioner |
| 12/11/2007 | Clerk: K. Reinke |
| 12/11/2007 | Bailiff: B. Cate |
| 12/11/2007 | Court Reporter: Tina O'Rourke |
| 12/11/2007 | People represented by George W. McFetridge Jr., Deputy District Attorney, present. |
| 12/11/2007 | Douglas Myers makes a special appearance for Lloyd Freeberg, Retained Attorney. Defendant present. |
| 12/11/2007 | All Parties being advised of their right to have this matter heard by a Judge of the court have stipulated that the matter be heard by Commissioner Gregory W. Jones. |
| 12/11/2007 | Stipulation for Court Commissioner filed. |
| 12/11/2007 | Defendant advised of and waives the following: |

# MINUTES

Case : 06HF2202

Name : [REDACTED]

02/01/2019 10:01:46 AM

| Date of Action | Text |
|---|---|
| 12/11/2007 | - The right to a trial by Jury. |
| 12/11/2007 | - The right to confront and cross-examine witnesses. |
| 12/11/2007 | - The right against self incrimination. |
| 12/11/2007 | Defendant waives the right to subpoena and present evidence. |
| 12/11/2007 | Defendant's motion to WITHDRAW NOT GUILTY PLEA to count(s) 11, 16, 21, 24, 40, 46, 54 granted. |
| 12/11/2007 | Court finds defendant intelligently and voluntarily waives legal and constitutional rights to jury trial, confront and examine witnesses, and to remain silent. |
| 12/11/2007 | To the First Amended Complaint defendant pleads GUILTY as to count(s) 11, 16, 21, 24, 40, 46, 54. |
| 12/11/2007 | Defendant's written waiver of legal and constitutional rights for guilty plea received and ordered filed. |
| 12/11/2007 | Addendum to the Advisement and Waiver of Rights for a Felony Guilty Plea filed. |
| 12/11/2007 | Letter from Wings program, Memo from District Attorney's office filed. |
| 12/11/2007 | Court finds factual basis and accepts plea. |
| 12/11/2007 | Defendant advised of the possible consequences of plea affecting deportation and citizenship. |
| 12/11/2007 | Defendant advised of maximum possible sentence. |
| 12/11/2007 | Defendant advised of consequences of violating probation and parole. |
| 12/11/2007 | This constitutes a prior conviction. |
| 12/11/2007 | Counsel joins in waivers, pleas, and admissions. |
| 12/11/2007 | Defendant waives arraignment for sentencing. |
| 12/11/2007 | Defendant requests immediate sentencing. |
| 12/11/2007 | Probation report waived. |
| 12/11/2007 | No legal cause why judgment should not be pronounced and defendant having been convicted of 530.5(a) PC as charged in count 11, defendant is sentenced to STATE PRISON for Middle term of 2 Year(s) . |
| 12/11/2007 | Defendant has also Pled Guilty to the additional charge of 470b PC in count 16 and is sentenced to STATE PRISON for 1/3 the mid term of 8 Months. Sentence imposed to be served consecutive 1/3 non-violent to count 11. |
| 12/11/2007 | Defendant has also Pled Guilty to the additional charge of 496(a) PC in count 21 and is sentenced to STATE PRISON for 1/3 the mid term of 8 Months. Sentence imposed to be served consecutive 1/3 non-violent to count 11. |
| 12/11/2007 | Defendant has also Pled Guilty to the additional charge of 470(d) PC in count 24 and is sentenced to STATE PRISON for 1/3 the mid term of 8 Months. Sentence imposed to be served consecutive 1/3 non-violent to count 11. |
| 12/11/2007 | Defendant has also Pled Guilty to the additional charge of 459-460(b) PC in count 40 and is sentenced to STATE PRISON for 1/3 the mid term of 8 Months. Sentence imposed to be served consecutive 1/3 non-violent to count 11. |
| 12/11/2007 | Defendant has also Pled Guilty to the additional charge of 459-460(b) PC in count 46 and is sentenced to STATE PRISON for 1/3 the mid term of 8 Months. Sentence imposed to be served consecutive 1/3 non-violent to count 11. |
| 12/11/2007 | Defendant has also Pled Guilty to the additional charge of 459-460(b) PC in count 54 and is sentenced to STATE PRISON for 1/3 the mid term of 8 Months. Sentence imposed to be served consecutive 1/3 non-violent to count 11. |

# MINUTES

Case : 06HF2202

Name :  ███████████

02/01/2019 10:01:46 AM

| Date of Action | Text |
|---|---|
| 12/11/2007 | Execution of State Prison sentence is suspended and defendant is placed on 3 Year(s) FORMAL PROBATION as to count(s) 11, 16, 21, 24, 40, 46, 54 on the following terms and conditions: |
| 12/11/2007 | Violate no law. |
| 12/11/2007 | Serve 408 Day(s) Orange County Jail as to count(s) 11, 16, 21, 24, 40, 46, 54. |
| 12/11/2007 | Credit for time served: 272 actual, 136 conduct, totaling 408 days. |
| 12/11/2007 | Pay $200.00 Restitution Fine pursuant to Penal Code 1202.4 or Penal Code 1202.4(b). |
| 12/11/2007 | Pay Security Fee(s) pursuant to Penal Code 1465.8 totaling $140.00. |
| 12/11/2007 | Pay $200.00 Probation Revocation Restitution Fine pursuant to Penal Code 1202.44. Restitution fine stayed, to become effective only upon final revocation of probation. |
| 12/11/2007 | All fees payable through the Probation Department. |
| 12/11/2007 | Court finds restitution has been paid in full in the amount of $29, 395.36 |
| 12/11/2007 | Submit to DNA testing pursuant to Penal Code 296. |
| 12/11/2007 | Use no unauthorized drugs, narcotics, or controlled substances. Submit to drug or narcotic testing as directed by Probation Officer or Police Officer. |
| 12/11/2007 | Submit your person and property including any residence, premises, container, or vehicle under your control to search and seizure at any time of the day or night by any law enforcement or probation officer with or without a warrant, and with or without reasonable cause or reasonable suspicion. |
| 12/11/2007 | Cooperate with Probation Officer in any plan for psychiatric, psychological, alcohol and/or drug treatment, or counseling. |
| 12/11/2007 | Do not possess any other persons' personal identifying information or personal financial information unless approved in advance by your probation officer. |
| 12/11/2007 | Do not have blank checks in your possession, nor write any portion of any checks, nor have checking account, nor use or possess credit cards or open credit accounts unless approved. |
| 12/11/2007 | Do not own, use, or possess any type of dangerous or deadly weapon including any firearms or ammunition. |
| 12/11/2007 | Defendant provided a copy of "Prohibited Persons Notice Form and Power of Attorney for Firearms and Disposal" pursuant to Penal Code 12021(d)(2). |
| 12/11/2007 | Obey all laws, orders, rules, and regulations of the Court, Jail, and Probation. |
| 12/11/2007 | Disclose terms and conditions of probation when asked by any law enforcement or probation officer. |
| 12/11/2007 | Defendant will complete teh Nancy Clerk rehabilitation program for one year |
| 12/11/2007 | Pay the costs of probation based on the ability to pay as directed by the Probation Officer. |
| 12/11/2007 | Defendant is required to complete a new financial disclosure form if money is still owing on a restitution order or fine 120 days before the scheduled release from probation. Defendant is required to file the form with the court at least 90 days before the scheduled release from probation. |
| 12/11/2007 | Count(s) 1, 2, 3, 4, 5, 6, 7, 8, 9, 10 DISMISSED - Motion of People. |
| 12/11/2007 | Count(s) 12, 13, 14, 15, 17, 18, 19, 20 DISMISSED - Motion of People. |
| 12/11/2007 | Count(s) 22, 23, 25, 26, 27, 28, 29, 30 DISMISSED - Motion of People. |
| 12/11/2007 | Count(s) 31, 32, 33, 34, 35, 36, 37, 38, 39 DISMISSED - Motion of People. |
| 12/11/2007 | Count(s) 41, 42, 43, 44, 45, 47, 48, 49, 50 DISMISSED - Motion of People. |

# MINUTES

Case : 06HF2202

Name :

02/01/2019 10:01:46 AM

| Date of Action | Text |
|---|---|
| 12/11/2007 | Count(s) 51, 52, 53, 55, 56, 57, 58, 59, 60 DISMISSED - Motion of People. |
| 12/11/2007 | Complete 1 year Nancy Clark program |
| 12/11/2007 | Defendant accepts terms and conditions of probation. |
| 12/11/2007 | Court orders bail bond # S100-01136444 exonerated. |
| 12/11/2007 | DMV Request Deleted. DMV interface DD1 request deleted - No violations to report |
| 12/15/2007 | DOJ Initial Abstract sent. |
| 03/11/2008 | Case calendared on 03/11/08 at 09:30 AM in H2 for MTN MOP. |
| 03/11/2008 | Hearing held on 03/11/2008 at 09:30:00 AM in Department H2 for Motion Modification of Probation. |
| 03/11/2008 | Officiating Judge: James Odriozola, Commissioner |
| 03/11/2008 | Clerk: M. Johnson |
| 03/11/2008 | Bailiff: I. Hamdallah |
| 03/11/2008 | Court Reporter: Marcia Gahring |
| 03/11/2008 | People represented by Chris Kralick, Deputy District Attorney, present. |
| 03/11/2008 | Defendant present in Court without counsel. |
| 03/11/2008 | Motion by Defense to complete Southern California Community Recovery Center in lieu of Nancy Clark Program |
| 03/11/2008 | Motion granted. |
| 03/11/2008 | Defendant to complete the Southern California Community Recovery Center Program |
| 03/11/2008 | Memorandum from Probation filed. |
| 03/11/2008 | Correspondence from Southern California Community Recovery Center filed. |
| 03/11/2008 | All terms and conditions of probation are to remain the same. |
| 04/10/2009 | Probation Violation re: Arraignment set on 04/13/2009 at 09:00 AM in Department C58. |
| 04/10/2009 | Defendant's release status updated to reflect: In Custody. |
| 04/10/2009 | Court orders bail set at NO BAIL. |
| 04/10/2009 | Probation Violation Petition dated 04/09/2009 filed. |
| 04/13/2009 | Hearing held on 04/13/2009 at 09:00:00 AM in Department C58 for Probation Violation Arraignment. |
| 04/13/2009 | # 5 on calendar. |
| 04/13/2009 | Officiating Judge: Robert R. Fitzgerald, Judge |
| 04/13/2009 | Clerk: B. Ard |
| 04/13/2009 | Bailiff: D. Scrip |
| 04/13/2009 | Court Reporter: Caryl Axton |
| 04/13/2009 | People represented by Amy Swanson, Deputy District Attorney, present. |
| 04/13/2009 | Defendant present in Court with counsel Freeberg, Lloyd, Retained Attorney. |
| 04/13/2009 | This case is an execution of sentence suspended and is being returned to the sentencing Judge. Judge Gregory Jones. |
| 04/13/2009 | Probation Violation re: Arraignment set on 05/01/2009 at 09:00 AM in Department H2. |
| 04/13/2009 | Probation ordered revoked as to count(s) 11, 16, 21, 24, 40, 46, 54. |
| 04/13/2009 | Defendant ordered to appear. |
| 04/13/2009 | Defendant remanded to the custody of the Sheriff. |

# MINUTES

Case : 06HF2202

Name : ▇▇▇▇▇▇▇▇                                    02/01/2019 10:01:46 AM

| Date of Action | Text |
|---|---|
| 04/13/2009 | Current bail set for defendant to remain. |
| 04/13/2009 | Notice to Sheriff issued. |
| 05/01/2009 | Hearing held on 05/01/2009 at 09:00:00 AM in Department H2 for Probation Violation Arraignment. |
| 05/01/2009 | Officiating Judge: Gregory W. Jones, Judge |
| 05/01/2009 | Clerk: K. Reinke |
| 05/01/2009 | Bailiff: B. Cate |
| 05/01/2009 | Court Reporter: Donna Wagner |
| 05/01/2009 | Erin Rowe made a special appearance for District Attorney Jan Christie. |
| 05/01/2009 | Defendant present in Court with counsel Freeberg, Lloyd, Retained Attorney. |
| 05/01/2009 | Probation Violation re: Arraignment continued to 05/29/2009 at 08:30 AM in Department H2 at request of Defense. |
| 05/01/2009 | Defendant waives statutory time for Hearing. |
| 05/01/2009 | Counsel joins in waivers. |
| 05/01/2009 | Defendant ordered to return. |
| 05/01/2009 | Current bail set for defendant to remain. |
| 05/01/2009 | Defendant remanded to the custody of the Sheriff. |
| 05/01/2009 | Notice to Sheriff issued. |
| 05/01/2009 | Keep with companion cases(s) 07HF0020. |
| 05/29/2009 | Hearing held on 05/29/2009 at 08:30:00 AM in Department H2 for Probation Violation Arraignment. |
| 05/29/2009 | Officiating Judge: Karen L. Robinson, Judge |
| 05/29/2009 | Clerk: L. Lesar |
| 05/29/2009 | Bailiff: C. S. Rozean |
| 05/29/2009 | Court Reporter: Donna Wagner |
| 05/29/2009 | Van C. Ho, certified law clerk, appearing specially on the behalf of George McFettride, District Attorney |
| 05/29/2009 | Defendant present in Court with counsel Freeberg, Lloyd, Retained Attorney. |
| 05/29/2009 | Probation Violation re: Arraignment continued to 06/12/2009 at 08:30 AM in Department H2 at request of Defense. |
| 05/29/2009 | Defendant waives statutory time for Sentencing. |
| 05/29/2009 | Counsel joins in waivers. |
| 05/29/2009 | Defendant ordered to return. |
| 05/29/2009 | Current bail set for defendant to remain. |
| 05/29/2009 | Defendant remanded to the custody of the Sheriff. |
| 05/29/2009 | Notice to Sheriff issued. |
| 05/29/2009 | Keep with companion cases(s) 07HF0020. |
| 05/29/2009 | Minutes entered by K. Reinke. |
| 06/12/2009 | Hearing held on 06/12/2009 at 08:30:00 AM in Department H2 for Probation Violation Arraignment. |
| 06/12/2009 | Officiating Judge: Karen L. Robinson, Judge |
| 06/12/2009 | Clerk: L. Lesar |

SUPERIOR COURT OF CALIFORNIA, COUNTY OF ORANGE

# MINUTES

Case : 06HF2202

Name : ████████████

02/01/2019 10:01:46 AM

| Date of Action | Text |
|---|---|
| 06/12/2009 | Bailiff: C. S. Rozean |
| 06/12/2009 | Court Reporter: Donna Wagner |
| 06/12/2009 | Van Ha, Law Clerk present under supervision of Erin Rowe, Deputy District Attorney specially appearing for George McFettride, Deputy District Attorney |
| 06/12/2009 | Erin Rowe made a special appearance for District Attorney George W. McFetridge Jr.. |
| 06/12/2009 | Probation Violation re: Arraignment continued to 06/15/2009 at 08:30 AM in Department H2 by stipulation of all parties. |
| 06/12/2009 | Defendant waives statutory time for Hearing. |
| 06/12/2009 | Counsel joins in waivers. |
| 06/12/2009 | Defendant ordered to appear. |
| 06/12/2009 | Defendant remanded to the custody of the Sheriff. |
| 06/12/2009 | Current bail set for defendant to remain. |
| 06/12/2009 | Notice to Sheriff issued. |
| 06/12/2009 | Keep with companion cases(s) 07HF0020. |
| 06/15/2009 | Hearing held on 06/15/2009 at 08:30:00 AM in Department H2 for Probation Violation Arraignment. |
| 06/15/2009 | Officiating Judge: Gregory W. Jones, Judge |
| 06/15/2009 | Clerk: C. Le |
| 06/15/2009 | Bailiff: I. Hamdallah |
| 06/15/2009 | Court Reporter: Starlette Soniega-Armijo |
| 06/15/2009 | Van Ha, Certified Law Clerk, appearing specially on behalf of George McFettride, Deputy District Attorney. |
| 06/15/2009 | Defendant present in Court with counsel Lloyd Freeberg, Retained Attorney. |
| 06/15/2009 | Defendant advised of legal and constitutional rights. |
| 06/15/2009 | Defendant waives right to probation hearing. Defendant admits violation of probation as to count(s) 11, 16, 21, 24, 40, 46, 54. |
| 06/15/2009 | Court finds defendant in violation of probation. |
| 06/15/2009 | Defendant waives arraignment for sentencing. |
| 06/15/2009 | Counsel joins in waivers. |
| 06/15/2009 | Defendant waives statutory time for Sentencing. |
| 06/15/2009 | Sentencing set on 08/07/2009 at 08:30 AM in Department H2. |
| 06/15/2009 | Defendant ordered to appear. |
| 06/15/2009 | Current bail set for defendant to remain. |
| 06/15/2009 | Defendant remanded to the custody of the Sheriff. |
| 06/15/2009 | Notice to Sheriff issued. |
| 06/15/2009 | Keep with companion cases(s) 07HF0020. |
| 06/15/2009 | Probation Department ordered to prepare a Probation & Sentencing report to be made available to court and counsel 5 days prior to Sentencing. |
| 06/15/2009 | Drug Information from Sav-On Pharmacy filed. |
| 06/15/2009 | Correspondence from Theodore G Williams, M.D filed. |
| 06/15/2009 | Forensic Psychological Evaluations from James Gruver, Ph. D., Licensed Psychologist, Dated 05-23-09, placed in confidential envelope and filed. |

SUPERIOR COURT OF CALIFORNIA, COUNTY OF ORANGE

# MINUTES

Case : 06HF2202

Name : Ashaary, Kiarash

02/01/2019 10:01:46 AM

| Date of Action | Text |
|---|---|
| 08/07/2009 | Hearing held on 08/07/2009 at 08:30:00 AM in Department H2 for Sentencing. |
| 08/07/2009 | Officiating Judge: Gregory W. Jones, Judge |
| 08/07/2009 | Clerk: L. Trottier |
| 08/07/2009 | Bailiff: B. Cate |
| 08/07/2009 | Court Reporter: Donna Wagner |
| 08/07/2009 | Minutes entered by T. Lewis. |
| 08/07/2009 | People represented by Beth Carmichael, Deputy District Attorney, present. |
| 08/07/2009 | Defendant present in Court with counsel Freeberg, Lloyd, Retained Attorney. |
| 08/07/2009 | Sentencing continued to 08/21/2009 at 08:30 AM in Department H2 at request of Defense. |
| 08/07/2009 | Defendant ordered to return. |
| 08/07/2009 | Defendant waives statutory time for Hearing. |
| 08/07/2009 | Current bail set for defendant to remain. |
| 08/07/2009 | Defendant remanded to the custody of the Sheriff. |
| 08/07/2009 | Notice to Sheriff issued. |
| 08/07/2009 | Keep with companion cases(s) 07HF0020. |
| 08/21/2009 | Hearing held on 08/21/2009 at 08:30:00 AM in Department H2 for Sentencing. |
| 08/21/2009 | Officiating Judge: Gregory W. Jones, Judge |
| 08/21/2009 | Clerk: M. Johnson |
| 08/21/2009 | Bailiff: C. F. Cisneros |
| 08/21/2009 | Court Reporter: Donna Cox |
| 08/21/2009 | People represented by Erin Rowe, Deputy District Attorney, present. |
| 08/21/2009 | Defendant present in Court with counsel Freeberg, Lloyd, Retained Attorney. |
| 08/21/2009 | Sentencing continued to 09/25/2009 at 08:30 AM in Department H2 by stipulation of all parties. |
| 08/21/2009 | Defendant waives statutory time for Sentencing. |
| 08/21/2009 | Probation & Sentencing report filed. |
| 08/21/2009 | Counsel joins in waivers. |
| 08/21/2009 | Current bail set for defendant to remain. |
| 08/21/2009 | Defendant remanded to the custody of the Sheriff. |
| 08/21/2009 | Notice to Sheriff issued. |
| 09/25/2009 | Hearing held on 09/25/2009 at 08:30:00 AM in Department H2 for Sentencing. |
| 09/25/2009 | Officiating Judge: James Odriozola, Commissioner |
| 09/25/2009 | Clerk: L. K. Mc Donald |
| 09/25/2009 | Bailiff: B. Lohrman |
| 09/25/2009 | Court Reporter: Donna Cox |
| 09/25/2009 | People represented by George W. McFetridge Jr., Deputy District Attorney, present. |
| 09/25/2009 | Laura Lindley makes a special appearance for Lloyd Freeberg, Retained Attorney. Defendant present. |
| 09/25/2009 | Probation Violation re: Sentencing set on 10/16/2009 at 08:30 AM in Department H2. |
| 09/25/2009 | Defendant waives statutory time for Sentencing. |

SUPERIOR COURT OF CALIFORNIA, COUNTY OF ORANGE

# MINUTES

Case : 06HF2202

Name : ███████████

02/01/2019 10:01:46 AM

| Date of Action | Text |
| --- | --- |
| 09/25/2009 | Counsel joins in waivers. |
| 09/25/2009 | Defendant ordered to appear. |
| 09/25/2009 | Current bail set for defendant to remain at $0.00. |
| 09/25/2009 | Defendant remanded to the custody of the Sheriff. |
| 09/25/2009 | Notice to Sheriff issued. |
| 09/25/2009 | Keep with companion cases(s) 07HF0020. |
| 10/16/2009 | Hearing held on 10/16/2009 at 08:30:00 AM in Department H2 for Probation Violation Sentencing. |
| 10/16/2009 | Officiating Judge: Gregory W. Jones, Judge |
| 10/16/2009 | Clerk: T. Lewis |
| 10/16/2009 | Bailiff: B. Cate |
| 10/16/2009 | Court Reporter: Donna Cox |
| 10/16/2009 | People represented by George W. McFetridge Jr., Deputy District Attorney, present. |
| 10/16/2009 | Tracee May-Brewster makes a special appearance for Lloyd Freeberg, Retained Attorney. Defendant present. |
| 10/16/2009 | Probation Violation re: Sentencing continued to 10/22/2009 at 08:30 AM in Department H2 at request of Defense. |
| 10/16/2009 | Defendant ordered to return. |
| 10/16/2009 | Current bail set for defendant to remain at $0.00. |
| 10/16/2009 | Defendant remanded to the custody of the Sheriff. |
| 10/16/2009 | Notice to Sheriff issued. |
| 10/16/2009 | Keep with companion cases(s) 07HF0020. |
| 10/22/2009 | Hearing held on 10/22/2009 at 08:30:00 AM in Department H2 for Probation Violation Sentencing. |
| 10/22/2009 | Officiating Judge: Gregory W. Jones, Judge |
| 10/22/2009 | Clerk: L. Sanchez |
| 10/22/2009 | Bailiff: C. S. Rozean |
| 10/22/2009 | Court Reporter: Donna Cox |
| 10/22/2009 | People represented by Stefanie Marangi, Deputy District Attorney, present. |
| 10/22/2009 | Defendant present in Court with counsel Freeberg, Lloyd, Retained Attorney. |
| 10/22/2009 | Probation Violation re: Sentencing continued to 11/13/2009 at 08:30 AM in Department H2 by stipulation of all parties. |
| 10/22/2009 | Defendant waives statutory time for Probation Violation. |
| 10/22/2009 | Current bail set for defendant to remain at $0.00. |
| 10/22/2009 | Defendant ordered to appear. |
| 10/22/2009 | Counsel joins in waivers. |
| 10/22/2009 | Defendant remanded to the custody of the Sheriff. |
| 10/22/2009 | Notice to Sheriff issued. |
| 11/13/2009 | Hearing held on 11/13/2009 at 08:30:00 AM in Department H2 for Probation Violation Sentencing. |
| 11/13/2009 | Officiating Judge: Gregory W. Jones, Judge |
| 11/13/2009 | Clerk: L. Trottier |

SUPERIOR COURT OF CALIFORNIA, COUNTY OF ORANGE

# MINUTES

Case : 06HF2202

Name : █████████

02/01/2019 10:01:46 AM

| Date of Action | Text |
|---|---|
| 11/13/2009 | Bailiff: B. Cate |
| 11/13/2009 | Court Reporter: Donna Cox |
| 11/13/2009 | People represented by George W. McFetridge Jr., Deputy District Attorney, present. |
| 11/13/2009 | Defendant present in Court with counsel Freeberg, Lloyd, Retained Attorney. |
| 11/13/2009 | Probation Violation re: Sentencing continued to 11/24/2009 at 08:30 AM in Department H2 at request of Defense. |
| 11/13/2009 | Defendant ordered to appear. |
| 11/13/2009 | Counsel joins in waivers. |
| 11/13/2009 | Current bail set for defendant to remain at $0.00. |
| 11/13/2009 | Defendant remanded to the custody of the Sheriff. |
| 11/13/2009 | Notice to Sheriff issued. |
| 11/13/2009 | Keep with companion cases(s) 07HF0020. |
| 11/24/2009 | Hearing held on 11/24/2009 at 08:30:00 AM in Department H2 for Probation Violation Sentencing. |
| 11/24/2009 | Officiating Judge: Robert Gannon, Judge |
| 11/24/2009 | Clerk: L. Taylor |
| 11/24/2009 | Bailiff: C. S. Rozean |
| 11/24/2009 | Court Reporter: Donna Cox |
| 11/24/2009 | People represented by Cheryl Gold, Deputy District Attorney, present. |
| 11/24/2009 | Defendant present in Court with counsel Freeberg, Lloyd, Retained Attorney. |
| 11/24/2009 | Defendant waives statutory time for Sentencing. |
| 11/24/2009 | Defendant requests immediate sentencing. |
| 11/24/2009 | Court orders probation reinstated and modified as to count(s) 11, 16, 21, 24, 40, 46, 54 as follows: |
| 11/24/2009 | STATE PRISON sentence previously suspended on 12/11/2007 as to count(s) 11 now IMPOSED. |
| 11/24/2009 | STATE PRISON sentence previously suspended on 12/11/2007 as to count(s) 16 now IMPOSED. |
| 11/24/2009 | STATE PRISON sentence previously suspended on 12/11/2007 as to count(s) 21 now IMPOSED. |
| 11/24/2009 | STATE PRISON sentence previously suspended on 12/11/2007 as to count(s) 24 now IMPOSED. |
| 11/24/2009 | STATE PRISON sentence previously suspended on 12/11/2007 as to count(s) 40 now IMPOSED. |
| 11/24/2009 | STATE PRISON sentence previously suspended on 12/11/2007 as to count(s) 46 now IMPOSED. |
| 11/24/2009 | STATE PRISON sentence previously suspended on 12/11/2007 as to count(s) 54 now IMPOSED. |
| 11/24/2009 | Total term to be served in State Prison is 6 Year(s)  . |
| 11/24/2009 | COURT ORDERS State Prison sentence VACATED. (Entered NUNC_PRO_TUNC on 07/05/11) |
| 11/24/2009 | The Court orders State Prison sentence credit ordered on 12/11/2007 vacated. (Entered NUNC_PRO_TUNC on 07/05/11) |

Case : 06HF2202

Name : ▮▮▮▮▮▮▮▮

02/01/2019 10:01:46 AM

| Date of Action | Text |
|---|---|
| 11/24/2009 | No legal cause why judgment should not be pronounced and defendant having been convicted of 530.5(a) PC as charged in count 11, defendant is sentenced to STATE PRISON for Middle term of 2 Year(s) 0 Months. (Entered NUNC_PRO_TUNC on 07/05/11) |
| 11/24/2009 | Defendant has also Pled Guilty to the additional charge of 470b PC in count 16 and is sentenced to STATE PRISON for 1/3 the mid term of 0 Year(s) 8 Months. Sentence imposed to be served consecutive 1/3 non-violent to count 11. (Entered NUNC_PRO_TUNC on 07/05/11) |
| 11/24/2009 | Defendant has also Pled Guilty to the additional charge of 496(a) PC in count 21 and is sentenced to STATE PRISON for Middle term of 2 Year(s) 0 Months. Sentence imposed to be served concurrent to count 11. (Entered NUNC_PRO_TUNC on 07/05/11) |
| 11/24/2009 | Defendant has also Pled Guilty to the additional charge of 470(d) PC in count 24 and is sentenced to STATE PRISON for Middle term of 2 Year(s) 0 Months. Sentence imposed to be served concurrent to count 11. (Entered NUNC_PRO_TUNC on 07/05/11) |
| 11/24/2009 | Defendant has also Pled Guilty to the additional charge of 459-460(b) PC in count 40 and is sentenced to STATE PRISON for Middle term of 2 Year(s) 0 Months. Sentence imposed to be served concurrent to count 11. (Entered NUNC_PRO_TUNC on 07/05/11) |
| 11/24/2009 | Defendant has also Pled Guilty to the additional charge of 459-460(b) PC in count 46 and is sentenced to STATE PRISON for Middle term of 2 Year(s) 0 Months. Sentence imposed to be served concurrent to count 11. (Entered NUNC_PRO_TUNC on 07/05/11) |
| 11/24/2009 | Defendant has also Pled Guilty to the additional charge of 459-460(b) PC in count 54 and is sentenced to STATE PRISON for Middle term of 2 Year(s) 0 Months. Sentence imposed to be served concurrent to count 11. (Entered NUNC_PRO_TUNC on 07/05/11) |
| 11/24/2009 | Credit for time served: 485 actual, 242 conduct, totaling 727 days pursuant to Penal Code 2933(e)(1). (Entered NUNC_PRO_TUNC on 07/05/11) |
| 11/24/2009 | defendant is also awarded 367 days credit for the completed treatment program. Total custody credits are 1, 094 days. (Entered NUNC_PRO_TUNC on 07/05/11) |
| 11/24/2009 | Total term to be served in State Prison is 2 Year(s) 8 Months. (Entered NUNC_PRO_TUNC on 07/05/11) |
| 11/24/2009 | Defendant's prison term has been served. (Entered NUNC_PRO_TUNC on 07/05/11) |
| 11/24/2009 | COURT ORDERS State Prison sentence VACATED. (Entered NUNC_PRO_TUNC on 08/21/12) |
| 11/24/2009 | The Court orders State Prison sentence credit ordered on 11/24/2009 vacated. (Entered NUNC_PRO_TUNC on 08/21/12) |
| 11/24/2009 | No legal cause why judgment should not be pronounced and defendant having been convicted of 530.5(a) PC as charged in count 11, defendant is sentenced to STATE PRISON for Middle term of 2 Year(s) 0 Months. (Entered NUNC_PRO_TUNC on 08/21/12) |
| 11/24/2009 | Defendant has also Pled Guilty to the additional charge of 470b PC in count 16 and is sentenced to STATE PRISON for 1/3 the mid term of 0 Year(s) 8 Months. Sentence imposed to be served consecutive 1/3 non-violent to count 11. (Entered NUNC_PRO_TUNC on 08/21/12) |

SUPERIOR COURT OF CALIFORNIA, COUNTY OF ORANGE

# MINUTES

Case : 06HF2202

Name [redacted]                                                    02/01/2019 10:01:46 AM

| Date of Action | Text |
|---|---|
| 11/24/2009 | Defendant has also Pled Guilty to the additional charge of 496(a) PC in count 21 and is sentenced to STATE PRISON for Low term of 1 Year(s) 4 Months. Sentence imposed to be served concurrent to count 11. (Entered NUNC_PRO_TUNC on 08/21/12) |
| 11/24/2009 | Defendant has also Pled Guilty to the additional charge of 470(d) PC in count 24 and is sentenced to STATE PRISON for Low term of 1 Year(s) 4 Months. Sentence imposed to be served concurrent to count 11. (Entered NUNC_PRO_TUNC on 08/21/12) |
| 11/24/2009 | Defendant has also Pled Guilty to the additional charge of 459-460(b) PC in count 40 and is sentenced to STATE PRISON for Low term of 1 Year(s) 4 Months. Sentence imposed to be served concurrent to count 11. (Entered NUNC_PRO_TUNC on 08/21/12) |
| 11/24/2009 | Defendant has also Pled Guilty to the additional charge of 459-460(b) PC in count 46 and is sentenced to STATE PRISON for Low term of 1 Year(s) 4 Months. Sentence imposed to be served concurrent to count 11. (Entered NUNC_PRO_TUNC on 08/21/12) |
| 11/24/2009 | Defendant has also Pled Guilty to the additional charge of 459-460(b) PC in count 54 and is sentenced to STATE PRISON for Low term of 1 Year(s) 4 Months. Sentence imposed to be served concurrent to count 11. (Entered NUNC_PRO_TUNC on 08/21/12) |
| 11/24/2009 | Credit for time served: 485 actual, 242 conduct, totaling 727 days pursuant to Penal Code 2933(e)(1). (Entered NUNC_PRO_TUNC on 08/21/12) |
| 11/24/2009 | Defendant is also awarded 367 days credit for the treatment program completed, for total custody credits of 1, 094 days (Entered NUNC_PRO_TUNC on 08/21/12) |
| 11/24/2009 | Total term to be served in State Prison is 2 Year(s) 8 Months. (Entered NUNC_PRO_TUNC on 08/21/12) |
| 11/24/2009 | Defendant's prison term has been served. (Entered NUNC_PRO_TUNC on 08/21/12) |
| 11/24/2009 | Court awards custody credits as follows: 485 days Actual time 242 days Good Time Work Time 367 days program credit Totaling 1, 094 days |
| 11/24/2009 | Court deems 6 year State Prison Sentence Served |
| 11/24/2009 | Defendant to submit to DNA testing pursuant to Penal Code 296. |
| 11/24/2009 | Defendant provided a copy of "Prohibited Persons Notice Form and Power of Attorney for Firearms and Disposal" pursuant to Penal Code 12021(d)(2). |
| 11/24/2009 | Pay $200.00 Restitution Fine pursuant to Penal Code 1202.4 or Penal Code 1202.4(b). |
| 11/24/2009 | Pay $200.00 Parole Revocation Restitution Fine pursuant to Penal Code 1202.45. Parole Revocation Restitution Fine suspended unless parole is revoked. |
| 11/24/2009 | Pay $30.00 Security Fee per convicted count pursuant to Penal Code 1465.8. |
| 11/24/2009 | Pay Criminal Conviction Assessment Fee per convicted count of $30.00 per misdemeanor/felony and $35.00 per infraction pursuant to Government Code 70373(a)(1). |
| 11/24/2009 | Court orders all fees payable through the Department of Corrections. |
| 11/24/2009 | Defendant released on this case only. Release issued. |
| 11/24/2009 | Notice to Sheriff issued. |

SUPERIOR COURT OF CALIFORNIA, COUNTY OF ORANGE

# MINUTES

Case : 06HF2202

Name : ▮▮▮▮▮▮▮▮▮▮▮                                      02/01/2019 10:01:46 AM

| Date of Action | Text |
|---|---|
| 11/24/2009 | Defendant ordered to report to Department of Corrections Parole Department located at:<br>1600 No. Main St.<br>Santa Ana, Ca 92702 within 72 hours of release. |
| 11/24/2009 | Court orders probation terminated as to count(s) 11, 16, 21, 24, 40, 46, 54. |
| 11/24/2009 | Notice to Sheriff issued. |
| 11/25/2009 | Defendant released on this case only. Release issued. |
| 11/25/2009 | Notice to Sheriff issued. |
| 11/29/2009 | DOJ Subsequent Abstract sent. |
| 11/29/2009 | DOJ Subsequent Abstract sent. |
| 11/29/2009 | Case closed. |
| 12/01/2009 | Original State Prison Abstract of Judgment - Prison Commitment, Determinate document filed and conformed copy mailed to California Department of Corrections and Rehabilitation, Division of Adult Institutions; Legal Processing Unit. |
| 01/12/2011 | Hearing held on 01/12/2011 at 09:00 AM in Department H5 for Hearing. |
| 01/12/2011 | Judicial Officer: Robert Gannon, Judge |
| 01/12/2011 | Clerk: L. Fields |
| 01/12/2011 | Bailiff:. Present |
| 01/12/2011 | Court Reporter: Karen Puckett |
| 01/12/2011 | People represented by Nikki Chambers, Deputy District Attorney, present. |
| 01/12/2011 | Defendant not present in Court represented by Lloyd Freeberg, Retained Attorney. |
| 01/12/2011 | Hearing continued to 02/02/2011 at 08:30 AM in Department H5 by stipulation of all parties. |
| 01/12/2011 | To address the State Prison Credits |
| 01/12/2011 | Defendant ordered to appear. |
| 02/02/2011 | Hearing held on 02/02/2011 at 08:30:00 AM in Department H5 for Hearing. |
| 02/02/2011 | Judicial Officer: Robert Gannon, Judge |
| 02/02/2011 | Clerk: L. Fields |
| 02/02/2011 | Bailiff: A. M. Fletcher |
| 02/02/2011 | Court Reporter: None |
| 02/02/2011 | Appearance made by George W. McFetridge, Deputy District Attorney, by telephone |
| 02/02/2011 | Laura Lindley makes a special appearance for Lloyd Freeberg, Retained Attorney. Defendant present. |
| 02/02/2011 | Court finds good cause for a continuance due to illness of defense counsel |
| 02/02/2011 | Hearing continued to 03/03/2011 at 08:30 AM in Department H5 at request of Defense. |
| 02/02/2011 | Defendant ordered to appear. |
| 03/03/2011 | Hearing held on 03/03/2011 at 08:30:00 AM in Department H5 for Hearing. |
| 03/03/2011 | Judicial Officer: Robert Gannon, Judge |
| 03/03/2011 | Clerk: L. Fields |
| 03/03/2011 | Bailiff: A. M. Fletcher |
| 03/03/2011 | Court Reporter: None |
| 03/03/2011 | District Attorney not present in Court. |

SUPERIOR COURT OF CALIFORNIA, COUNTY OF ORANGE

# MINUTES

Case : 06HF2202

Name : ███████████                                           02/01/2019 10:01:46 AM

| Date of Action | Text |
|---|---|
| 03/03/2011 | Defendant present in Court with counsel Freeberg, Lloyd, Retained Attorney. |
| 03/03/2011 | Hearing continued to 03/28/2011 at 08:30 AM in Department H5 at request of Defense. |
| 03/03/2011 | Defendant ordered to appear. |
| 03/03/2011 | Court orders defendant released on own recognizance. |
| 03/03/2011 | Agreement for Release on Own Recognizance signed and filed. |
| 03/28/2011 | Hearing held on 03/28/2011 at 08:30:00 AM in Department H5 for Hearing. |
| 03/28/2011 | Judicial Officer: Robert Gannon, Judge |
| 03/28/2011 | Clerk: L. Fields |
| 03/28/2011 | Bailiff: A. M. Fletcher |
| 03/28/2011 | Court Reporter: None |
| 03/28/2011 | People represented by Pete Pierce, Deputy District Attorney, present. |
| 03/28/2011 | Appearance made by Pete Pierce, Deputy District Attorney, by telephone |
| 03/28/2011 | Sheri R Sandecki makes a special appearance for Lloyd Freeberg, Retained Attorney. Defendant present. |
| 03/28/2011 | Hearing continued to 04/07/2011 at 08:30 AM in Department H5 at request of Defense. |
| 03/28/2011 | Defendant waives statutory time for Hearing. |
| 03/28/2011 | Counsel joins in waivers. |
| 03/28/2011 | Defendant ordered to appear. |
| 03/28/2011 | Defendant's release on own recognizance continued. |
| 04/06/2011 | Calendar Line for HRG transferred from H5 on 04/07/2011 at 08:30 AM to H2 on 04/07/2011 at 08:30 AM. |
| 04/07/2011 | Hearing held on 04/07/2011 at 08:30:00 AM in Department H2 for Hearing. |
| 04/07/2011 | Judicial Officer: Robert Gannon, Judge |
| 04/07/2011 | Clerk: L. Fields |
| 04/07/2011 | Bailiff:. Present |
| 04/07/2011 | Court Reporter: Donna Cox |
| 04/07/2011 | District Attorney not present in Court. |
| 04/07/2011 | Defendant present in Court with counsel Freeberg, Lloyd, Retained Attorney. |
| 04/07/2011 | Hearing continued to 05/17/2011 at 08:30 AM in Department H5 at request of Defense. |
| 04/07/2011 | Defendant ordered to appear. |
| 04/07/2011 | Defendant's release on own recognizance continued. |
| 04/07/2011 | Agreement for Release on Own Recognizance signed and filed. |
| 05/17/2011 | Hearing held on 05/17/2011 at 08:30:00 AM in Department H5 for Hearing. |
| 05/17/2011 | Judicial Officer: Robert Gannon, Judge |
| 05/17/2011 | Clerk: L. Fields |
| 05/17/2011 | Bailiff: A. M. Fletcher |
| 05/17/2011 | Court Reporter: Kristy Damron |
| 05/17/2011 | Nikki Chambers made a special appearance for District Attorney George William McFetridge Jr. |
| 05/17/2011 | Defendant present in Court with counsel Freeberg, Lloyd, Retained Attorney. |
| 05/17/2011 | Hearing continued to 05/31/2011 at 09:00 AM in Department H5 at request of Defense. |

# MINUTES

Case : 06HF2202

Name : ████████████

02/01/2019 10:01:46 AM

| Date of Action | Text |
|---|---|
| 05/17/2011 | Defendant ordered to appear. |
| 05/17/2011 | Defendant's release on own recognizance continued. |
| 05/17/2011 | Agreement for Release on Own Recognizance signed and filed. |
| 05/31/2011 | Hearing held on 05/31/2011 at 09:00:00 AM in Department H5 for Hearing. |
| 05/31/2011 | Judicial Officer: Robert Gannon, Judge |
| 05/31/2011 | Clerk: L. Fields |
| 05/31/2011 | Bailiff: A. M. Fletcher |
| 05/31/2011 | Court Reporter: Karen Puckett |
| 05/31/2011 | People represented by George William McFetridge Jr, Deputy District Attorney, present. |
| 05/31/2011 | Defendant present in Court with counsel Freeberg, Lloyd, Retained Attorney. |
| 05/31/2011 | Hearing continued to 06/03/2011 at 08:30 AM in Department H5 at request of Defense. |
| 05/31/2011 | Defendant ordered to appear. |
| 05/31/2011 | Defendant's release on own recognizance continued. |
| 06/03/2011 | Hearing held on 06/03/2011 at 08:30:00 AM in Department H5 for Hearing. |
| 06/03/2011 | Judicial Officer: Robert Gannon, Judge |
| 06/03/2011 | Clerk: L. Fields |
| 06/03/2011 | Bailiff: A. M. Fletcher |
| 06/03/2011 | Court Reporter: Marcia Gahring |
| 06/03/2011 | People represented by George William McFetridge Jr, Deputy District Attorney, present. |
| 06/03/2011 | Defendant present in Court with counsel Freeberg, Lloyd, Retained Attorney. |
| 06/03/2011 | Stipulation re: defendant's state prison credits filed. |
| 06/03/2011 | District Attorney and defense counsel stipulate to withdraw the previously filed stipulation |
| 06/03/2011 | Hearing continued to 06/14/2011 at 09:00 AM in Department H5 by stipulation of all parties. |
| 06/03/2011 | Defendant ordered to appear. |
| 06/03/2011 | Defendant's release on own recognizance continued. |
| 06/14/2011 | Hearing held on 06/14/2011 at 09:00:00 AM in Department H5 for Hearing. |
| 06/14/2011 | Judicial Officer: Robert Gannon, Judge |
| 06/14/2011 | Clerk: L. Fields |
| 06/14/2011 | Bailiff: A. M. Fletcher |
| 06/14/2011 | Court Reporter: Marcia Gahring |
| 06/14/2011 | People represented by George William McFetridge Jr, Deputy District Attorney, present. |
| 06/14/2011 | Defendant present in Court with counsel Freeberg, Lloyd, Retained Attorney. |
| 06/14/2011 | Hearing continued to 06/29/2011 at 09:00 AM in Department H5 by stipulation of all parties. |
| 06/14/2011 | Defendant ordered to appear. |
| 06/14/2011 | Defendant's release on own recognizance continued. |
| 06/14/2011 | Agreement for Release on Own Recognizance signed and filed. |

# MINUTES

Case : 06HF2202

Name : ▮▮▮▮▮▮▮▮▮                                    02/01/2019 10:01:46 AM

| Date of Action | Text |
| --- | --- |
| 06/17/2011 | Hearing held on 06/17/2011 at 04:00 PM in Department H5 for Chambers Work. |
| 06/17/2011 | Judicial Officer: Robert Gannon, Judge |
| 06/17/2011 | Clerk: L. Fields |
| 06/17/2011 | Bailiff:. Present |
| 06/17/2011 | Court Reporter: None |
| 06/17/2011 | District Attorney not present in Court. |
| 06/17/2011 | Defendant not present in court. |

Case : 06HF2202

Name :  ▓▓▓▓▓▓▓▓▓▓                                          02/01/2019 10:01:46 AM

| Date of Action | Text |
|---|---|
| 06/17/2011 | In a first amended complaint filed on May 7, 2007, defendant was charged with 59 felony counts and 1 misdemeanor count. Pursuant to a plea agreement negotiated with the District Attorney, on December 11, 2007 defendant entered guilty pleas to 7 felony counts, and was sentenced to a total of 6 years in state prison, with a 2 year sentence on count 11, and terms of 8 months consecutive on each of 6 additional felony counts (counts 16, 21, 24, 40, 46, and 54). Execution of sentence was suspended, defendant was placed on 3 years formal probation on conditions which included serving 408 days in the Orange County jail, and completion of the one-year Nancy Clark treatment program. Defendant was given credit for 272 actual days served and 136 conduct for a total credit of 408 days. |
| | On April 9, 2009, a Probation Violation petition was filed, and probation was revoked on April 13, 2009. On June 15, 2009, defendant was found in violation of probation. Sentencing was continued several times at defendant?s request with the concurrence of the District Attorney. On November 24, 2009, defendant was sentenced to a total of 6 years in state prison, with total credits of 1094 days. |
| | At the time of sentencing on November 24, 2009, it was represented to the sentencing court that the parties had agreed, with the concurrence of a different judge who had found defendant in violation of probation, that defendant should serve in custody a term corresponding to a term with total credits of 1094 days, which the parties then believed also corresponded to the sentence of 6 years. Relying on this representation, the sentencing court sentenced defendant to a term of 6 years, awarded credits of 1094 days, and deemed the 6 year sentence to have been served. |
| | A letter dated December 17, 2010 from the Department of Corrections and Rehabilitation was sent to the court. The letter advised that the awarding of 1094 days credit did not correspond to a 6 year sentence, and that, given the then applicable formula for calculating credits, 2191 days credit would be the correct amount of credited time corresponding to a sentence of 6 years. |
| | It is now apparent that the previously agreed upon calculation that total credits of 1094 days corresponded to a 6 year sentence was in error. |
| | Under Penal Code, section 1170 subdivision (d), a trial court at any time upon the recommendation of the Director of Corrections, may recall a sentence and commitment and ?resentence the defendant in the same manner as if he or she had not previously been sentenced, provided the new sentence, if any, is no greater than the initial sentence.? People v. Hill,   185 Cal.App.3d 831, 834 (1986). |
| | As to the terms of imprisonment only, the court hereby re-sentences defendant, nunc pro tunc, to a term of two years on count 11, and 8 months consecutive on count 16, and 8 months concurrent on each of the following counts: counts 21, 24, 40, 46, and 54, for a total term of imprisonment of 2 years, 8 months. Defendant is awarded credits of 485 days actual custody time with 242 days conduct credits, and 367 days credit for the treatment program defendant completed, for total credits of 1094 days. Defendant is deemed to have served the custody sentence imposed in this re-sentencing. |
| | The clerk is directed to prepare an Amended Abstract of Judgment reflecting the terms of the re-sentencing, and to forward a copy of same to the Department of Corrections and Rehabilitation. |
| | The clerk is also directed to give written notice of this ruling to the parties. |
| 06/17/2011 | Hearing for 06/29/2011 09:00 AM in H5 to remain. |
| 06/17/2011 | Minute Order sent to Deputy District Attorney and Defense Counsel. |
| 06/29/2011 | Hearing held on 06/29/2011 at 09:00:00 AM in Department H5 for Hearing. |
| 06/29/2011 | Judicial Officer: Robert Gannon, Judge |
| 06/29/2011 | Clerk: L. Fields |
| 06/29/2011 | Bailiff:. Present |

# MINUTES

Case : 06HF2202

Name : ███████████                                       02/01/2019 10:01:46 AM

| Date of Action | Text |
|---|---|
| 06/29/2011 | Court Reporter: None |
| 06/29/2011 | People represented by George William McFetridge Jr, Deputy District Attorney, present. |
| 06/29/2011 | Defendant present in Court with counsel Freeberg, Lloyd, Retained Attorney. |
| 06/29/2011 | Court orders minutes of 11/24/09 nun pro tunc'd to reflect amended state prison sentence |
| 06/29/2011 | Court orders an amended state prison abstract be prepared |
| 07/05/2011 | Nunc Pro Tunc entry(s) made on this date for 11/24/2009. |
| 07/05/2011 | Nunc Pro Tunc entry(s) made on this date for 11/24/2009 12:00:00 AM. |
| 09/20/2011 | Amended State Prison Abstract of Judgment - Prison Commitment, Determinate document filed and conformed copy mailed to California Department of Corrections and Rehabilitation, Division of Adult Institutions; Legal Processing Unit. |
| 10/18/2011 | Letter from the Department of Corrections and Rehabilitation - Division of Adult Institutuions forwarded to Harbor Justice Center - Newport Beach Facility from Central Justice Center. |
| 10/20/2011 | Case referred to Department H5 for review. |
| 10/26/2011 | Hearing held on 10/26/2011 at 09:00 AM in Department H5 for Chambers Work. |
| 10/26/2011 | Judicial Officer: Robert Gannon, Judge |
| 10/26/2011 | Clerk: L. Fields |
| 10/26/2011 | Bailiff:. Present |
| 10/26/2011 | Court Reporter: None |
| 10/26/2011 | District Attorney not present in Court. |
| 10/26/2011 | Defendant not present in court. |
| 10/26/2011 | Court read and considered Letter from Department of Corrections and Rahabilitation dated 9/29/11. |
| 10/26/2011 | Response letter sent to Linda Ledford at Department of Corrections and Rahabilitation via fax and mail, awaiting clarification of discrepancy |
| 03/09/2012 | Hearing held on 03/09/2012 at 08:30 AM in Department H5 for Hearing. |
| 03/09/2012 | Judicial Officer: Robert Gannon, Judge |
| 03/09/2012 | Clerk: L. Fields |
| 03/09/2012 | Bailiff: R. T. Cruz |
| 03/09/2012 | Court Reporter: None |
| 03/09/2012 | People represented by George William McFetridge Jr, Deputy District Attorney, present. |
| 03/09/2012 | Defendant present in Court with counsel Freeberg, Lloyd, Retained Attorney. |
| 03/09/2012 | Hearing continued to 04/13/2012 at 01:30 PM in Department H5 by stipulation of all parties. |
| 03/09/2012 | Re: Writ to be filed or stipulated sentence modification/ correction |
| 03/09/2012 | Electronic Minute Order sent to the Probation Department. |
| 04/13/2012 | Hearing held on 04/13/2012 at 01:30:00 PM in Department H5 for Hearing. |
| 04/13/2012 | Judicial Officer: Robert Gannon, Judge |
| 04/13/2012 | Clerk: L. Fields |
| 04/13/2012 | Bailiff: C. H. Joyce |

SUPERIOR COURT OF CALIFORNIA, COUNTY OF ORANGE

# MINUTES

Case : 06HF2202

Name : █████████████

02/01/2019 10:01:46 AM

| Date of Action | Text |
|---|---|
| 04/13/2012 | Court Reporter: None |
| 04/13/2012 | Appearance made by George McFetridge, Deputy District Attorney by telephone. |
| 04/13/2012 | Appearance made by Lloyd Freeberg Retained Attorney by telephone. |
| 04/13/2012 | Due to illness of defense counsel |
| 04/13/2012 | Hearing continued to 05/01/2012 at 01:30 PM in Department H5 by stipulation of all parties. |
| 05/01/2012 | Hearing held on 05/01/2012 at 01:30:00 PM in Department H5 for Hearing. |
| 05/01/2012 | Judicial Officer: Robert Gannon, Judge |
| 05/01/2012 | Clerk: L. Fields |
| 05/01/2012 | Bailiff: R. O. Coleman |
| 05/01/2012 | Court Reporter: None |
| 05/01/2012 | Appearance made by George William McFetridge Deputy District Attorney by telephone. |
| 05/01/2012 | Appearance made by Lloyd Freeberg Retained Attorney by telephone. |
| 05/01/2012 | Hearing continued to 06/01/2012 at 01:30 PM in Department H5 by stipulation of all parties. |
| 06/01/2012 | Hearing held on 06/01/2012 at 01:30:00 PM in Department H5 for Hearing. |
| 06/01/2012 | Judicial Officer: Robert Gannon, Judge |
| 06/01/2012 | Clerk: L. Fields |
| 06/01/2012 | Bailiff: J. Ellison |
| 06/01/2012 | Court Reporter: None |
| 06/01/2012 | People represented by George William McFetridge Jr, Deputy District Attorney, present. |
| 06/01/2012 | Defendant present in Court without counsel. |
| 06/01/2012 | In open court at 01:58 PM |
| 06/01/2012 | Court notes no contact by defense counsel |
| 06/01/2012 | Sentencing set on 06/07/2012 at 02:00 PM in Department H5. |
| 06/01/2012 | Defendant ordered to appear. |
| 06/07/2012 | Hearing held on 06/07/2012 at 02:00:00 PM in Department H5 for Sentencing. |
| 06/07/2012 | Judicial Officer: Robert Gannon, Judge |
| 06/07/2012 | Clerk: L. Fields |
| 06/07/2012 | Bailiff: J. A. Monroe |
| 06/07/2012 | Court Reporter: Kristy Damron |
| 06/07/2012 | People represented by George William McFetridge Jr, Deputy District Attorney, present. |
| 06/07/2012 | Defendant present in Court with counsel Freeberg, Lloyd, Retained Attorney. |
| 06/07/2012 | In open court at 02:13 PM |

| Date of Action | Text |
|---|---|
| 06/07/2012 | In a first amended complaint filed on May 7, 2007, defendant was charged with 59 felony counts and 1 misdemeanor count. Pursuant to a plea agreement negotiated with the District Attorney, on December 11, 2007 defendant entered guilty pleas to 7 felony counts, and was sentenced to a total of 6 years in state prison, with a 2 year sentence on count 11, and terms of 8 months consecutive on each of 6 additional felony counts (counts 16, 21, 24, 40, 46, and 54). Execution of sentence was suspended, defendant was placed on 3 years formal probation on conditions which included serving 408 days in the Orange County jail, and completion of the one-year Nancy Clark treatment program. Defendant was given credit for 272 actual days served and 136 conduct for a total credit of 408 days.<br>On April 9, 2009, a Probation Violation petition was filed, and probation was revoked on April 13, 2009. On June 15, 2009, defendant was found in violation of probation. Sentencing was continued several times at defendant?s request with the concurrence of the District Attorney. On November 24, 2009, defendant was sentenced to a total of 6 years in state prison, with total credits of 1094 days.<br>At the time of sentencing on November 24, 2009, it was represented to the sentencing court that the parties had agreed, with the concurrence of a different judge who had found defendant in violation of probation, that defendant should serve in custody a term corresponding to a term with total credits of 1094 days, which the parties then believed also corresponded to the sentence of 6 years. Relying on this representation, the sentencing court sentenced defendant to a term of 6 years, awarded credits of 1094 days, and deemed the 6 year sentence to have been served.<br>A letter dated December 17, 2010 from the Department of Corrections and Rehabilitation was sent to the court. The letter advised that the awarding of 1094 days credit did not correspond to a 6 year sentence, and that, given the then applicable formula for calculating credits, 2191 days credit would be the correct amount of credited time corresponding to a sentence of 6 years.<br>It is now apparent that the previously agreed upon calculation that total credits of 1094 days corresponded to a 6 year sentence was in error.<br>Under Penal Code, section 1170 subdivision (d), a trial court at any time upon the recommendation of the Director of Corrections, may recall a sentence and commitment and resentence the defendant in the same manner as if he or she had not previously been sentenced, provided the new sentence, if any, is no greater than the initial sentence. People v. Hill, 185 Cal.App.3d 831, 834 (1986).<br>As to the terms of imprisonment only, the court hereby re-sentences defendant, nunc pro tunc, to a term of two years on count 11, and 8 months consecutive on count 16, and 16 months concurrent on each of the following counts: counts 21, 24, 40, 46, and 54, for a total term of imprisonment of 2 years, 8 months. Defendant is awarded credits of 485 days actual custody time with 242 days conduct credits, and 367 days credit for the treatment program defendant completed, for total credits of 1094 days. Defendant is deemed to have served the custody sentence imposed in this re-sentencing. |
| 06/07/2012 | Court orders and Amended Abstract of Judgment reflecting the terms of the re-sentencing, and to forward a copy of the same to the Department of Corrections and Rehabilitation |
| 08/21/2012 | Nunc Pro Tunc entry(s) made on this date for 11/24/2009. |
| 08/22/2012 | Amended Felony Abstract of Judgment State Prison Commitment, Determinate document filed and conformed copy mailed to California Department of Corrections and Rehabilitation, Division of Adult Institutions; Legal Processing Unit. |
| 05/22/2018 | Pay FEE of $150.00 Change of Plea Fee pursuant to Penal Code 1203.4, 1203.41 & 1203.42. |
| 05/22/2018 | Remittance from receipt # 16248022 received in the amount of $ 150.00. |
| 05/22/2018 | Defense Motion to Dismiss (PC1203.4) filed. |
| 05/22/2018 | petiton for relief under penal code 1203.4, 1203.4a, 1203.41, 1203.42 filed. |

# MINUTES

Case : 06HF2202

Name :

02/01/2019 10:01:46 AM

| Date of Action | Text |
|---|---|
| 05/22/2018 | Proof of Service filed. |
| 05/22/2018 | Motion re: Dismiss [Penal Code 1203.4/1203.4a/1203.41] set on 07/06/2018 at 08:30 AM in Department C53. |
| 07/06/2018 | Hearing held on 07/06/2018 at 08:30:00 AM in Department C53 for Motion Dismiss [Penal Code 1203.4/1203.4a/1203.41/1203.42]. |
| 07/06/2018 | Judicial Officer: Gary M Pohlson, Judge |
| 07/06/2018 | Clerk: A. Garcia |
| 07/06/2018 | Bailiff: J. L. Mc Million |
| 07/06/2018 | Court Reporter: Kimberly R Moore |
| 07/06/2018 | District Attorney waives appearance. |
| 07/06/2018 | Defendant present in Court with counsel Saif Rahman, Retained Attorney. |
| 07/06/2018 | Oral motion by Defense for the motion to be continued, heard. |
| 07/06/2018 | Motion granted. |
| 07/06/2018 | Motion re: Dismiss [Penal Code 1203.4/1203.4a/1203.41/1203.42] continued to 07/20/2018 at 08:30 AM in Department C53 at request of Defense. |
| 07/20/2018 | Hearing held on 07/20/2018 at 08:30:00 AM in Department C53 for Motion Dismiss [Penal Code 1203.4/1203.4a/1203.41/1203.42]. |
| 07/20/2018 | Judicial Officer: Gary M Pohlson, Judge |
| 07/20/2018 | Clerk: N. Robles |
| 07/20/2018 | Bailiff: E. F. Richardson |
| 07/20/2018 | Court Reporter: Andrea Gaunt |
| 07/20/2018 | People represented by George William McFetridge Jr, Deputy District Attorney, present. |
| 07/20/2018 | Defendant present in Court with counsel Saif Rahman, Retained Attorney. |
| 07/20/2018 | Motion re: Dismiss [Penal Code 1203.4/1203.4a/1203.41/1203.42] continued to 09/14/2018 at 09:00 AM in Department C49 by stipulation of all parties. |
| 07/20/2018 | Motion re: Dismiss [Penal Code 1203.4/1203.4a/1203.41/1203.42] on 09/14/2018 at 09:00 AM in C49 entered in error. (Entered NUNC_PRO_TUNC on 08/30/18) |
| 07/20/2018 | Motion re: Dismiss [Penal Code 1203.4/1203.4a/1203.41/1203.42] continued to 09/14/2018 at 08:30 AM in Department C53 by stipulation of all parties. (Entered NUNC_PRO_TUNC on 08/30/18) |
| 07/20/2018 | Minutes entered by E. Villela on 07/20/2018. |
| 08/30/2018 | Nunc Pro Tunc entry(s) made on this date for 07/20/2018. |
| 09/14/2018 | Hearing held on 09/14/2018 at 08:30:00 AM in Department C53 for Motion Dismiss [Penal Code 1203.4/1203.4a/1203.41/1203.42]. |
| 09/14/2018 | Judicial Officer: Gary M Pohlson, Judge |
| 09/14/2018 | Clerk: N. Robles |
| 09/14/2018 | Bailiff: E. F. Richardson |
| 09/14/2018 | Court Reporter: Wendy Tatreau |
| 09/14/2018 | Susan Lee made a special appearance for District Attorney George William McFetridge Jr. |
| 09/14/2018 | Defendant not present in Court represented by Saif Rahman, Retained Attorney. |
| 09/14/2018 | Motion re: Dismiss [Penal Code 1203.4/1203.4a/1203.41/1203.42] continued to 09/28/2018 at 08:30 AM in Department C53 at request of Defense. |

SUPERIOR COURT OF CALIFORNIA, COUNTY OF ORANGE

# MINUTES

Case : 06HF2202

Name : ███████████████

02/01/2019 10:01:46 AM

| Date of Action | Text |
|---|---|
| 09/28/2018 | Hearing held on 09/28/2018 at 08:30:00 AM in Department C53 for Motion Dismiss [Penal Code 1203.4/1203.4a/1203.41/1203.42]. |
| 09/28/2018 | Judicial Officer: Gary M Pohlson, Judge |
| 09/28/2018 | Clerk: N. Robles |
| 09/28/2018 | Bailiff: E. F. Richardson |
| 09/28/2018 | Court Reporter: Kimberly R Moore |
| 09/28/2018 | People represented by George William McFetridge Jr, Deputy District Attorney, present. |
| 09/28/2018 | Defendant present in Court with counsel Saif Rahman, Retained Attorney. |
| 09/28/2018 | Motion re: Dismiss [Penal Code 1203.4/1203.4a/1203.41/1203.42] continued to 11/02/2018 at 08:30 AM in Department C53 by stipulation of all parties. |
| 11/02/2018 | Hearing held on 11/02/2018 at 08:30:00 AM in Department C53 for Motion Dismiss [Penal Code 1203.4/1203.4a/1203.41/1203.42]. |
| 11/02/2018 | Judicial Officer: Gary M Pohlson, Judge |
| 11/02/2018 | Clerk: N. Robles |
| 11/02/2018 | Bailiff: E. F. Richardson |
| 11/02/2018 | Court Reporter: Wendy Tatreau |
| 11/02/2018 | People represented by George William McFetridge Jr, Deputy District Attorney, present. |
| 11/02/2018 | Defendant not present in Court represented by Saif Rahman, Retained Attorney. |
| 11/02/2018 | Court read and considered Petition for Dismissal of case Pursuant to 1203.4. |
| 11/02/2018 | Oral motion by Defense to withdraw motion. |
| 11/02/2018 | Motion granted. |
| 11/02/2018 | Motion withdrawn. |
| 11/30/2018 | At the request of Defense Counsel, case calendared on 11/30/18 at 08:30 AM in C53 for MTN PC1203.4. |
| 11/30/2018 | Hearing held on 11/30/2018 at 08:30:00 AM in Department C53 for Motion Dismiss [Penal Code 1203.4/1203.4a/1203.41/1203.42]. |
| 11/30/2018 | Judicial Officer: Gary M Pohlson, Judge |
| 11/30/2018 | Clerk: N. Robles |
| 11/30/2018 | Bailiff: E. F. Richardson |
| 11/30/2018 | Court Reporter: Shelley Hill |
| 11/30/2018 | People represented by George William McFetridge Jr, Deputy District Attorney, present. |
| 11/30/2018 | Defendant not present in Court represented by Saif Rahman, Retained Attorney. |
| 11/30/2018 | Defense Motion to Dismiss (PC1203.4) filed. |
| 11/30/2018 | Motion Pursuantn to 1473.7 filed in case 07HF0020 |
| 11/30/2018 | Court read and considered Motion to Withdraw Plea and Dismiss Case Under Penal Code Section 1203.4. |
| 11/30/2018 | People submit(s). |
| 11/30/2018 | Motion granted. |

# MINUTES

Case : 06HF2202

Name : ███████████

02/01/2019 10:01:46 AM

| Date of Action | Text |
|---|---|
| 11/30/2018 | Court finds Court finds finds the defendant was not advised of their immigration consequences and grants the motion pursuant to Penal Code 1473.7. The defendant withdraws his guilty plea(s). People state they are unable to proceed at this time. Defense requests the Court dismiss this case in the furtherance of justice. The Court orders this case dismissed pursuant to Penal Code 1385. |
| 11/30/2018 | Defendant's motion to WITHDRAW GUILTY PLEA to count(s) 11, 16, 21, 24, 40, 46, 54 granted. |
| 11/30/2018 | Count(s) 11, 16, 21, 24, 40, 46, 54 DISMISSED - pursuant to Penal Code 1385 - Furtherance of justice. |
| 11/30/2018 | Order Vacating Conviction Under Penal Code 1473.7 signed and filed. |

Orange County Superior Court Docket Sheet - 07HF0020

# Superior Court of California
## County of Orange

Case Number : 07HF0020
Copy Request: 3930508
Request Type: Case Documents
Prepared for: KA

Number of documents: 1
Number of pages: 13

# MINUTES

Case : 07HF0020

Name :

12/14/2018 15:34:53 PM

| Date of Action | Text |
|---|---|
| 01/02/2007 | Original Complaint filed on 01/02/2007 by Orange County District Attorney. |
| 01/02/2007 | Name filed: Ashaary, Kiarash |
| 01/02/2007 | FELONY charge of 11377(a) HS filed as count 1. Date of violation: 12/05/2006. |
| 01/02/2007 | MISDEMEANOR charge of 11364 HS filed as count 2. Date of violation: 12/05/2006. |
| 01/02/2007 | Case calendared on 01/09/07 at 08:30 AM in H2 for ARGN. |
| 01/02/2007 | Police/Arrest Report filed. |
| 01/03/2007 | Case in pending status, awaiting bail. |
| 01/09/2007 | Hearing held on 01/09/2007 at 08:30:00 AM in Department H2 for Arraignment. |
| 01/09/2007 | Officiating Judge: Peter J. Polos, Judge |
| 01/09/2007 | Clerk: M. Johnson |
| 01/09/2007 | Bailiff: L. Martinez |
| 01/09/2007 | Court Reporter: Marcia Gahring |
| 01/09/2007 | People represented by Matthew Zandi, Deputy District Attorney, present. |
| 01/09/2007 | Defendant not present in Court represented by Robert M Brodney, Retained Attorney. |
| 01/09/2007 | Defendant inadvertenly brought to Central Justice Center |
| 01/09/2007 | Court reporter waived by all parties. |
| 01/09/2007 | Bench warrant ordered issued and held for the defendant to 01/12/2007, for Arraignment re: Warrant Hold at 08:30 AM in Department H2. Bail set at $25, 000.00, Mandatory Appearance. |
| 01/09/2007 | Keep with companion cases(s) 06HF2202, 03SF0869. |
| 01/12/2007 | Hearing held on 01/12/2007 at 08:30:00 AM in Department H2 for Arraignment Warrant Hold. |
| 01/12/2007 | Officiating Judge: Peter J. Polos, Judge |
| 01/12/2007 | Clerk: M. Johnson |
| 01/12/2007 | Bailiff: J. Winovich |
| 01/12/2007 | Court Reporter: Marcia Gahring |
| 01/12/2007 | People represented by George W. McFetridge Jr., Deputy District Attorney, present. |
| 01/12/2007 | Defendant present in Court with counsel Brodney, Robert M, Retained Attorney. |
| 01/12/2007 | Defendant waives reading and advisement of the Original Complaint. |
| 01/12/2007 | Counsel acknowledges receipt of the complaint. |
| 01/12/2007 | To the Original Complaint defendant pleads NOT GUILTY to all counts. |
| 01/12/2007 | Defense reserves all motions. |
| 01/12/2007 | Pre Trial set on 02/15/2007 at 08:30 AM in Department H2. |
| 01/12/2007 | Court finds the defendant understandingly, knowingly, and voluntarily waives the right to a Preliminary Hearing within 10 court days of arraignment. |
| 01/12/2007 | Court orders bail set in the amount of $25, 000.00. |
| 01/12/2007 | Notice to Sheriff issued. |
| 01/12/2007 | Fingerprint card is received and filed. |
| 01/12/2007 | Keep with companion cases(s) 06HF2202 & 03SF0869. |
| 01/12/2007 | Minutes entered by R. Hume. |
| 02/15/2007 | Hearing held on 02/15/2007 at 08:30:00 AM in Department H2 for Pre Trial. |
| 02/15/2007 | Officiating Judge: Peter J. Polos, Judge |

SUPERIOR COURT OF CALIFORNIA, COUNTY OF ORANGE

# MINUTES

Case : 07HF0020

Name :

12/14/2018 15:34:53 PM

| Date of Action | Text |
|---|---|
| 02/15/2007 | Clerk: T. Hauck |
| 02/15/2007 | Bailiff: J. Winovich |
| 02/15/2007 | Court Reporter: Marcia Gahring |
| 02/15/2007 | People represented by George W. McFetridge Jr., Deputy District Attorney, present. |
| 02/15/2007 | Susan L. Angell makes a special appearance for Robert M Brodney, Retained Attorney. Defendant present. |
| 02/15/2007 | Warrant issued on 01/09/2007 withdrawn for defendant. |
| 02/15/2007 | Pre Trial continued to 03/27/2007 at 08:30 AM in Department H2 at request of Defense. |
| 02/15/2007 | Court finds the defendant understandingly, knowingly, and voluntarily waives the right to a Preliminary Hearing within 60 calendar days of arraignment. |
| 02/15/2007 | Counsel joins in waivers. |
| 02/15/2007 | Defendant ordered to appear. |
| 02/15/2007 | Defendant remanded to the custody of the Sheriff. |
| 02/15/2007 | Current bail set for defendant to remain. |
| 02/15/2007 | Notice to Sheriff issued. |
| 02/15/2007 | Keep with companion cases(s) 06HF2202, 03SF0869. |
| 03/27/2007 | Hearing held on 03/27/2007 at 08:30:00 AM in Department H2 for Pre Trial. |
| 03/27/2007 | Officiating Judge: Peter J. Polos, Judge |
| 03/27/2007 | Clerk: K. Reinke |
| 03/27/2007 | Bailiff: J. Winovich |
| 03/27/2007 | Court Reporter: Marcia Gahring |
| 03/27/2007 | People represented by George W. McFetridge Jr., Deputy District Attorney, present. |
| 03/27/2007 | Defendant present in Court with counsel Brodney, Robert M, Retained Attorney. |
| 03/27/2007 | Pre Trial set on 05/07/2007 at 08:30 AM in Department H2. |
| 03/27/2007 | Defendant waives statutory time for Preliminary Hearing. |
| 03/27/2007 | Counsel joins in waivers. |
| 03/27/2007 | Defendant ordered to return. |
| 03/27/2007 | Current bail set for defendant to remain. |
| 03/27/2007 | Defendant remanded to the custody of the Sheriff. |
| 03/27/2007 | Notice to Sheriff issued. |
| 03/27/2007 | Keep with companion cases(s) 03SF0869 and 06HF2202. |
| 03/27/2007 | Letter from defendant's mother filed. |
| 03/27/2007 | Notice to Sheriff issued. |
| 04/23/2007 | Bail Bond Number S25 01219046 posted in the amount of $25000.00 by GOLDB of SENEC. |
| 04/23/2007 | Bail Bond posted per Sheriff Bail Bond report. Bond to be filed when received. |
| 04/23/2007 | Surety Bond # S25 01219046 filed. |
| 04/23/2007 | Surety Bond # S25 01219046 filed. |
| 05/07/2007 | Hearing held on 05/07/2007 at 08:30:00 AM in Department H2 for Pre Trial. |
| 05/07/2007 | Officiating Judge: Peter J. Polos, Judge |
| 05/07/2007 | Clerk: C. B. Henderson |

# MINUTES

Case : 07HF0020

Name : ▮▮▮▮▮▮▮                                        12/14/2018 15:34:53 PM

| Date of Action | Text |
|---|---|
| 05/07/2007 | Bailiff: J. Winovich |
| 05/07/2007 | Court Reporter: Marcia Gahring |
| 05/07/2007 | People represented by George W. McFetridge Jr., Deputy District Attorney, present. |
| 05/07/2007 | Brian Cretney makes a special appearance for Robert M Brodney, Retained Attorney. Defendant present. |
| 05/07/2007 | Pre Trial set on 05/21/2007 at 08:30 AM in Department H2. |
| 05/07/2007 | Preliminary Hearing set on 06/05/2007 at 08:30 AM in Department H2. |
| 05/07/2007 | Defendant waives statutory time for Preliminary Hearing. |
| 05/07/2007 | Counsel joins in waivers. |
| 05/07/2007 | Defendant ordered to appear. |
| 05/07/2007 | Present bail deemed sufficient and continued. |
| 05/07/2007 | Keep with companion cases(s) 06HF2202 and 03SF0869. |
| 05/21/2007 | Hearing held on 05/21/2007 at 08:30:00 AM in Department H2 for Pre Trial. |
| 05/21/2007 | Officiating Judge: Kelly MacEachern, Judge |
| 05/21/2007 | Clerk: C. B. Henderson |
| 05/21/2007 | Bailiff: J. Winovich |
| 05/21/2007 | Court Reporter: Marcia Gahring |
| 05/21/2007 | People represented by George W. McFetridge Jr., Deputy District Attorney, present. |
| 05/21/2007 | Lloyd Freeberg, Retained Attorney, substituting in as Attorney of Record. |
| 05/21/2007 | Robert M Brodney relieved as Counsel of Record. |
| 05/21/2007 | Defendant present in Court with counsel Lloyd Freeberg, Retained Attorney. |
| 05/21/2007 | Pre Trial set on 06/07/2007 at 08:30 AM in Department H2. |
| 05/21/2007 | Preliminary Hearing set on 06/28/2007 at 08:30 AM in Department H2. |
| 05/21/2007 | Defendant waives statutory time for Preliminary Hearing. |
| 05/21/2007 | Defendant ordered to appear. |
| 05/21/2007 | Present bail deemed sufficient and continued. |
| 05/21/2007 | Preliminary Hearing vacated for 06/05/2007 at 08:30 AM in H2. |
| 05/21/2007 | Keep with companion cases(s) 06HF2202 and 03SF0869. |
| 06/07/2007 | Hearing held on 06/07/2007 at 08:30:00 AM in Department H2 for Pre Trial. |
| 06/07/2007 | Officiating Judge: Peter J. Polos, Judge |
| 06/07/2007 | Clerk: T. Hauck |
| 06/07/2007 | Bailiff: J. Winovich |
| 06/07/2007 | Court Reporter: Marcia Gahring |
| 06/07/2007 | People represented by George W. McFetridge Jr., Deputy District Attorney, present. |
| 06/07/2007 | Martin Joseph Heneghan makes a special appearance for Lloyd Freeberg, Retained Attorney. Defendant present. |
| 06/07/2007 | Pretrial off calendar, Preliminary Hearing set on 06/28/2007 at 08:30 AM in H2 to remain. |
| 06/07/2007 | Defendant ordered to appear. |
| 06/07/2007 | Present bail deemed sufficient and continued. |
| 06/07/2007 | Keep with companion cases(s) 06HF2202, 03SF0869. |

# MINUTES

Case : 07HF0020

Name : ▮▮▮▮▮▮▮▮▮▮                                    12/14/2018 15:34:53 PM

| Date of Action | Text |
|---|---|
| 06/28/2007 | Hearing held on 06/28/2007 at 08:30:00 AM in Department H2 for Preliminary Hearing. |
| 06/28/2007 | Officiating Judge: Peter J. Polos, Judge |
| 06/28/2007 | Clerk: C. B. Henderson |
| 06/28/2007 | Bailiff: P. Ada |
| 06/28/2007 | Court Reporter: Marcia Gahring |
| 06/28/2007 | People represented by George W. McFetridge Jr., Deputy District Attorney, present. |
| 06/28/2007 | James Sweeney makes a special appearance for Lloyd Freeberg, Retained Attorney. Defendant present. |
| 06/28/2007 | Pre Trial set on 08/01/2007 at 08:30 AM in Department H2. |
| 06/28/2007 | Defendant waives reasonable time. (Entered NUNC_PRO_TUNC on 07/02/07) |
| 06/28/2007 | Defendant ordered to appear. |
| 06/28/2007 | Present bail deemed sufficient and continued. |
| 06/28/2007 | Keep with companion cases(s) 06HF2202 and 03SF0869. |
| 07/02/2007 | Nunc Pro Tunc entry(s) made on this date for 06/28/2007. |
| 08/01/2007 | Hearing held on 08/01/2007 at 08:30:00 AM in Department H2 for Pre Trial. |
| 08/01/2007 | Officiating Judge: Kelly MacEachern, Judge |
| 08/01/2007 | Clerk: T. Hauck |
| 08/01/2007 | Bailiff: L. Martinez |
| 08/01/2007 | Court Reporter: Lori Shepherd |
| 08/01/2007 | People represented by George W. McFetridge Jr., Deputy District Attorney, present. |
| 08/01/2007 | Defendant present in Court with counsel Freeberg, Lloyd, Retained Attorney. |
| 08/01/2007 | Pre Trial set on 10/04/2007 at 08:30 AM in Department H2. |
| 08/01/2007 | Probation Department ordered to prepare a Pre-Plea report to be made available to court and counsel 5 days prior to Sentencing. |
| 08/01/2007 | Defendant is ordered to pay for probation report as determined by the Probation Department. |
| 08/01/2007 | Defendant waives statutory time for Preliminary Hearing. |
| 08/01/2007 | Counsel joins in waivers. |
| 08/01/2007 | Defendant ordered to appear. |
| 08/01/2007 | Present bail deemed sufficient and continued. |
| 08/01/2007 | Keep with companion cases(s) 06HF2202, 03SF0869. |
| 10/04/2007 | Hearing held on 10/04/2007 at 08:30:00 AM in Department H2 for Pre Trial. |
| 10/04/2007 | Officiating Judge: James Odriozola, Commissioner |
| 10/04/2007 | Clerk: C. Le |
| 10/04/2007 | Bailiff:. Present |
| 10/04/2007 | Court Reporter: Michelle Lott-Megenhofer |
| 10/04/2007 | Minutes entered by s. Bartush. |
| 10/04/2007 | People represented by George W. McFetridge Jr., Deputy District Attorney, present. |
| 10/04/2007 | Defendant present in Court with counsel Lloyd Freeberg, Retained Attorney. |
| 10/04/2007 | Pre Trial set on 11/06/2007 at 08:30 AM in Department H2. |
| 10/04/2007 | Defendant waives statutory time for Preliminary Hearing. |

# MINUTES

Case : 07HF0020

Name : ▮▮▮▮▮▮▮▮▮▮

12/14/2018 15:34:53 PM

| Date of Action | Text |
|---|---|
| 10/04/2007 | Present bail deemed sufficient and continued. |
| 10/04/2007 | Keep with companion cases(s) 06HF2202 03SF0869. |
| 10/04/2007 | Pre Plea filed. |
| 11/06/2007 | Hearing held on 11/06/2007 at 08:30:00 AM in Department H2 for Pre Trial. |
| 11/06/2007 | Officiating Judge: Gregory W. Jones, Commissioner |
| 11/06/2007 | Clerk: M. Johnson |
| 11/06/2007 | Bailiff: I. Hamdallah |
| 11/06/2007 | Court Reporter: Karen Puckett |
| 11/06/2007 | People represented by George W. McFetridge Jr., Deputy District Attorney, present. |
| 11/06/2007 | Defendant present in Court with counsel Freeberg, Lloyd, Retained Attorney. |
| 11/06/2007 | Pre Trial continued to 11/29/2007 at 08:30 AM in Department H2 at request of Defense. |
| 11/06/2007 | Court finds the defendant understandingly, knowingly, and voluntarily waives the right to a Preliminary Hearing within 60 calendar days of arraignment. |
| 11/06/2007 | Counsel joins in waivers. |
| 11/06/2007 | Defendant ordered to return. |
| 11/06/2007 | Present bail deemed sufficient and continued. |
| 11/29/2007 | Hearing held on 11/29/2007 at 08:30:00 AM in Department H2 for Pre Trial. |
| 11/29/2007 | Officiating Judge: James Odriozola, Commissioner |
| 11/29/2007 | Clerk: K. Reinke |
| 11/29/2007 | Bailiff: I. Hamdallah |
| 11/29/2007 | Court Reporter: Roxanne Drake |
| 11/29/2007 | People represented by George W. McFetridge Jr., Deputy District Attorney, present. |
| 11/29/2007 | Defendant present in Court with counsel Freeberg, Lloyd, Retained Attorney. |
| 11/29/2007 | Pre Trial set on 12/11/2007 at 08:30 AM in Department H2. |
| 11/29/2007 | Defendant waives reasonable time. |
| 11/29/2007 | Counsel joins in waivers. |
| 11/29/2007 | Defendant ordered to return. |
| 11/29/2007 | Present bail deemed sufficient and continued. |
| 12/11/2007 | Hearing held on 12/11/2007 at 08:30:00 AM in Department H2 for Pre Trial. |
| 12/11/2007 | Officiating Judge: Gregory W. Jones, Commissioner |
| 12/11/2007 | Clerk: K. Reinke |
| 12/11/2007 | Bailiff: B. Cate |
| 12/11/2007 | Court Reporter: Tina O'Rourke |
| 12/11/2007 | People represented by George W. McFetridge Jr., Deputy District Attorney, present. |
| 12/11/2007 | Douglas Myers makes a special appearance for Lloyd Freeberg, Retained Attorney. Defendant present. |
| 12/11/2007 | All Parties being advised of their right to have this matter heard by a Judge of the court have stipulated that the matter be heard by Commissioner Gregory W. Jones. |
| 12/11/2007 | Stipulation for Court Commissioner filed. |
| 12/11/2007 | Defendant advised of and waives the following: |
| 12/11/2007 | - The right to a trial by Jury. |

# MINUTES

Case : 07HF0020

Name : ████████████

12/14/2018 15:34:53 PM

| Date of Action | Text |
|---|---|
| 12/11/2007 | - The right to confront and cross-examine witnesses. |
| 12/11/2007 | - The right against self incrimination. |
| 12/11/2007 | Defendant waives the right to subpoena and present evidence. |
| 12/11/2007 | Defendant's motion to WITHDRAW NOT GUILTY PLEA to count(s) 1 granted. |
| 12/11/2007 | Court finds defendant intelligently and voluntarily waives legal and constitutional rights to jury trial, confront and examine witnesses, and to remain silent. |
| 12/11/2007 | To the Original Complaint defendant pleads GUILTY as to count(s) 1. |
| 12/11/2007 | Defendant's written waiver of legal and constitutional rights for guilty plea received and ordered filed. |
| 12/11/2007 | Court finds factual basis and accepts plea. |
| 12/11/2007 | Defendant advised of the possible consequences of plea affecting deportation and citizenship. |
| 12/11/2007 | Defendant advised of maximum possible sentence. |
| 12/11/2007 | Defendant advised of consequences of violating probation and parole. |
| 12/11/2007 | This constitutes a prior conviction. |
| 12/11/2007 | Counsel joins in waivers, pleas, and admissions. |
| 12/11/2007 | Defendant waives arraignment for sentencing. |
| 12/11/2007 | Defendant requests immediate sentencing. |
| 12/11/2007 | Probation report waived. |
| 12/11/2007 | No legal cause why judgment should not be pronounced and defendant having been convicted of 11377(a) HS as charged in count 1, defendant is sentenced to STATE PRISON for 1/3 the mid term for a sentence of 8 Months, consecutive 1/3 non-violent to case # 06HF2202. |
| 12/11/2007 | Execution of State Prison sentence is suspended and defendant is placed on 3 Year(s) FORMAL PROBATION as to count(s) 1 on the following terms and conditions: |
| 12/11/2007 | Violate no law. |
| 12/11/2007 | Serve 408 Day(s) Orange County Jail as to count(s) 1. |
| 12/11/2007 | Credit for time served: 272 actual, 136 conduct, totaling 408 days. |
| 12/11/2007 | Pay $200.00 Restitution Fine pursuant to Penal Code 1202.4 or Penal Code 1202.4(b). |
| 12/11/2007 | Pay $200.00 Probation Revocation Restitution Fine pursuant to Penal Code 1202.44. Restitution fine stayed, to become effective only upon final revocation of probation. |
| 12/11/2007 | Pay Security Fee(s) pursuant to Penal Code 1465.8 totaling $20.00. |
| 12/11/2007 | All fees payable through the Probation Department. |
| 12/11/2007 | Register pursuant to Health & Safety Code 11590. |
| 12/11/2007 | Submit to DNA testing pursuant to Penal Code 296. |
| 12/11/2007 | Use no unauthorized drugs, narcotics, or controlled substances. Submit to drug or narcotic testing as directed by Probation Officer or Police Officer. |
| 12/11/2007 | Submit your person and property including any residence, premises, container, or vehicle under your control to search and seizure at any time of the day or night by any law enforcement or probation officer with or without a warrant, and with or without reasonable cause or reasonable suspicion. |
| 12/11/2007 | Cooperate with Probation Officer in any plan for psychiatric, psychological, alcohol and/or drug treatment, or counseling. |

# MINUTES

Case : 07HF0020

Name : ██████████                                      12/14/2018 15:34:53 PM

| Date of Action | Text |
|---|---|
| 12/11/2007 | Submit your person and property including any residence, premises, container, or vehicle under your control to search and seizure at any time of the day or night by any law enforcement or probation officer with or without a warrant, and with or without reasonable cause or reasonable suspicion. |
| 12/11/2007 | Do not have blank checks in your possession, nor write any portion of any checks, nor have checking account, nor use or possess credit cards or open credit accounts unless approved. |
| 12/11/2007 | Do not possess any other persons' personal identifying information or personal financial information unless approved in advance by your probation officer. |
| 12/11/2007 | Do not own, use, or possess any type of dangerous or deadly weapon including any firearms or ammunition. |
| 12/11/2007 | Defendant provided a copy of "Prohibited Persons Notice Form and Power of Attorney for Firearms and Disposal" pursuant to Penal Code 12021(d)(2). |
| 12/11/2007 | Obey all laws, orders, rules, and regulations of the Court, Jail, and Probation. |
| 12/11/2007 | Disclose terms and conditions of probation when asked by any law enforcement or probation officer. |
| 12/11/2007 | Defendant is required to complete a new financial disclosure form if money is still owing on a restitution order or fine 120 days before the scheduled release from probation. Defendant is required to file the form with the court at least 90 days before the scheduled release from probation. |
| 12/11/2007 | Pay the costs of probation based on the ability to pay as directed by the Probation Officer. |
| 12/11/2007 | Count(s) 2 DISMISSED - Motion of People. |
| 12/11/2007 | Complete 1 year Nancy Clark Program |
| 12/11/2007 | Defendant accepts terms and conditions of probation. |
| 12/11/2007 | Court orders bail bond # S25 01219046 exonerated. |
| 12/11/2007 | DD1-GJ sent to DMV. Return Code: 800 |
| 12/15/2007 | DOJ Initial Abstract sent. |
| 03/11/2008 | Case calendared on 03/11/08 at 09:30 AM in H2 for MTN MOP. |
| 03/11/2008 | Hearing held on 03/11/2008 at 09:30:00 AM in Department H2 for Motion Modification of Probation. |
| 03/11/2008 | Officiating Judge: James Odriozola, Commissioner |
| 03/11/2008 | Clerk: M. Johnson |
| 03/11/2008 | Bailiff: I. Hamdallah |
| 03/11/2008 | Court Reporter: Marcia Gahring |
| 03/11/2008 | People represented by Chris Kralick, Deputy District Attorney, present. |
| 03/11/2008 | Defendant present in Court without counsel. |
| 03/11/2008 | Motion by Defense to complete Southern California Community Recovery Center in lieu of Nancy Clark Program |
| 03/11/2008 | Motion granted. |
| 03/11/2008 | Defendant to complete the Southern California Community Recovery Center Program |
| 03/11/2008 | Memorandum from Probation filed. |
| 03/11/2008 | Correspondence from Southern California Community Recovery Center filed. |
| 03/11/2008 | All terms and conditions of probation are to remain the same. |

# MINUTES

Case : 07HF0020

Name : ███████████          12/14/2018 15:34:53 PM

| Date of Action | Text |
|---|---|
| 04/10/2009 | Probation Violation re: Arraignment set on 04/13/2009 at 09:00 AM in Department C58. |
| 04/10/2009 | Defendant's release status updated to reflect: In Custody. |
| 04/10/2009 | Court orders bail set at NO BAIL. |
| 04/10/2009 | Probation Violation Petition dated 04/09/2009 filed. |
| 04/13/2009 | Hearing held on 04/13/2009 at 09:00:00 AM in Department C58 for Probation Violation Arraignment. |
| 04/13/2009 | # 8 on calendar. |
| 04/13/2009 | Officiating Judge: Robert R. Fitzgerald, Judge |
| 04/13/2009 | Clerk: B. Ard |
| 04/13/2009 | Bailiff: D. Scrip |
| 04/13/2009 | Court Reporter: Caryl Axton |
| 04/13/2009 | People represented by Amy Swanson, Deputy District Attorney, present. |
| 04/13/2009 | Defendant present in Court with counsel Freeberg, Lloyd, Retained Attorney. |
| 04/13/2009 | This case is an execution of sentence suspended and is being returned to the sentencing Judge. Judge Gregory Jones. |
| 04/13/2009 | Probation Violation re: Arraignment set on 05/01/2009 at 09:00 AM in Department H2. |
| 04/13/2009 | Defendant ordered to appear. |
| 04/13/2009 | Probation ordered revoked as to count(s) 1. |
| 04/13/2009 | Defendant remanded to the custody of the Sheriff. |
| 04/13/2009 | Current bail set for defendant to remain. |
| 04/13/2009 | Notice to Sheriff issued. |
| 05/01/2009 | Hearing held on 05/01/2009 at 09:00:00 AM in Department H2 for Probation Violation Arraignment. |
| 05/01/2009 | Officiating Judge: Gregory W. Jones, Judge |
| 05/01/2009 | Clerk: K. Reinke |
| 05/01/2009 | Bailiff: B. Cate |
| 05/01/2009 | Court Reporter: Donna Wagner |
| 05/01/2009 | Erin Rowe made a special appearance for District Attorney Jan Christie. |
| 05/01/2009 | Defendant present in Court with counsel Freeberg, Lloyd, Retained Attorney. |
| 05/01/2009 | Probation Violation re: Arraignment continued to 05/29/2009 at 08:30 AM in Department H2 at request of Defense. |
| 05/01/2009 | Defendant waives statutory time for Hearing. |
| 05/01/2009 | Counsel joins in waivers. |
| 05/01/2009 | Defendant ordered to return. |
| 05/01/2009 | Current bail set for defendant to remain. |
| 05/01/2009 | Defendant remanded to the custody of the Sheriff. |
| 05/01/2009 | Notice to Sheriff issued. |
| 05/01/2009 | Keep with companion cases(s) 06HF2202. |
| 05/29/2009 | Hearing held on 05/29/2009 at 08:30:00 AM in Department H2 for Probation Violation Arraignment. |
| 05/29/2009 | Officiating Judge: Karen L. Robinson, Judge |

# MINUTES

Case : 07HF0020

Name : ████████████

12/14/2018 15:34:53 PM

| Date of Action | Text |
|---|---|
| 05/29/2009 | Clerk: L. Lesar |
| 05/29/2009 | Bailiff: C. S. Rozean |
| 05/29/2009 | Court Reporter: Donna Wagner |
| 05/29/2009 | Van C. Ho, certified law clerk, appearing specially on the behalf of George McFettride, District Attorney |
| 05/29/2009 | Defendant present in Court with counsel Freeberg, Lloyd, Retained Attorney. |
| 05/29/2009 | Probation Violation re: Arraignment continued to 06/12/2009 at 08:30 AM in Department H2 at request of Defense. |
| 05/29/2009 | Defendant waives statutory time for Sentencing. |
| 05/29/2009 | Counsel joins in waivers. |
| 05/29/2009 | Defendant ordered to return. |
| 05/29/2009 | Current bail set for defendant to remain. |
| 05/29/2009 | Defendant remanded to the custody of the Sheriff. |
| 05/29/2009 | Notice to Sheriff issued. |
| 05/29/2009 | Keep with companion cases(s) 06HF2202. |
| 05/29/2009 | Minutes entered by K. Reinke. |
| 06/11/2009 | Order to Permit Inmate Visitation signed and filed. |
| 06/12/2009 | Hearing held on 06/12/2009 at 08:30:00 AM in Department H2 for Probation Violation Arraignment. |
| 06/12/2009 | Officiating Judge: Karen L. Robinson, Judge |
| 06/12/2009 | Clerk: L. Lesar |
| 06/12/2009 | Bailiff: C. S. Rozean |
| 06/12/2009 | Court Reporter: Donna Wagner |
| 06/12/2009 | Van Ha, Law Clerk present under supervision of Erin Rowe, Deputy District Attorney specially appearing for George McFettride, Deputy District Attorney |
| 06/12/2009 | Erin Rowe made a special appearance for District Attorney George W. McFetridge Jr.. |
| 06/12/2009 | Probation Violation re: Arraignment continued to 06/15/2009 at 08:30 AM in Department H2 by stipulation of all parties. |
| 06/12/2009 | Defendant waives statutory time for Hearing. |
| 06/12/2009 | Counsel joins in waivers. |
| 06/12/2009 | Defendant ordered to appear. |
| 06/12/2009 | Defendant remanded to the custody of the Sheriff. |
| 06/12/2009 | Current bail set for defendant to remain. |
| 06/12/2009 | Notice to Sheriff issued. |
| 06/12/2009 | Keep with companion cases(s) 06HF2202. |
| 06/15/2009 | Hearing held on 06/15/2009 at 08:30:00 AM in Department H2 for Probation Violation Arraignment. |
| 06/15/2009 | Officiating Judge: Gregory W. Jones, Judge |
| 06/15/2009 | Clerk: C. Le |
| 06/15/2009 | Bailiff: I. Hamdallah |
| 06/15/2009 | Court Reporter: Starlette Soniega-Armijo |

SUPERIOR COURT OF CALIFORNIA, COUNTY OF ORANGE

# MINUTES

Case : 07HF0020

Name : ▮▮▮▮▮▮▮▮▮▮

12/14/2018 15:34:53 PM

| Date of Action | Text |
|---|---|
| 06/15/2009 | Van Ha, Certified Law Clerk, appearing specially on behalf of George McFettride, Deputy District Attorney. |
| 06/15/2009 | Defendant present in Court with counsel Lloyd Freeberg, Retained Attorney. |
| 06/15/2009 | Probation Violation re: Arraignment continued to 08/07/2009 at 08:30 AM in Department H2 by stipulation of all parties. |
| 06/15/2009 | Defendant waives statutory time for Hearing. |
| 06/15/2009 | Defendant ordered to appear. |
| 06/15/2009 | Current bail set for defendant to remain. |
| 06/15/2009 | Defendant remanded to the custody of the Sheriff. |
| 06/15/2009 | Notice to Sheriff issued. |
| 06/15/2009 | Keep with companion cases(s) 06HF2202. |
| 08/07/2009 | Hearing held on 08/07/2009 at 08:30:00 AM in Department H2 for Probation Violation Arraignment. |
| 08/07/2009 | Officiating Judge: Gregory W. Jones, Judge |
| 08/07/2009 | Clerk: L. Trottier |
| 08/07/2009 | Bailiff: B. Cate |
| 08/07/2009 | Court Reporter: Donna Wagner |
| 08/07/2009 | Minutes entered by T. Lewis. |
| 08/07/2009 | People represented by Beth Carmichael, Deputy District Attorney, present. |
| 08/07/2009 | Defendant present in Court with counsel Freeberg, Lloyd, Retained Attorney. |
| 08/07/2009 | Probation Violation re: Arraignment continued to 08/21/2009 at 08:30 AM in Department H2 by stipulation of all parties. |
| 08/07/2009 | Defendant ordered to return. |
| 08/07/2009 | Defendant waives statutory time for Hearing. |
| 08/07/2009 | Current bail set for defendant to remain. |
| 08/07/2009 | Defendant remanded to the custody of the Sheriff. |
| 08/07/2009 | Notice to Sheriff issued. |
| 08/07/2009 | Keep with companion cases(s) 06HF2202. |
| 08/07/2009 | Probation Addendum Report filed. |
| 08/21/2009 | Hearing held on 08/21/2009 at 08:30:00 AM in Department H2 for Probation Violation Arraignment. |
| 08/21/2009 | Officiating Judge: Gregory W. Jones, Judge |
| 08/21/2009 | Clerk: M. Johnson |
| 08/21/2009 | Bailiff: C. F. Cisneros |
| 08/21/2009 | Court Reporter: Donna Cox |
| 08/21/2009 | People represented by Erin Rowe, Deputy District Attorney, present. |
| 08/21/2009 | Defendant present in Court with counsel Freeberg, Lloyd, Retained Attorney. |
| 08/21/2009 | Probation Violation re: Arraignment continued to 09/25/2009 at 08:30 AM in Department H2 by stipulation of all parties. |
| 08/21/2009 | Defendant waives statutory time for Hearing. |
| 08/21/2009 | Counsel joins in waivers. |

# MINUTES

Case : 07HF0020

Name : ███████████

12/14/2018 15:34:53 PM

| Date of Action | Text |
|---|---|
| 08/21/2009 | Defendant ordered to return. |
| 08/21/2009 | Current bail set for defendant to remain. |
| 08/21/2009 | Defendant remanded to the custody of the Sheriff. |
| 08/21/2009 | Notice to Sheriff issued. |
| 09/25/2009 | Hearing held on 09/25/2009 at 08:30:00 AM in Department H2 for Probation Violation Arraignment. |
| 09/25/2009 | Officiating Judge: James Odriozola, Commissioner |
| 09/25/2009 | Clerk: L. K. Mc Donald |
| 09/25/2009 | Bailiff: B. Lohrman |
| 09/25/2009 | Court Reporter: Donna Cox |
| 09/25/2009 | People represented by George W. McFetridge Jr., Deputy District Attorney, present. |
| 09/25/2009 | Laura Lindley makes a special appearance for Lloyd Freeberg, Retained Attorney. Defendant present. |
| 09/25/2009 | Probation Violation re: Arraignment continued to 10/16/2009 at 08:30 AM in Department H2 by stipulation of all parties. |
| 09/25/2009 | Defendant waives statutory time for Hearing. |
| 09/25/2009 | Counsel joins in waivers. |
| 09/25/2009 | Defendant ordered to appear. |
| 09/25/2009 | Current bail set for defendant to remain at $0.00. |
| 09/25/2009 | Defendant remanded to the custody of the Sheriff. |
| 09/25/2009 | Notice to Sheriff issued. |
| 09/25/2009 | Keep with companion cases(s) 06HF2202. |
| 10/15/2009 | Transferred from: Ashaary, Kiarash |
| 10/16/2009 | Hearing held on 10/16/2009 at 08:30:00 AM in Department H2 for Probation Violation Arraignment. |
| 10/16/2009 | Officiating Judge: Gregory W. Jones, Judge |
| 10/16/2009 | Clerk: T. Lewis |
| 10/16/2009 | Bailiff: B. Cate |
| 10/16/2009 | Court Reporter: Donna Cox |
| 10/16/2009 | People represented by George W. McFetridge Jr., Deputy District Attorney, present. |
| 10/16/2009 | Tracee May-Brewster makes a special appearance for Lloyd Freeberg, Retained Attorney. Defendant present. |
| 10/16/2009 | Probation Violation re: Arraignment continued to 10/22/2009 at 08:30 AM in Department H2 at request of Defense. |
| 10/16/2009 | Defendant ordered to return. |
| 10/16/2009 | Current bail set for defendant to remain at $0.00. |
| 10/16/2009 | Defendant remanded to the custody of the Sheriff. |
| 10/16/2009 | Notice to Sheriff issued. |
| 10/16/2009 | Keep with companion cases(s) 06HF2202. |
| 10/22/2009 | Hearing held on 10/22/2009 at 08:30:00 AM in Department H2 for Probation Violation Arraignment. |
| 10/22/2009 | Officiating Judge: Gregory W. Jones, Judge |

# MINUTES

Case : 07HF0020

Name : ███████████                                      12/14/2018 15:34:53 PM

| Date of Action | Text |
| --- | --- |
| 10/22/2009 | Clerk: L. Sanchez |
| 10/22/2009 | Bailiff: C. S. Rozean |
| 10/22/2009 | Court Reporter: Donna Cox |
| 10/22/2009 | People represented by Stefanie Marangi, Deputy District Attorney, present. |
| 10/22/2009 | Defendant present in Court with counsel Freeberg, Lloyd, Retained Attorney. |
| 10/22/2009 | Probation Violation re: Arraignment continued to 11/13/2009 at 08:30 AM in Department H2 by stipulation of all parties. |
| 10/22/2009 | Defendant waives statutory time for Probation Violation. |
| 10/22/2009 | Current bail set for defendant to remain at $0.00. |
| 10/22/2009 | Counsel joins in waivers. |
| 10/22/2009 | Defendant ordered to appear. |
| 10/22/2009 | Defendant remanded to the custody of the Sheriff. |
| 10/22/2009 | Notice to Sheriff issued. |
| 11/13/2009 | Hearing held on 11/13/2009 at 08:30:00 AM in Department H2 for Probation Violation Arraignment. |
| 11/13/2009 | Officiating Judge: Gregory W. Jones, Judge |
| 11/13/2009 | Clerk: L. Trottier |
| 11/13/2009 | Bailiff: B. Cate |
| 11/13/2009 | Court Reporter: Donna Cox |
| 11/13/2009 | People represented by George W. McFetridge Jr., Deputy District Attorney, present. |
| 11/13/2009 | Defendant present in Court with counsel Freeberg, Lloyd, Retained Attorney. |
| 11/13/2009 | Probation Violation re: Arraignment continued to 11/24/2009 at 08:30 AM in Department H2 at request of Defense. |
| 11/13/2009 | Defendant ordered to appear. |
| 11/13/2009 | Counsel joins in waivers. |
| 11/13/2009 | Current bail set for defendant to remain at $0.00. |
| 11/13/2009 | Defendant remanded to the custody of the Sheriff. |
| 11/13/2009 | Notice to Sheriff issued. |
| 11/13/2009 | Keep with companion cases(s) 06HF2202. |
| 11/24/2009 | Hearing held on 11/24/2009 at 08:30:00 AM in Department H2 for Probation Violation Arraignment. |
| 11/24/2009 | Officiating Judge: Robert Gannon, Judge |
| 11/24/2009 | Clerk: L. Taylor |
| 11/24/2009 | Bailiff: C. S. Rozean |
| 11/24/2009 | Court Reporter: Donna Cox |
| 11/24/2009 | People represented by Cheryl Gold, Deputy District Attorney, present. |
| 11/24/2009 | Defendant present in Court with counsel Freeberg, Lloyd, Retained Attorney. |
| 11/24/2009 | Defendant advised of legal and constitutional rights. |
| 11/24/2009 | Defendant advised of and waives the following: |
| 11/24/2009 | - The right to confront and cross-examine witnesses. |
| 11/24/2009 | - The right against self incrimination. |
| 11/24/2009 | Defendant waives the right to subpoena and present evidence. |

# MINUTES

Case : 07HF0020

Name :                                                      12/14/2018 15:34:53 PM

| Date of Action | Text |
|---|---|
| 11/24/2009 | Defendant waives right to probation hearing. Defendant admits violation of probation as to count(s) 1. |
| 11/24/2009 | Court orders probation reinstated and modified as to count(s) 1 as follows: |
| 11/24/2009 | Court orders STATE PRISON imposed on 12/11/2007 VACATED as to count(s) 1 and related enhancement(s). |
| 11/24/2009 | Court orders probation terminated as to count(s) 1. |
| 11/24/2009 | Defendant released on this case only. Release issued. |
| 11/24/2009 | Notice to Sheriff issued. |
| 11/29/2009 | DOJ Subsequent Abstract sent. |
| 11/29/2009 | DOJ Subsequent Abstract sent. |
| 11/29/2009 | DOJ Subsequent Abstract sent. |
| 11/29/2009 | Case closed. |
| 11/03/2013 | Case closed. |
| 11/30/2018 | At the request of Defense Counsel, case calendared on 11/30/18 at 08:30 AM in C53 for PET. |
| 11/30/2018 | Hearing held on 11/30/2018 at 08:30:00 AM in Department C53 for Petition. |
| 11/30/2018 | Judicial Officer: Gary M Pohlson, Judge |
| 11/30/2018 | Clerk: N. Robles |
| 11/30/2018 | Bailiff: E. F. Richardson |
| 11/30/2018 | Court Reporter: Shelley Hill |
| 11/30/2018 | People represented by George William McFetridge Jr, Deputy District Attorney, present. |
| 11/30/2018 | Defendant not present in Court represented by Saif Rahman, Retained Attorney. |
| 11/30/2018 | Defense Motion to Withdraw Plea Pursuant to Penal Code 1473.7 filed. |
| 11/30/2018 | Court read and considered Petition for Relief Under Penal Code 1473.7. |
| 11/30/2018 | People submit(s). |
| 11/30/2018 | Motion granted. |
| 11/30/2018 | Court finds finds the defendant was not advised of their immigration consequences and grants the motion pursuant to Penal Code 1473.7. The defendant withdraws his guilty plea(s). People state they are unable to proceed at this time. Defense requests the Court dismiss this case in the furtherance of justice. The Court orders this case dismissed pursuant to Penal Code 1385. |
| 11/30/2018 | Defendant's motion to WITHDRAW GUILTY PLEA to count(s) 1 granted. |
| 11/30/2018 | Case dismissed - pursuant to Penal Code 1385 - Furtherance of justice. |
| 11/30/2018 | Order Vacating Conviction Under Penal Code 1473.7 signed and filed. |
| 11/30/2018 | Minutes of 11/30/2018 entered on 12/03/2018. |
| 12/05/2018 | Deleted DD1 - Abstract of Conviction abstract from case. |
| 12/05/2018 | Deleted DD1 - Abstract of Conviction abstract from case. |
| 12/06/2018 | Case closed. |

EXHIBIT '21'

Orange County Superior Court Docket Sheet - IRM322200

Home » Online Services » Case Access » Case Detail

Case Detail - IRM322200

Case Search Home

# Case Detail - IRM322200

## Case Summary

| Case No. | Case Category | Case Level/Type | Plaintiff Person/Business Name | Party Role |
|---|---|---|---|---|

IRM322200 Criminal/Traffic Infraction          People █████████████

**Filing Date Case Status Case Status Date Destruction Date File Location**
08/27/2008 Closed          02/08/2009

## Case Detail

| Charge | Charge Date | Charge Dispo Date | Charge Dispo Type |
| --- | --- | --- | --- |
| 21655.5(b) VC | 08/27/2008 | 02/05/2009 | Pled Guilty |
| 21655.8(a) VC | 08/27/2008 | 02/05/2009 | Pled Guilty |

© 2014 Superior Court of Orange County

EXHIBIT '22'

Orange County Superior Court Docket Sheet - SH889199

- Jury Services
- Juvenile
- Probate/Mental Health
- Small Claims
- Traffic & Infractions
- General Info
  - ADA
  - Appearances in Court
  - Bids/Solicitations
  - Budget and Filing / Workload Information
  - Children's Chambers
  - Court Governance
  - Court Holidays
  - Court Locations, Hours & Phone Numbers
  - Community Outreach/Education
  - DUI Court
  - Employment
  - Government Claim Forms
  - Judicial Officers
  - Lawyers and Litigants
  - Media Relations
  - Online Services
  - Records
  - Temporary Judge Program

Home » Online Services » Case Access » Case Detail

- Online Services
  - Account Services
  - Cases on Calendar
  - Case Access
  - Case Index Search
  - Case Name Search
  - Civil-Reserve A Motion Date
  - Court Reporter Transcript Requests
  - eFiling
  - eJuror
  - My Court Portal-Traffic & Criminal
  - Probate Notes
  - Tentative Rulings

Case Detail - SH889199

Case Search Home

# Case Detail - SH889199

## Case Summary

**Case No.  Case Category  Case Level/Type  Plaintiff Person/Business Name  Party Role**

SH889199 Criminal/Traffic Infraction          People ███████████

**Filing Date Case Status Case Status Date Destruction Date File Location**
05/05/2012  Closed          11/15/2013

## Case Detail

**Charge   Charge Date Charge Dispo Date   Charge Dispo Type**
22350 VC 04/24/2012   03/12/2013                Traffic School Completed

Back to Results   New Search

- Jury Services
- Juvenile
- Probate/Mental Health
- Small Claims
- Traffic & Infractions
- General Info
  - ADA
  - Appearances in Court
  - Bids/Solicitations
  - Budget and Filing / Workload Information
  - Children's Chambers
  - Court Governance
  - Court Holidays
  - Court Locations, Hours & Phone Numbers
  - Community Outreach/Education
  - DUI Court
  - Employment
  - Government Claim Forms
  - Judicial Officers
  - Lawyers and Litigants
  - Media Relations
  - Online Services
  - Records
  - Temporary Judge Program

Home » Online Services » Case Access » Case Detail

- Online Services
  - Account Services
  - Cases on Calendar
  - Case Access
  - Case Index Search
  - Case Name Search
  - Civil-Reserve A Motion Date
  - Court Reporter Transcript Requests
  - eFiling
  - eJuror
  - My Court Portal-Traffic & Criminal
  - Probate Notes
  - Tentative Rulings

Case Detail - 13465TU

Case Search Home

# Case Detail - 13465TU

## Case Summary

**Case No. Case Category Case Level/Type Plaintiff Person/Business Name Party Role**

13465TU Criminal/Traffic Infraction        People        ████████████████

**Filing Date Case Status Case Status Date Destruction Date File Location**
06/12/2015  Closed        02/18/2016

## Case Detail

**Charge      Charge Date Charge Dispo Date    Charge Dispo Type**
22349(a) VC 06/06/2015    02/17/2016         Traffic School Completed

Back to Results   New Search

© 2014 Superior Court of Orange County
Locations Telephone Numbers Employment Sitemap RSS Privacy Policy Webmaster

www.ingramcontent.com/pod-product-compliance
Lightning Source LLC
Chambersburg PA
CBHW051753200326
41597CB00025B/4544